VOLUME 13

OLD TESTAMENT

THE NEW COLLEGEVILLE BIBLE COMMENTARY

ISAIAH

Leslie J. Hoppe, O.F.M.

SERIES EDITOR

Daniel Durken, O.S.B.

LITURGICAL PRESS

Collegeville, Minnesota

www.litpress.org

Nihil Obstat: Reverend Robert Harren, *Censor deputatus.*

Imprimatur: ✠ Most Reverend John F. Kinney, J.C.D., D.D., Bishop of Saint Cloud, Minnesota, May 11, 2012.

Design by Ann Blattner.

Cover illustration: detail by *Vision of Isaiah* by Donald Jackson. © 2007 *The Saint John's Bible,* Order of Saint Benedict, Collegeville, Minnesota, USA. Used with permission. All rights reserved.

Photos: pages 10, 41, Wikimedia Commons; page 22, Photos.com; page 93, Thinkstock/iStockphotos; page 144, David Manahan, OSB; page 167, Thinkstock/Ingram Publishing.

Maps created by Robert Cronan of Lucidity Information Design, LLC.

1	2	3	4	5	6	7	8	9

Library of Congress Cataloging-in-Publication Data

Hoppe, Leslie J.
    Isaiah / Leslie J. Hoppe.
       p. cm. — (New Collegeville Bible commentary. Old Testament ; v. 13)
    Includes index.
    ISBN 978-0-8146-2847-8
    1. Bible. O.T. Isaiah—Commentaries.   I. Title.

    BS1515.53.H67   2012
    224'.1077—dc23   2012014491

CONTENTS

ABBREVIATIONS

Books of the Bible

Acts—Acts of the Apostles
Amos—Amos
Bar—Baruch
1 Chr—1 Chronicles
2 Chr—2 Chronicles
Col—Colossians
1 Cor—1 Corinthians
2 Cor—2 Corinthians
Dan—Daniel
Deut—Deuteronomy
Eccl (or Qoh)—Ecclesiastes
Eph—Ephesians
Esth—Esther
Exod—Exodus
Ezek—Ezekiel
Ezra—Ezra
Gal—Galatians
Gen—Genesis
Hab—Habakkuk
Hag—Haggai
Heb—Hebrews
Hos—Hosea
Isa—Isaiah
Jas—James
Jdt—Judith
Jer—Jeremiah
Job—Job
Joel—Joel
John—John
1 John—1 John
2 John—2 John
3 John—3 John
Jonah—Jonah
Josh—Joshua
Jude—Jude
Judg—Judges
1 Kgs—1 Kings

2 Kgs—2 Kings
Lam—Lamentations
Lev—Leviticus
Luke—Luke
1 Macc—1 Maccabees
2 Macc—2 Maccabees
Mal—Malachi
Mark—Mark
Matt—Matthew
Mic—Micah
Nah—Nahum
Neh—Nehemiah
Num—Numbers
Obad—Obadiah
1 Pet—1 Peter
2 Pet—2 Peter
Phil—Philippians
Phlm—Philemon
Prov—Proverbs
Ps(s)—Psalms
Rev—Revelation
Rom—Romans
Ruth—Ruth
1 Sam—1 Samuel
2 Sam—2 Samuel
Sir—Sirach
Song—Song of Songs
1 Thess—1 Thessalonians
2 Thess—2 Thessalonians
1 Tim—1 Timothy
2 Tim—2 Timothy
Titus—Titus
Tob—Tobit
Wis—Wisdom
Zech—Zechariah
Zeph—Zephaniah

The Book of Isaiah

By any measure the book of Isaiah is among the world's greatest works of religious literature. It probes the mystery of a people's life with God. It is unrelenting in its insistence that the foundation of that life is God's commitment to Jerusalem—God's unwillingness to make judgment on the city's infidelity the last word that its people would hear. The book makes use of a variety of literary techniques—both prose and poetry—to move people to see that Jerusalem did have a future with God. The book's principal characters—the Holy One of Israel, the virgin daughter Zion, and the Servant of the Lord—engage the reader in a drama of great emotion and intensity. Other personalities appear as the book's reflection on Israel's life with God oscillates between judgment and salvation. These include the prophet Isaiah and his two strangely named sons; King Ahaz and his son Hezekiah; Cyrus the Persian; the owner of an unproductive vineyard; the Assyrian army; the nations; the poor; and Immanuel. Justice for the poor is a motif that continually surfaces throughout the book, leading the reader to conclude that Israel's relationship with its God is indirect—that it is a by-product of the creation and maintenance of a just society.

Those who read this book from beginning to end will experience a range of emotions that testify to the book's complexity. They will sympathize with the prophet's friend who expected to find a good harvest of grapes in his vineyard (Isa 5). They will be in awe with the prophet as he experiences the majesty of God (Isa 6). They will puzzle at the obtuseness of Ahaz (Isa 7). They will reel at the intense hatred of the oracles against the nations (Isa 13–27). They will be relieved as they hear of Jerusalem's liberation (Isa 40). They will be shocked at the suffering of the Servant of the Lord (52:13–53:12). They will be happy for mother Zion embraced by her husband and surrounded by her children again (Isa 62, 66). And they will be disappointed by the book's ending (66:24). The last verse is so depressing that when the final verses of Isaiah are read in the synagogue, by custom the reader repeats verse 23, with its more upbeat tone after reading verse 24 so that the book does not end on a negative note.

The book of Isaiah continues to have a profound influence on its readers—especially those who belong to two of the religious traditions that developed from the religion of ancient Israel: Judaism and Christianity. The book of Isaiah is often read in the synagogue as the *Haftarah*, the reading that is meant to parallel and illuminate the reading from the torah. Also, the significance of Jerusalem in the book of Isaiah has helped shaped Judaism's attitude toward this city. Especially significant is the vision of justice and peace with which the city will be blessed (see 2:2-4; 11:6-9).

The Christian confession of Jesus as the Messiah has been shaped significantly by the book of Isaiah. Among the more significant references to Isaiah in the New Testament is Matthew's citation of the Immanuel prophecy (Isa 7:14; Matt 2:23), Luke's use of elements from the fourth Servant Song to explain the necessity of Jesus' suffering and death (e.g., Isa 53:7-9; Luke 33:27; Acts 8:32-33), and the idea of the New Jerusalem in the book of Revelation (Isa 65:18; Rev 21:2). The church's early theologians referred to the book of Isaiah as "the fifth gospel," because they discerned the significance of this book for the New Testament, which cites Isaiah more often than any book of the Hebrew Bible except the book of Psalms. Isaiah continues to exercise its influence in the church. Passages from Isaiah are read frequently in both the Sunday and weekday lectionaries. The Second Vatican Council cited Isaiah 2:4 and 32:17 in its Constitution on the Church in the Modern World when speaking on social justice and peace (*Gaudium et spes*, 70). Finally, the book's vision for the future has provided liberation theologians with a biblical foundation for their advocacy on behalf of the poor and oppressed.

Modern scholarly interpretation of Isaiah has been shaped by the recognition that the book is a composite work that reflects three different periods of Jerusalem's history. Chapters 1–23 and 28–39 contain material relating to the ministry of the eighth-century prophet, Isaiah, son of Amoz (1:1-2). He condemned the social, political, and economic system of the kingdom of Judah because it created a two-tiered society made up of the very rich and very poor. The rich acquired and maintained their position in Judahite society by taking advantage of the poor. What was even worse was that the temple and its liturgy were used to assure the oppressors that God would continue to protect Judah despite its manifest failure to maintain a community of justice. The prophet believed that the aggressively militaristic Assyrian Empire was God's instrument of judgment on the kingdom of Judah. Chapters 36–39 are taken for the most part from 2 Kings 18:13–20:19, which describes the Assyrian siege of Jerusalem.

Isaiah 40–55 are the product of an anonymous prophet whose ministry took place about 125 years after that of Isaiah, son of Amoz. The message of these chapters is that there is a future for Jerusalem beyond the disaster that occurred when Nabuchadnezzar, king of Babylon, captured Jerusalem, destroyed the temple, ended the Judahite monarchy and national state, and led off many leading citizens into exile. The rise of Cyrus, the Persian, convinced the anonymous prophet of the exile that Judah's time of judgment was over and that Cyrus was God's chosen instrument to rebuild Jerusalem and its temple (Isa 45). The prophet's exquisite poems helped the people of Judah to make sense of the disaster they experienced and to see that there was a future beyond judgment.

Isaiah 56–66 are a collection of poems that reflected the disillusionment of some when the hopes engendered by Isaiah 40–55 did not materialize. While the temple had been rebuilt, the national state was not restored, the economy was in shambles, and the conflict between the wealthy and the poor resurfaced. Despite the disappointment, the poems of chapters 56–66 expect a full and glorious restoration for Judah (Isa 60).

The final component of Isaiah is found in chapters 24–27. These chapters look forward to a day of judgment when God will finally defeat the powers of evil, vindicate the just, and punish evildoers. The day of judgment will end with all God's people, scattered about the world, returning to worship God in Jerusalem (Isa 27:13).

The circumstances under which the book of Isaiah took the form it now has are not entirely clear. Three fairly complete copies of the book of Isaiah were found among the Dead Sea Scrolls so the book in its present form existed prior to the second century B.C. when the community that produced the scrolls settled near the Dead Sea. The latest components of the book (chs. 24–27) probably date from no later than the fourth century. More precision than this is not possible at present. The book of Isaiah, then, took the form it now has sometime between the fourth and the second centuries B.C., though the earliest components of the book come from the eighth century B.C. What is clear is the book's purpose: to give the people of Judah and Jerusalem hope for the future and the will to re-embrace their ancestral religious traditions. Of course, there were other similar attempts. For example, the Deuteronomic tradition tries to persuade Judah that its future is tied up with careful observance of the norms of traditional Israelite morality as articulated in the book of Deuteronomy. The Chronicler asserts that Judah's future depends upon the legitimacy of its temple rituals as marked by their continuity with preexilic liturgical traditions. The book of Isaiah sees Jerusalem's future as God's "creative redemption." Jerusalem's response to this new act of God is to create and maintain a society based on justice and equity.

While this commentary assumes the composite character of the book, it will approach the work as a whole with a literary and theological integrity of its own. The divisions of the book adopted here are not those reflecting the history of its composition but its literary shape. The book falls into five parts of approximately the same length, which usually begin with an oracle of judgment on pride and arrogance and end with a word of salvation. Also, each of these sections is addressed to Jerusalem. These five sections are chapters 1–12: Jerusalem's Future; chapters 13–27: Jerusalem and the Nations; chapters 28–39: Judgment and Salvation for Jerusalem; chapters 40–55: Jerusalem's Liberation; and chapters 56–66: The New Jerusalem.

There are two principal motifs that are the literary and theological linch-pins of the book of Isaiah. The first flows from the distinctive title the book of Isaiah gives for God: "the Holy One of Israel." This unique Isaianic way of speaking about Jerusalem's God was formulated to expand the people's notion of deity. The Lord was unlike any other god and did not act as Jerusalem expected God to act. The holiness of God, then, was not a "moral" quality. It was God's otherness and singularity. It was manifest in the way God acted toward Jerusalem and the nations. In the first three sections of the book (1–12; 13–27; 28–39), God demands that Jerusalem create and maintain a society based on justice. The consequence for failing to do this will be severe judgment including the loss of the state, dynasty, temple, and land. In the fourth section of the book (40–55), there are several instances when "Holy One" is followed by the term "redeemer" (41:14; 43:14; 47:4; 48:17). In the last section, the nations will recognize the holiness of Israel's God because of Jerusalem's commitment to justice (57:15; 60:9, 14).

The second principal motif of the book is Jerusalem/Zion. The portrait that the prophet paints of the city contrasts sharply with that of the "Holy One of Israel." While the Lord demands justice for the poor, Jerusalem and its leaders crush them. While God's holiness has been made known to Israel throughout its history, Jerusalem seeks its security in alliances with other nations and through the worship of other gods. When God declares that Jerusalem has paid for its sins, the people are hesitant to believe. Despite this, God never stops loving Jerusalem and its people. God is determined to provide Jerusalem with a glorious future. The interaction between the Holy One of Israel and Jerusalem is the engine that drives Isaiah.

To appreciate the book's achievement, it is best to read the text straight through first without the commentary. This will allow the reader to get a sense of the book as a whole. Such a sustained reading will evoke from the reader a variety of responses. Reading the commentary then will help the reader probe more deeply into parts of the text that are particularly intriguing, inspiring, or puzzling. The most creative interaction with the text will result from the reader's recognition that the book is an expression of faith—faith in the Holy One of Israel and in the future of Jerusalem. The book is confident that judgment, though deserved by the city, is never God's last word to Jerusalem. The Jewish reader still looks to the final redemption of Jerusalem, while the book's Christian reader looks for the coming of the new and heavenly Jerusalem. The faith of both has been shaped decisively by the book of Isaiah.

The Book of Isaiah

I. Isaiah 1–39

A. Indictment of Israel and Judah

1 ¹The vision which Isaiah, son of Amoz, saw concerning Judah and Jerusalem in the days of Uzziah, Jotham, Ahaz and Hezekiah, kings of Judah.

JERUSALEM'S FUTURE

Isaiah 1:1–12:6

The first section of the book of Isaiah begins with an indictment of Jerusalem's infidelity (1:2-9) and ends with a prayer of thanksgiving for its restoration in the future (12:1-6). Between these two poles, Isaiah alternates between harsh and explicit descriptions of the judgment that awaits Jerusalem for its role in creating an unjust society, and lyrical and touching images of the future beyond judgment that God has for the city and its people. The genius of the prophet was not only his ability to appreciate the realities of the political and military crises in Jerusalem's immediate future but especially his ability to see beyond these to a glorious future for Zion. Still, Isaiah was no Pollyanna as his words make clear. He was certain that Jerusalem was to undergo a severe crisis that included political impotence and military defeat. Even more devastating would be the loss of and exile from the land that God promised to ancient Israel's ancestors. But beyond this judgment on Jerusalem was the promise of a new city ruled by a good king who led a people committed to justice.

1:1 The prophet's name

The book identifies itself as the "vision of Isaiah." It is a vision—the prophet's dream—of what he imagined Jerusalem's future to be. The prophet's name clarifies that vision. The name "Isaiah" means "the Lord saves." The naming of four Judahite kings asserts that what follows was first proclaimed in the eighth century B.C. when Jerusalem faced severe political, economic, and military crises.

11

Michelangelo's Isaiah in the Sistine Chapel, Vatican.

Accusation and Appeal. ²Hear,
O heavens, and listen, O earth,
for the LORD speaks:
Sons have I raised and reared,
but they have rebelled against
me!
³An ox knows its owner,
and an ass, its master's manger;
But Israel does not know,
my people has not understood.
⁴Ah! Sinful nation, people laden
with wickedness,
evil offspring, corrupt children!
They have forsaken the LORD,
spurned the Holy One of Israel,
apostatized,
⁵Why would you yet be struck,
that you continue to rebel?

The whole head is sick,
the whole heart faint.
⁶From the sole of the foot to the head
there is no sound spot in it;
Just bruise and welt and oozing
wound,
not drained, or bandaged,
or eased with salve.
⁷Your country is waste,
your cities burnt with fire;
Your land—before your eyes
strangers devour it,
a waste, like the devastation of
Sodom.
⁸And daughter Zion is left
like a hut in a vineyard,
Like a shed in a melon patch,
like a city blockaded.

1:2-9 God's judgment

The prophet's words begin with a poignant cry of betrayal. That the prophet identifies God as the parent betrayed and Israel as God's guilty children implies that judgment will not be God's last word to Israel. Like the love of parents for their children, God's love for Israel does not fail because of Israel's failures. The second comparison, likening Israel with beasts of burden, suggests that Israel acted out of ignorance, not appreciating the nature of its relationship with God. This also suggests some mitigation of Israel's guilt. Still, this will not prevent Israel from experiencing God's judgment for its infidelity. What the prophet cannot understand is the reason Israel has not learned from experience. Its infidelity continued until its cities were destroyed, its land desolate, and Jerusalem abandoned. Still, God did not allow Israel to destroy itself, but kept a few survivors alive. These survivors have accepted their situation as the Lord's doing, and they recognize the miracle that God worked in keeping them alive.

In verse 9, the prophet introduces what will be a significant theme in the book: the remnant. The survival of the "small remnant" prevented Jerusalem and the other cities of Judah from sharing the fate of Sodom and Gomorrah (see Gen 19:24-25). Paul quotes verse 9 in the course of his impassioned discourse on God's continuing love for the Jewish people (Rom 9:27-29).

▶ This symbol indicates a cross reference number in the *Catechism of the Catholic Church*. See page 178 for number citations.

⁹If the LORD of hosts had not
    left us a small remnant,
We would have become as Sodom,
    would have resembled
        Gomorrah.

◄ ¹⁰Hear the word of the LORD,
    princes of Sodom!
Listen to the instruction of our God,
    people of Gomorrah!
¹¹What do I care for the multitude
    of your sacrifices?
    says the LORD.
I have had enough of whole-burnt
    rams
    and fat of fatlings;
In the blood of calves, lambs, and
    goats
    I find no pleasure.
¹²When you come to appear before
    me,
    who asks these things of you?
¹³Trample my courts no more!
    To bring offerings is useless;
    incense is an abomination to me.
New moon and sabbath, calling
    assemblies—
    festive convocations with
        wickedness—
    these I cannot bear.
¹⁴Your new moons and festivals I
    detest;
    they weigh me down, I tire of
        the load.

¹⁵When you spread out your hands,
    I will close my eyes to you;
Though you pray the more,
    I will not listen.
Your hands are full of blood!
    ¹⁶Wash yourselves clean! ►
Put away your misdeeds from
        before my eyes;
    cease doing evil;
    ¹⁷learn to do good. ►
Make justice your aim: redress the
        wronged,
    hear the orphan's plea, defend
        the widow.

¹⁸Come now, let us set things right,
    says the LORD:
Though your sins be like scarlet,
    they may become white as snow;
Though they be red like crimson,
    they may become white as wool.
¹⁹If you are willing, and obey,
    you shall eat the good things of
        the land;
²⁰But if you refuse and resist,
    you shall be eaten by the sword:
    for the mouth of the LORD has
        spoken!

The Purification of Jerusalem. ²¹How
    she has become a prostitute,
    the faithful city, so upright!
Justice used to lodge within her,
    but now, murderers.

1:10-20 Israel's worship

Taking on the persona of God, the prophet picks up on the reference to Sodom and Gomorrah in verse 9 to introduce a critique of Israel's liturgy that has few parallels in comprehensiveness and intensity. God rejects Israel's religious festivals, sacrifices, and acts of personal piety because Israel has not maintained a just society. Without justice, Israel's worship of the Lord is an empty shell. The book of Isaiah ends with another stinging critique of ritual activity (66:1-4). The book, then, is framed by bitter and comprehensive criticisms of ritual because the prophet believed Israel's communal worship facilitated its selective obedience. Israel believed that

²²Your silver is turned to dross,
   your wine is mixed with water.
²³Your princes are rebels
   and comrades of thieves;
Each one of them loves a bribe
   and looks for gifts.
The fatherless they do not defend,
   the widow's plea does not reach
      them.
²⁴Now, therefore, says the Lord,
   the LORD of hosts, the Mighty
      One of Israel:

Ah! I will take vengeance on my
      foes
   and fully repay my enemies!
²⁵I will turn my hand against you,
   and refine your dross in the
      furnace,
   removing all your alloy.
²⁶I will restore your judges as at first,
   and your counselors as in the
      beginning;
After that you shall be called
   city of justice, faithful city.

God must be pleased with it because of its liturgy even though its social, political, and economic life was a mockery of justice. Still, God's judgment is not final because God asks Israel to consider what it has done. Israel has to choose between life and death. Obedience is not a matter of knowledge. It is a matter of will. If Israel chooses to live in obedience, then red can become white. Sin can be countered by repentance.

To put the apocalyptic vision recorded in the book of Revelation into words, John studied the book of Isaiah. In describing the devastation of Jerusalem at the end of the age, John alludes to verse 10 and the application of the name Sodom to Jerusalem (Rev 11:8). As a book of prophecy, Isaiah assumes that the people of Judah are in control of their future: the choices *they* make will create their future. The prophet's task is to help the people appreciate the consequences of their choices. Because they have created a society based on injustice and oppression, that society will collapse. The book also affirms that judgment will not be the last word that God will address to Judah. God will restore Jerusalem, giving the people another opportunity to create a just society in which all will enjoy God's peace.

The book of Revelation is an example of an apocalyptic worldview that does not envision the triumph of divine justice in *this* world. Apocalyptic looks forward to a new world to be created by the power of God. The climax of the book of Revelation occurs in chapter 21 with its vision of a "*new* heaven and a *new* earth" (Rev 21:1; emphasis added). But like the book of Isaiah, Revelation identifies Jerusalem as the focal point of the new earth (Rev 21:9-27).

1:21-26 Jerusalem's future

At one time, Jerusalem's social and economic system was just. What once was, however, is no more, and the city faces divine judgment. Its political

²⁷Zion shall be redeemed by justice,
    and her repentant ones by
        righteousness.
²⁸Rebels and sinners together shall
    be crushed,
    those who desert the LORD shall
        be consumed.

Judgment on the Sacred Groves. ²⁹You
    shall be ashamed of the
        terebinths which you
        desired,

and blush on account of the
    gardens which you chose.
³⁰You shall become like a terebinth
    whose leaves wither,
    like a garden that has no water.
³¹The strong tree shall turn to
    tinder,
    and the one who tends it shall
        become a spark;
Both of them shall burn together,
    and there shall be none to
        quench them.

---

leadership is venal (1:26). The city's leaders should have been protecting the economically vulnerable, but they have used their position to exploit the poor to enrich themselves and thereby have become God's enemies. However, the goal of God's judgment against Jerusalem's elite is not mere vengeance, but the elimination of the city's corrupt political system. With new leadership, Jerusalem can once again be a just and faithful city. Still, the prophet is clear that Zion's current leadership provoked the divine judgment that was coming on Jerusalem. But one day God will provide the city with leaders who have a measure of integrity. The prophet insists that Jerusalem's standing before God is not a consequence of its unique status as the dwelling place of God on earth. Jerusalem's salvation lies in the doing of justice. The city's fate then will be a consequence of its people's commitment to maintaining a just and equitable economic system that protects the most vulnerable people. The future of Jerusalem is in the hands of its people and leaders.

1:29-31 False worship

These verses are likely veiled references to the worship of the goddess Asherah, whose rituals may have involved trees in some way (see Jer 17:2). Asherah was the wife of El, the supreme deity of the Ugaritic pantheon. An inscription found on the Sinai Peninsula suggests that some worshipers of the Lord honored Asherah as the Lord's consort. The prophet objects to worship related to Asherah explicitly in 17:8 and 27:9, and the third part of the book (40–55) is filled with parodies of idol worship. Such worship provided ideological support for an unjust social system based on an elite who controlled the economic lives of the poor. The Lord, however, is a God who takes the side of the poor against those who exploit them.

15

2 ¹This is what Isaiah, son of Amoz, saw concerning Judah and Jerusalem.

Zion, the Royal City of God. ²In days to come,
The mountain of the LORD's house
shall be established as the
highest mountain
and raised above the hills.
All nations shall stream toward it.
³Many peoples shall come and
say:
"Come, let us go up to the LORD's
mountain,
to the house of the God of Jacob,
That he may instruct us in his ways,
and we may walk in his paths."
For from Zion shall go forth
instruction,
and the word of the LORD from
Jerusalem.

⁴He shall judge between the nations,
and set terms for many peoples.
They shall beat their swords into
plowshares
and their spears into pruning
hooks;
One nation shall not raise the
sword against another,
nor shall they train for war again.
⁵House of Jacob, come,
let us walk in the light of the
LORD!

The Lord's Day of Judgment on Pride.
⁶You have abandoned your people,
the house of Jacob!
Because they are filled with diviners,
and soothsayers, like the
Philistines;
with foreigners they clasp
hands.

2:1-4 Jerusalem of the future

The prophet speaks not of the Jerusalem of his day but of Jerusalem in the distant future—a time after the city is purged by the coming judgment. Isaiah is convinced that the city's status will change in the future. However, that status will not be the consequence of God's presence in the temple, but of the city's role as the place to which all peoples will come to learn the torah. The prophet does not speak of the nations as enemies to be defeated but as peoples with whom Judah is to live in peace. The enemy that will be defeated is war. The universal observance of the torah will bring an era of peace. The fourth and fifth sections of the book (40–55; 56–66) develop the themes of the future of Jerusalem and Israel's relations with other peoples.

A variation of this oracle occurs in Micah 4:1-4, while Joel 4:10 turns the oracle's imagery inside out. The book of Isaiah returns to the imagery and thought of 2:1-4 several times, e.g., 5:25; 9:6; 11:6-9; 30:27-28; 51:4; 56:6-8; 60:11-14. These passages underscore the book's purpose of helping its readers appreciate what God has in store for Jerusalem.

2:5-22 The day of judgment

The refrain "the LORD alone will be exalted on that day" (2:11 and 17) sets the tone of this poem on the subject of what lies ahead for Jerusalem. Judgment is coming because of divination, Judah's "prosperity," and idolatry (2:5-11). The Bible is clear about divination: it is forbidden to Israel (Exod

⁷Their land is full of silver and gold,
　there is no end to their treasures;
Their land is full of horses,
　there is no end to their chariots.
⁸Their land is full of idols;
　they bow down to the works of
　　their hands,
　what their fingers have made.
⁹So all shall be abased,
　each one brought low.
　Do not pardon them!
¹⁰Get behind the rocks,
　hide in the dust,
From the terror of the Lord
　and the splendor of his majesty!
¹¹The eyes of human pride shall be
　lowered,
　the arrogance of mortals shall be
　　abased,
　and the Lord alone will be ex-
　　alted, on that day.
¹²For the Lord of hosts will have
　his day
　against all that is proud and
　　arrogant,
　against all that is high, and it
　　will be brought low;
¹³Yes, against all the cedars of
　Lebanon
　and against all the oaks of
　　Bashan,
¹⁴Against all the lofty mountains
　and all the high hills,

¹⁵Against every lofty tower
　and every fortified wall,
¹⁶Against all the ships of Tarshish
　and all stately vessels.
¹⁷Then human pride shall be abased,
　the arrogance of mortals
　　brought low,
And the Lord alone will be exalted
　on that day.
¹⁸The idols will vanish
　completely.
¹⁹People will go into caves in the
　rocks
　and into holes in the earth,
At the terror of the Lord
　and the splendor of his majesty,
　as he rises to overawe the earth.
²⁰On that day people shall throw to
　moles and bats
　their idols of silver and their
　　idols of gold
　which they made for themselves
　　to worship.
²¹And they shall go into caverns in
　the rocks
　and into crevices in the cliffs,
At the terror of the Lord
　and the splendor of his majesty,
　as he rises to overawe the earth.
²²As for you, stop worrying about
　mortals,
　in whose nostrils is but a breath;
　for of what worth are they?

22:17; Lev 20:27; Deut 18:10-11). The reason for this prohibition is that an unfavorable prediction was followed by the use of prayers and rituals to induce the gods to change the fate of those who have received an unfavorable omen. Judah cannot evade the judgment that is coming on it no matter what rituals may be used to deflect God's will for Israel's immediate future. The country's prosperity benefited the few people at the top of the social and economic hierarchy. The prophet condemned this "prosperity" because it was achieved at the expense of the poor. The worship of gods other than the Lord provided religious support for an unjust social and economic system.

The motif of "the day of the Lord" (2:12) appears frequently in the prophetic tradition (Isa 13:6; Amos 5:18-20; Jer 17:16-18; Ezek 30:3; Joel

3 **Judgment on Jerusalem and Judah.** [1]The Lord, the LORD of hosts,
    will take away from Jerusalem
        and from Judah
Support and staff—
    all support of bread,
    all support of water:
[2]Hero and warrior,
    judge and prophet, diviner and
        elder,
[3]The captain of fifty and the
        nobleman,
    counselor, skilled magician, and
        expert charmer.
[4]I will place boys as their princes;
    the fickle will govern them,
[5]And the people will oppress one
        another,
    yes, each one the neighbor.
The child will be insolent toward
        the elder,
    and the base toward the
        honorable.

[6]When anyone seizes a brother
    in their father's house, saying,
"You have clothes! Be our ruler,
    and take in hand this ruin!"—
[7]He will cry out in that day:
"I cannot be a healer,
    when there is neither bread nor
        clothing in my own
        house!
You will not make me a ruler of
        the people!"
[8]Jerusalem has stumbled, Judah has
        fallen;
    for their speech and deeds af-
        front the LORD,
    a provocation in the sight of his
        majesty.
[9]Their very look bears witness
        against them;
    they boast of their sin like
        Sodom,
They do not hide it.
    Woe to them!

1:15). That day was to witness God's final victory over every enemy. What the prophet asserts here is that Israel is among those who will experience God's judgment because of the injustice that the poor must endure. God's ultimate triumph will lead people to cease serving other deities as they finally recognize that Yahweh alone deserves their exclusive service. In describing the terrors of "the day of the Lord," the prophet asserts three times that people will hide themselves among caves and rocks in the attempt to escape judgment (2:10, 19, 21). The book of Revelation uses that same imagery in speaking of the terrors that it sees as coming at the end of the age (Rev 6:15).

3:1-12 The collapse of the political order

The exaltation of the Lord means the collapse of Jerusalem's political order. The country's leaders will be unable to insure that people have the basic necessities for life: bread and water. One consequence will be the breakdown of society's basic structure. Judah will be without competent leaders. This will result in serious and destructive social conflict. The ensuing situation will be so bad that no one will want to accept a position of leadership.

They deal out evil to
themselves.
[10]Happy the just, for it will go well
with them,
the fruit of their works they will
eat.
[11]Woe to the wicked! It will go ill
with them,
with the work of their hands
they will be repaid.
[12]My people—infants oppress them,
women rule over them!
My people, your leaders deceive
you,
they confuse the paths you
should follow.

[13]The LORD rises to accuse,
stands to try his people.
[14]The Lord enters into judgment
with the people's elders and
princes:
You, you who have devoured the
vineyard;

the loot wrested from the poor
is in your houses.
[15]What do you mean by crushing
my people,
and grinding down the faces of
the poor?
says the Lord, the GOD of hosts.

The Haughty Women of Zion. [16]The
LORD said:
Because the daughters of Zion
are haughty,
and walk with necks
outstretched,
Ogling and mincing as they go,
their anklets tinkling with every
step,
[17]The Lord shall cover the scalps of
Zion's daughters with scabs,
and the LORD shall lay bare their
heads.
[18]On that day the LORD will do away
with the finery of the anklets, sunbursts,
and crescents; [19]the pendants, bracelets,

The prophet makes it clear that the cause of this anarchy was the failure of Judah's leaders to maintain a just society. While there were individuals who conducted their affairs with justice, the society as a whole was a distortion of what God wanted Judah to become. While the just can expect to survive the coming judgment, God means to remake Judahite society by eliminating those responsible for its corruption. In particular, Jerusalem's leaders bear the primary responsibility for the chaos that gripped Judah.

3:13–4:1 Judgment upon the wealthy

The prophet was convinced that the fall of Judah and Jerusalem was the inevitable consequence of decisions made by the people of means. To demonstrate their responsibility, the prophet pictures them on trial before God, who accuses them of oppressing the poor. The prophet singles out rich women flaunting their wealth for all to see. When judgment comes, God will destroy every single bit of finery with which these women flaunt the prosperity gained at the expense of the poor. The rich have stolen from the poor to give themselves the best of everything. Judgment is coming and they will lose everything. The rich will then learn what it means to be poor. War will rob Judah of its young people and plunge it into mourning.

and veils; ²⁰the headdresses, bangles, cinctures, perfume boxes, and amulets; ²¹the signet rings, and the nose rings; ²²the court dresses, wraps, cloaks, and purses; ²³the lace gowns, linen tunics, turbans, and shawls.

²⁴Instead of perfume there will be
    stench,
  instead of a girdle, a rope,
And instead of elaborate coiffure,
    baldness;
  instead of a rich gown, a
      sackcloth skirt.
Then, instead of beauty, shame.
²⁵Your men will fall by the sword,
  and your champions, in war;
²⁶Her gates will lament and mourn,
  as the city sits desolate on the
    ground.
4 ¹Seven women will take hold of one
    man
  on that day, saying:

"We will eat our own food
  and wear our own clothing;
Only let your name be given us,
  put an end to our disgrace!"

Jerusalem Purified. ²On that day,
The branch of the LORD will be
    beauty and glory,
  and the fruit of the land will be
    honor and splendor
  for the survivors of Israel.
³Everyone who remains in Zion,
  everyone left in Jerusalem
Will be called holy:
  everyone inscribed for life in
    Jerusalem.
⁴When the Lord washes away
  the filth of the daughters of
    Zion,
And purges Jerusalem's blood from
    her midst
  with a blast of judgment, a
    searing blast,
⁵Then will the LORD create,

Judah's losses in war will turn its women into widows who will contend with one another for the chance to marry the few remaining men.

4:2-6 Jerusalem's restoration

Though the prophet warns Jerusalem of the judgment that is coming upon it, he never claims that judgment is God's last word to the city. On the contrary, Isaiah was able to see beyond the immediate crisis. Of course, the corruption of the city's leadership and the idleness of its wealthy class evoke a purifying visitation from God. Still, the prophet envisions a new city, one that God will create following the terrible judgment that is coming on an economy founded on injustice toward the poor. What the immediate future holds for Jerusalem is the purging that will come with "searing judgment," leaving only a remnant in the city. God will protect those who survive this judgment and then refound Zion.

The temple does not appear to have a significant place in the prophet's vision of a new Jerusalem. Isaiah envisions the Zion of the future with God present not in some grandiose structure but in the humble shelter of the peasant farmer. The judgment that is coming on Jerusalem is not vindictiveness but has as its purpose the preparation of the purified remnant. This

over the whole site of Mount
     Zion
and over her place of assembly,
A smoking cloud by day
     and a light of flaming fire by
          night.
⁶For over all, his glory will be
     shelter and protection:
     shade from the parching heat of
          day,
     refuge and cover from storm
          and rain.

5 **The Song of the Vineyard.** ¹Now let me
sing of my friend,
     my beloved's song about his
          vineyard.
My friend had a vineyard
     on a fertile hillside;
²He spaded it, cleared it of stones,
     and planted the choicest vines;
Within it he built a watchtower,
     and hewed out a wine press.
Then he waited for the crop of
          grapes,
     but it yielded rotten grapes.
³Now, inhabitants of Jerusalem,
     people of Judah,

judge between me and my
     vineyard:
⁴What more could be done for my
     vineyard
     that I did not do?
Why, when I waited for the crop of
          grapes,
     did it yield rotten grapes?
⁵Now, I will let you know
     what I am going to do to my
          vineyard:
Take away its hedge, give it to
          grazing,
     break through its wall, let it be
          trampled!
⁶Yes, I will make it a ruin:
     it shall not be pruned or hoed,
     but will be overgrown with
          thorns and briers;
I will command the clouds
     not to rain upon it.
⁷The vineyard of the LORD of hosts
     is the house of Israel,
     the people of Judah, his
          cherished plant;
He waited for judgment, but see,
     bloodshed!
     for justice, but hark, the outcry!

---

remnant will witness God's reestablishment of the city on the basis of justice and equity. While Isaiah condemns the Jerusalem of his day because of its exploitive social and economic system, he sees a new Jerusalem cleansed of the sins of its past.

5:1-7 The song of the vineyard

The prophet returns to words of judgment against Jerusalem and Judah, but this judgment is veiled in an allegory about his "friend's" vineyard (see also Hos 10:1; Jer 2:21; Ezek 19:10-14; Matt 21:33; Mark 12:1; Luke 20:10). The prophet's friend invested time and energy into his vineyard with the expectation of a return on this investment. For crops like grapes, full production did not begin for several years after the vines were planted. The owner of the vineyard had to have confidence and patience that a harvest would come one day. But the song is about disappointment. The anticipated results of the efforts do not materialize: the vineyard produces only bitter grapes. The

Oracles of Reproach. [8]Ah! Those who
    join house to house,
      who connect field with field,
    Until no space remains, and you
      alone dwell
        in the midst of the land!
[9]In my hearing the LORD of hosts
    has sworn:
      Many houses shall be in ruins,
      houses large and fine, with
        nobody living there.

[10]Ten acres of vineyard
    shall yield but one bath,
And a homer of seed
    shall yield but an ephah.
[11]Ah! Those who rise early in the
    morning
    in pursuit of strong drink,
lingering late
    inflamed by wine,
[12]Banqueting on wine with harp
    and lyre,

---

owner of the vineyard speaks directly to the reader, asking advice because he will have to make a decision about the future of the vineyard soon. The questioning reflects a degree of pathos, since the unspoken answer to the owner's questions is "nothing."

The owner will not tear up the vines and destroy them as one would expect but will rather remove his care and protection from the vineyard. The owner will stop the cultivation of the vineyard and will allow the natural course of events to take place. By tearing down the wall, the owner will open the vineyard to animals that will eat the grapes. Their grazing will put the plants at risk. The owner will not have the vines pruned. They will then grow too long to support the fruit. By failing to hoe, the owner makes it possible for weeds to grow and compete for nutrients and moisture. Eventually, the weeds will dominate the vineyard and the grapevines will become weak and stunted. The prophet implies that divine judgment on Jerusalem is the absence of God's sustaining presence, leaving the city prey to those who will take advantage of its weakness.

The people of Judah have not met God's expectations. They were to be a blessing to the world, i.e., they were to produce fruit. They were to fulfill their calling in the world as the people of God by maintaining a society whose values were shaped by righteousness and justice. The vineyard will be abandoned and without care or cultivation. It will be overrun and eventually destroyed. God will abandon Judah to those who would conquer it.

5:8-23 Judah's crimes

After the allegorical indictment found in the song of the vineyard, the prophet becomes specific. He begins by condemning the large estates of the wealthy (5:8-11). The people of means were able to acquire their large estates by taking advantage of the economic reverses of the poor and confiscating their land for the nonpayment of debts. The wealthy cultivated grapes and

"Now let me sing my beloved's song about his vineyard." (See Isaiah 5:1-7.)

timbrel and flute,
But the deed of the LORD they do
not regard,
the work of his hands they do
not see!
¹³Therefore my people go into exile
for lack of understanding,
Its nobles starving,
its masses parched with thirst.
¹⁴Therefore Sheol enlarges its throat
and opens its mouth beyond
measure;
Down into it go nobility and masses,
tumult and revelry.
¹⁵All shall be abased, each one
brought low,
and the eyes of the haughty
lowered,
¹⁶But the LORD of hosts shall be
exalted by judgment,
by justice the Holy God shown
holy.
¹⁷Lambs shall graze as at pasture,
young goats shall eat in the
ruins of the rich.
¹⁸Ah! Those who tug at guilt with
cords of perversity,
and at sin as if with cart ropes!
¹⁹Who say, "Let him make haste,

let him speed his work, that we
may see it;
On with the plan of the Holy One
of Israel!
let it come to pass, that we may
know it!"
²⁰Ah! Those who call evil good, and
good evil,
who change darkness to light,
and light into darkness,
who change bitter to sweet, and
sweet into bitter!
²¹Ah! Those who are wise in their
own eyes,
prudent in their own view!
²²Ah! Those who are champions at
drinking wine,
masters at mixing drink!
²³Those who acquit the guilty for
bribes,
and deprive the innocent of
justice!
²⁴Therefore, as the tongue of fire
licks up stubble,
as dry grass shrivels in the
flame,
Their root shall rot
and their blossom scatter like
dust;

---

olives on their land to increase production of wine and olive oil. The export and sale of these commodities were highly profitable. Because more land was given to the cultivation of crops for export, less land was available for growing grains to feed Judah's people. With less grain available for sale, the price of this staple rose, putting more economic pressure on the poor. This helped create a permanent underclass in Judah. This breach of traditional Israelite morality would bring terrible consequences. The prophet promises that the land will not yield the increase the wealthy were expecting. They will have to face the kind of economic pressures that were part of the daily experience of the poor.

The prophet condemns the extravagant lifestyle of the wealthy (5:11-17). Most Judahite farmers were able to raise enough crops to feed their families and animals, to set aside seed for the next planting, and to have something

For they have rejected the
  instruction of the LORD of
  hosts,
and scorned the word of the
  Holy One of Israel.

²⁵Therefore the wrath of the LORD
  blazes against his people,
he stretches out his hand to
  strike them;
The mountains quake,
  their corpses shall be like refuse
  in the streets.
For all this, his wrath is not turned
  back,
  his hand is still outstretched.

Invasion. ²⁶He will raise a signal to a
  far-off nation,
and whistle for it from the ends
  of the earth.
Then speedily and promptly
  they will come.

²⁷None among them is weary, none
  stumbles,
none will slumber, none will
  sleep.
None with waist belt loose,
  none with sandal thong broken.
²⁸Their arrows are sharp,
  and all their bows are bent,
The hooves of their horses like flint,
  and their chariot wheels like the
  whirlwind.
²⁹They roar like the lion,
  like young lions, they roar;
They growl and seize the prey,
  they carry it off and none can
  rescue.
³⁰They will growl over it, on that
  day,
like the growling of the sea,
Look to the land—
  darkness closing in,
  the light dark with clouds!

---

to offer at the shrines to thank God for the land's fertility. The wealthy lived in excess, but the prophet assures them that they will learn what it means to live on the subsistence level. The people of means were able to acquire their wealth by ignoring God's will, by perverting the values of traditional Israelite morality, by their conceit, and by bribery (5:18-22). Because they have ignored the torah, which makes God's will for Israel clear, they can expect only the worst. Unable to cope, they will die in record numbers and the poor will be able to reclaim their heritage. God will insure that justice triumphs.

5:24-30 The means of judgment

The divine judgment that Judah will experience is coming. The result will be the destruction of the nation that has injustice as its foundation. The prophet is aware of the expansionist policies of Judah's more powerful neighbors. He sees Judah falling to their military might. What the rich were doing to the poor, Judah's neighbors would shortly do to the nation as a whole. They will destroy a society whose social and economic values are so out of touch with traditional Israelite morality that they deserve the condemnation that the prophet pronounces on them in the name of God.

B. The Book of Emmanuel

6 The Sending of Isaiah. [1]In the year King Uzziah died, I saw the Lord seated on a high and lofty throne, with the train of his garment filling the temple. [2]Seraphim were stationed above; each of them had six wings: with two they covered their faces, with two they covered their feet, and with two they hovered. [3]One cried out to the other:

> "Holy, holy, holy is the Lord of hosts!
> All the earth is filled with his glory!"

[4]At the sound of that cry, the frame of the door shook and the house was filled with smoke.

[5]Then I said, "Woe is me, I am doomed! For I am a man of unclean lips, living among a people of unclean lips, and my eyes have seen the King, the Lord of hosts!" [6]Then one of the seraphim flew to me, holding an ember which he had taken with tongs from the altar.

[7]He touched my mouth with it. "See," he said, "now that this has touched your lips, your wickedness is removed, your sin purged."

[8]Then I heard the voice of the Lord saying, "Whom shall I send? Who will go for us?" "Here I am," I said; "send me!" [9]And he replied: Go and say to this people:

> Listen carefully, but do not understand!
> Look intently, but do not perceive!
> [10]Make the heart of this people sluggish,
> dull their ears and close their eyes;
> Lest they see with their eyes, and hear with their ears,
> and their heart understand,
> and they turn and be healed.

[11]"How long, O Lord?" I asked. And he replied:

> Until the cities are desolate,
> without inhabitants,
> Houses, without people,
> and the land is a desolate waste.
> [12]Until the Lord sends the people far away,
> and great is the desolation in the midst of the land.
> [13]If there remain a tenth part in it,
> then this in turn shall be laid waste;
> As with a terebinth or an oak
> whose trunk remains when its leaves have fallen.
> Holy offspring is the trunk.

6:1-13 The call of the prophet

Judgment upon Judah was necessary and inevitable. The prophet was to have a critical role in making the people of Judah aware of that judgment so that when it did come they would recognize it for what it was: judgment on a society whose values were a perversion of God's will for Israel. There was to be no mistaking what was to befall Judah as the result of the military strength of imperialistic neighbors or any inability of Israel's patron deity to protect it against this imperialism. On the contrary, what was to befall Judah was God's own doing, announced by prophets whom God commissioned to bring Judah God's message of judgment. To dramatize

The Syro-Ephraimite War

7 **Crisis in Judah.** ¹In the days of Ahaz, king of Judah, son of Jotham, son of Uzziah, Rezin, king of Aram, and Pekah, king of Israel, son of Remaliah, went up to attack Jerusalem, but they were not able to conquer it. ²When word came to the house of David that Aram had allied itself with Ephraim, the heart of the king and heart of the people trembled, as the trees of the forest tremble in the wind.

³Then the LORD said to Isaiah: Go out to meet Ahaz, you and your son Shear-jashub, at the end of the conduit of the upper pool, on the highway to the fuller's field, ⁴and say to him: Take care you

---

Isaiah's role in this terrible encounter between God and Judah, the tradition describes the "call of Isaiah."

The book supplies a date for this call to remind its readers that Isaiah's ministry took place at a turning point in Judah's history (6:1). The forty-year reign of Uzziah (783–742 B.C.) was over. It had been a time of economic expansion and prosperity, though only a few Judahites enjoyed any economic benefits from the boom times of Uzziah's reign. The peasants were left behind. But Judah's economy would never again be as strong as it was under Uzziah, and the specter of the powerful Assyrian army was on the horizon. Judgment was coming.

The setting for the story of Isaiah's call is in the temple. There the prophet sees God accompanied by seraphim. The name "seraphim" recalls the fiery serpents of the wilderness tradition (Num 21:6-9; Deut 8:15). The Hebrew word "seraphim" means "the burning ones" and was used as the name of snakes whose venom caused a burning sensation in a person bitten by them. According to the story in Numbers and Deuteronomy, God used these serpents to punish the Israelites for their murmuring. The seraphim that the prophet sees are harbingers of what is in store for Judah. Their song underscores the basic affirmation that the book makes: God is holy. This holiness requires the purging of all immorality from those who stand in God's presence. Isaiah recognizes this and believes that he will not survive his encounter with God. It is important to note that the prophet stands in solidarity with his people. He does not see himself as a morally upright person who has a right to stand in judgment over others, but the seraphs purge the prophet with a burning coal so that he can begin his mission of announcing God's intention to purge Judah.

In postbiblical Jewish tradition and in medieval Christian tradition, the seraphim form a class of angels. While Isaiah 6 presents the seraphim as winged creatures of the heavenly king, it envisions the seraphim as serpents—not angels. During the time of Isaiah, a bronze serpent was still part of the temple's liturgical accouterments. It was destroyed by King

remain calm and do not fear; do not let your courage fail before these two stumps of smoldering brands, the blazing anger of Rezin and the Arameans and of the son of Remaliah—⁵because Aram, with Ephraim and the son of Remaliah, has planned evil against you. They say, ⁶"Let us go up against Judah, tear it apart, make it our own by force, and appoint the son of Tabeel king there."

⁷Thus says the Lord GOD:
It shall not stand, it shall not be!
⁸The head of Aram is Damascus,
and the head of Damascus is Rezin;
⁹The head of Ephraim is Samaria,
and the head of Samaria is the son of Remaliah.
Within sixty-five years,
Ephraim shall be crushed, no longer a nation.

Hezekiah (see 2 Kgs 18:4). The loss of that image and the development of angelology led to the inclusion of seraphim among the "nine choirs of angels" in a non-canonical Jewish book known as *The Testament of Adam* (ch. 4). This latter work rather than the biblical text has shaped the image of the seraphim in Christian art.

What is the prophet's mission? The tradition is aware that Isaiah's ministry did not prevent the destruction of the temple, the scattering of its priesthood, the end of the dynasty nor the end of the national state. Experience has shown that the prophet was not called to keep Israel from its destiny but to make Israel aware of that destiny. The prophet's mission was to delay Israel's comprehension of the divine plan until generations later, after Israel's endurance of not one but two devastations of its land and two exiles. These bitter events whose significance is illuminated by the message of the prophet made it impossible for Israel to evade responsibility for its fate.

John, the visionary in the book of Revelation, sees the glory of God and the Lamb just as the prophet Isaiah did (6:2-3; Rev 4:6-8). Matthew cites verses 9-10 to explain the apparent failure of the crowds to respond to Jesus' mission (Matt 13:13-15), while the prophet's words are implicit in both Mark (4:12) and Luke (8:10). Luke has Paul recite this text at the climax of Acts. Rejected by the Jews of Rome, Paul turns to the Gentiles, convinced that they will listen (Acts 28:23-29). At the end of his narrative of Jesus' public ministry, the author of the Fourth Gospel (not to be confused with the author of Revelation) paraphrases verses 9-10 to explain the failure of Jesus to attract a wide following (John 12:39-41). God tells the prophet Isaiah that his message will fall on deaf ears. People will refuse to see the scenario of their future that the prophet describes. The New Testament sees this as true not only for Isaiah but also for Jesus and Paul.

Unless your faith is firm,
  you shall not be firm!

Emmanuel. ¹⁰Again the LORD spoke to Ahaz: ¹¹Ask for a sign from the LORD, your God; let it be deep as Sheol, or high as the sky! ¹²But Ahaz answered, "I will not ask! I will not tempt the LORD!" ¹³Then he said: Listen, house of David! Is it not enough that you weary human beings? Must you also weary my God? ¹⁴Therefore the Lord himself will give you a sign; the young woman, pregnant and about to bear a son, shall name him Emmanuel. ¹⁵Curds and honey he will eat so that he may learn to reject evil and choose good; ¹⁶for before the child learns to reject evil and choose good, the land of those two kings whom you dread shall be deserted.

¹⁷The LORD shall bring upon you and your people and your father's house such days as have not come since Ephraim seceded from Judah (the king of Assyria). ¹⁸On that day

The LORD shall whistle
  for the fly in the farthest streams
    of Egypt,
  and for the bee in the land of
    Assyria.
¹⁹All of them shall come and settle
  in the steep ravines and in the
    rocky clefts,
  on all thornbushes and in all
    pastures.

²⁰On that day the Lord shall shave with the razor hired from across the River (the king of Assyria) the head, and the hair of the feet; it shall also shave off the beard.

²¹On that day a man shall keep alive a young cow or a couple of sheep, ²²and from their abundant yield of milk he shall eat curds; curds and honey shall be the food of all who are left in the land. ²³On that day every place where there were a thousand vines worth a thousand pieces of silver shall become briers and thorns. ²⁴One shall have to go there with bow and arrows, for all the country shall be briers and thorns. ²⁵But as for all the hills which were hoed with a mattock, for fear of briers and thorns you will not go there; they shall become a place for cattle to roam and sheep to trample.

8 **A Son of Isaiah.** ¹The LORD said to me: Take a large tablet, and inscribe on it with an ordinary stylus, "belonging to Maher-shalal-hash-baz," ²and call reliable witnesses for me, Uriah the priest, and Zechariah, son of Jeberechiah.

³Then I went to the prophetess and she conceived and bore a son. The LORD said to me: Name him Maher-shalal-hash-baz, ⁴for before the child learns to say, "My father, my mother," the wealth of Damascus and the spoils of Samaria shall be carried off by the king of Assyria.

The Choice: The Lord or Assyria.
⁵Again the LORD spoke to me:

⁶Because this people has rejected
  the waters of Shiloah that flow
    gently,
And melts with fear at the display
  of Rezin and Remaliah's son,

7:1–8:10 Immanuel—God with us

Again after speaking in generalities, the prophet becomes specific. He just spoke about the purpose of his mission as delaying Judah's comprehension of the divine will until there could be no mistaking the divine

7Therefore the Lord is bringing up
against them
the waters of the River, great
and mighty,
the king of Assyria and all his
glory.
It shall rise above all its channels,
and overflow all its banks.
8It shall roll on into Judah,
it shall rage and pass on—
up to the neck it shall reach.
But his outspread wings will fill
the width of your land,
Emmanuel!
9Band together, O peoples, but be
shattered!
Give ear, all you distant lands!
Arm yourselves, but be
shattered! Arm your-
selves, but be shattered!
10Form a plan, it shall be thwarted;
make a resolve, it shall not be
carried out,
for "With us is God!"

intention. Now the prophet describes in detail one instance of that lack of comprehension. The prophet details his encounter with Ahaz, the embattled king of Judah, who was under intense pressure to join a coalition of small national states aligned against the imperial power of Assyria.

The king did not want to be dragged into any military action against Assyria, so he sought Assyria's help in maintaining Judah's independence of action. The prophet recognized that while Ahaz's overtures to Assyria would solve the immediate crisis, their long-term effects would be the opposite of the king's goal of keeping Judah independent. Isaiah advised Ahaz to ignore the threats made against him by the coalition aligned against Assyria since that coalition was certain to fail. The prophet's analysis of the political situation was more astute than that of Ahaz. But the king could not see it nor could he accept the prophet's advice. This he was fated to do (see 6:9-10) since God's goal was the destruction of the Judahite state because of its injustice toward its own citizens. The irony in this passage is the threefold repetition of the Hebrew phrase *immanu el*, which means "God is with us." God is with Judah, but before Judah can experience the saving power of God, it must experience God's judgment on its unjust social and economic system.

This passage is built around several word plays. The first involves the names of Isaiah's sons. God instructed the prophet to take his son and confront Ahaz (7:3). This son's name was *Shear-jashub*, which means "a remnant shall return." The boy's name implies both judgment and salvation for Judah. Only a few of its people will survive the judgment that will involve the end of Judah's political and religious institutions, but God will insure that there will be survivors who will return and begin again. The passage ends with the naming of another of the prophet's sons, *Maher-shalal-hash-baz*, which means "The spoil speeds, the prey hastens." The son who

Disciples of Isaiah. ¹¹For thus said the LORD—his hand strong upon me—warning me not to walk in the way of this people:

¹²Do not call conspiracy what this people calls conspiracy, nor fear what they fear, nor feel dread.

---

bears this unwieldy name is a living assurance to Ahaz that his fear of the coalition threatening him is baseless. That coalition will collapse before the child learns to say his first words (8:3-4).

Another wordplay occurs as the prophet concludes his words of assurance to Ahaz in verses 7b-9. One way to preserve that wordplay in English translation is to render verse 9b: "If you do not make yourself *firm* (in the Lord), you will not be *affirmed* (by the Lord)." Note the words for firm/ affirmed are forms of the Hebrew root *'mn*, which we know from the word "Amen." The prophet asserts that Ahaz need do nothing to save Judah but have confidence in God's words of assurance. With this confidence, Ahaz's own attempts to find security will come to nothing. But Ahaz felt that he had to do something. He was unwilling to accept the prophet's assurances that the Lord was going to protect Judah. A literal translation of Isaiah 65:16 identifies the Lord as "the God of Amen," i.e., the God of assurance, and Revelation 3:14 identifies Jesus as "The Amen."

The most important of the wordplays in this passage are those involving the Hebrew phrase *immanu el*, which occurs three times: 7:14; 8:8, 10. The prophet attempts to support his words of assurance (7:7-9) that those plotting against Judah are just human beings who will not succeed. Because Ahaz is not content with this assurance, the prophet supports them with a "sign." The prophet calls the king's attention to a pregnant woman that both apparently knew. Isaiah asserts that the crisis will pass before the child, who has yet to be born, is weaned. While the identity of the child is not clear, the significance of the sign is. The prophet advises the king to bide his time and the crisis will pass. He urges Ahaz to regard the birth of the child as a sign of God's presence that will protect Judah from external threats. Matthew (1:22-23) cites this text to underscore the significance of Jesus, whom the evangelist believes to be the very presence of God who has come to save Israel.

The second occurrence of *immanu el* in 8:8 is not as reassuring. The presence it signifies is not a saving presence but one that brings judgment. The prophet affirms that the real danger that Judah faces comes not from the nations allied against it but from an unexpected source. Because the prophet's message has been discounted by king and people, Judah will have to face threats from both Assyria and Egypt (7:18-25; 8:5-8). Still, the

31

¹³But conspire with the LORD of
hosts;
he shall be your fear, he shall be
your dread.
¹⁴He shall be a snare,
a stone for injury,
A rock for stumbling
to both the houses of Israel,
A trap and a snare
to those who dwell in Jerusalem;
¹⁵And many among them shall
stumble;
fallen and broken;
snared and captured.

¹⁶Bind up my testimony, seal the instruction with my disciples. ¹⁷I will trust in the LORD, who is hiding his face from the house of Jacob; yes, I will wait for him. ¹⁸Here am I and the children whom the LORD has given me: we are signs and portents in Israel from the LORD of hosts, who dwells on Mount Zion.

¹⁹And when they say to you, "Inquire of ghosts and soothsayers who chirp and mutter; should not a people inquire of their gods, consulting the dead on behalf of the living, ²⁰for instruction and testi-

---

prophet is convinced that God's last word to Judah will not be judgment but salvation. While Judah will experience God's judgment through the nations, God will not allow that judgment to consume Judah. The Lord will ever be *immanu el* for Judah (8:9-10).

8:11-15 The futility of intrigue

To recapitulate the message of 7:1–8:10, the prophet speaks about the folly of the political intrigue that Ahaz used to secure his country's future. Isaiah has clearly and forcefully conveyed God's assurances that Judah has nothing to fear from any perceived military or political threats to its existence. Rather than fearing political powers, Judah ought to fear God. It is God who is the enemy of Judah as long as its social and economic practices exploit and oppress its own citizens. Indeed, Judah will have to face an enemy but it will not be a human one. God has always been present to Israel as a rock of salvation. But because of its moral failures, the Lord will now become a "rock for stumbling" (8:14). Both Romans 9:33 and 1 Peter 2:8 quote this text to describe the failure of some people to accept Jesus as God's final word to Israel.

8:16-20 The book of the prophet

This passage gives us a glimpse into the beginnings of the book of Isaiah. The prophet asks that his supporters keep a record of what he said so that people will come to see the significance of his words. The many people who discounted the prophet's message turned to divination for insights into Judah's future. Isaiah wants his words to be preserved so that when his message is confirmed by events of Judah's future, people will know that prophets rather than diviners convey God's word to God's people.

mony?" Surely, those who speak like this are the ones for whom there is no dawn.

²¹He will pass through it
hard-pressed and hungry,
and when hungry, shall become
enraged,
and curse king and gods.
He will look upward,
²²and will gaze at the earth,
But will see only distress and
darkness,
oppressive gloom,
murky, without light.

The Promise of Salvation Under a New Davidic King. ²³There is no gloom where there had been distress. Where once he degraded the land of Zebulun and the land of Naphtali, now he has glorified the way of the Sea, the land across the Jordan, Galilee of the Nations.

9 ¹The people who walked in darkness
have seen a great light;
Upon those who lived in a land of
gloom
a light has shone.
²You have brought them abundant
joy
and great rejoicing;
They rejoice before you as people
rejoice at harvest,
as they exult when dividing the
spoils.
³For the yoke that burdened them,
the pole on their shoulder,
The rod of their taskmaster,
you have smashed, as on the
day of Midian.
⁴For every boot that tramped in
battle,
every cloak rolled in blood,
will be burned as fuel for fire.
⁵For a child is born to us, a son is
given to us;

Hebrews 2:13 quotes verses 17-18 in speaking about how Jesus was made perfect through his suffering.

8:23–9:6 From darkness to light

When the prophet envisions the future, he sees beyond the possibilities of the present to an ideal future. Here the prophet looks forward to the day when the two Israelite kingdoms will be united under the rule of a single, glorious ruler from the Davidic dynasty. The prophet begins his ode to Israel's future by mentioning territories in the far north which were among the first threatened by the Assyrians. He describes the rejoicing of the people saved from Assyrian power. The prophet uses several metaphors to describe God's new act of grace for Israel. It will be like the move from light to darkness and like the harvest that brings an end to the threat of hunger and starvation. The joy it brings will be like that of soldiers over the fruits of their victory. It will remind people of the victory of Gideon over the Midianites (Judg 7:15-25)—a victory that came without the need for striking even a single blow. Israel's future will be the result of a similar victory—so complete as to make the donning of warriors' armor no longer necessary.

The prophet's ode to Israel's future continues as he describes the enthronement of the king who will rule over the Israel created by God's new

upon his shoulder dominion
rests.
They name him Wonder-Counselor,
God-Hero,
Father-Forever, Prince of Peace.
⁶His dominion is vast
and forever peaceful,
Upon David's throne, and over his
kingdom,
which he confirms and sustains
By judgment and justice,
both now and forever.
The zeal of the LORD of hosts will
do this!

Judgment on the Northern Kingdom.
⁷The Lord has sent a word against
Jacob,
and it falls upon Israel;
⁸And all the people know it—
Ephraim and those who dwell
in Samaria—
those who say in arrogance and
pride of heart,
⁹"Bricks have fallen,
but we will rebuild with cut
stone;
Sycamores have been felled,

but we will replace them with
cedars."
¹⁰So the LORD raises up their foes
against them
and stirs up their enemies to
action—
¹¹Aram from the east and the
Philistines from the west—
they devour Israel with open
mouth.
For all this, his wrath is not turned
back,
and his hand is still outstretched!
¹²The people do not turn back to the
one who struck them,
nor do they seek the LORD of
hosts.
¹³So the LORD cuts off from Israel
head and tail,
palm branch and reed in one day.
¹⁴(The elder and the noble are the
head,
the prophet who teaches
falsehood is the tail.)
¹⁵Those who lead this people lead
them astray,
and those who are led are
swallowed up.

act of grace. This future king will do what Ahaz could not: he will trust in the fidelity and power of the Lord. This king will not need advisors because his faith will guide him wondrously. He will be an authentic representative of God on earth and will bring an all-embracing and a never-ending peace to God's people. His kingdom will be sustained by justice.

Luke 1:78-79 alludes to this text when he has Zechariah speak about what God will do for Israel. Matthew 4:15-16 cites 9:1-2 as he describes the beginning of Jesus' ministry in Galilee—the region where the territories of Zebulon and Naphtali were located.

9:7–10:4 Judgment on Israel

Again the prophet moves back from his vision of the future to his indictment of the present. Though he sees the two Israelite kingdoms united under the rule of the Davidic dynasty some day, for the present the kingdom of Israel has to face judgment. The indictment has four particulars each

¹⁶That is why the Lord does not
spare their young men,
and their orphans and widows
he does not pity;
For they are totally impious and
wicked,
and every mouth speaks folly.
For all this, his wrath is not turned
back,
his hand is still outstretched!
¹⁷For wickedness burns like fire,
devouring brier and thorn;
It kindles the forest thickets,
which go up in columns of
smoke.
¹⁸At the wrath of the LORD of hosts
the land quakes,
and the people are like fuel for
fire;
no one spares his brother.
¹⁹They hack on the right, but remain
hungry;

they devour on the left, but are
not filled.
Each devours the flesh of the
neighbor;
²⁰Manasseh devours Ephraim, and
Ephraim Manasseh,
together they turn on Judah.
For all this, his wrath is not turned
back,
his hand is still outstretched!

10 **Perversion of Justice.** ¹Ah! Those
who enact unjust statutes,
who write oppressive decrees,
²Depriving the needy of judgment,
robbing my people's poor of
justice,
Making widows their plunder,
and orphans their prey!
³What will you do on the day of
punishment,
when the storm comes from afar?

concluding with the same refrain: "For all this [God's] wrath is not turned back, / his hand is still outstretched!" (9:11, 16, 20; 10:4).

The first particular (9:7-11) denounces Israel for its arrogance. While the houses of the poor built with mud bricks and sycamore timber are collapsing, villas for the wealthy built from cedar and dressed stones are going up. This must end so God is stirring up Israel's neighbors whose military forays will destroy Israel and its corrupt economic and social system. The second particular (9:12-16) singles out Israel's elders and prophets who should have led the people with integrity. Their failure to meet their responsibilities will lead to devastation that will spare no one. Without competent leadership, society as a whole has become corrupt and will suffer under divine judgment.

The third particular (9:17-20) describes a society that is destroying itself through civil strife. Israel's social and economic system has degenerated to the extent that people see each other as enemies. They ought to have considered each other brothers and sisters with whom they are to share the bounty that God has granted the land. Instead of this, they compete with each other for control of the nation's economic resources—a competition that has brought Israel to disaster. The final particular (10:1-4) indicts Israel for creating an economic system that steals from the defenseless. People of

To whom will you flee for help?
  Where will you leave your
    wealth,
[4]Lest it sink beneath the captive
  or fall beneath the slain?
For all this, his wrath is not turned
    back,
  his hand is still outstretched!

Judgment on Assyria. [5]Ah! Assyria,
  the rod of my wrath,
    the staff I wield in anger.
[6]Against an impious nation I send
    him,
  and against a people under my
    wrath I order him
To seize plunder, carry off loot,
  and to trample them like the
    mud of the street.
[7]But this is not what he intends,
  nor does he have this in mind;
Rather, it is in his heart to destroy,
  to make an end of not a few
    nations.
[8]For he says, "Are not my
    commanders all kings?"
[9]"Is not Calno like Carchemish,
Or Hamath like Arpad,
  or Samaria like Damascus?
[10]Just as my hand reached out to
    idolatrous kingdoms
  that had more images than
    Jerusalem and Samaria—
[11]Just as I treated Samaria and her
    idols,
  shall I not do to Jerusalem and
    her graven images?"

[12]But when the Lord has brought to an
end all his work on Mount Zion and in
Jerusalem,

I will punish the utterance
  of the king of Assyria's proud
    heart,
  and the boastfulness of his
    haughty eyes.
[13]For he says:
"By my own power I have done it,
  and by my wisdom, for I am
    shrewd.
I have moved the boundaries of
    peoples,
  their treasures I have pillaged,
  and, like a mighty one, I have
    brought down the
    enthroned.
[14]My hand has seized, like a nest,
  the wealth of nations.
As one takes eggs left alone,
  so I took in all the earth;
No one fluttered a wing,
  or opened a mouth, or chirped!"
[15]Will the ax boast against the one
  who hews with it?
Will the saw exalt itself above
  the one who wields it?
As if a rod could sway the one who
    lifts it,
  or a staff could lift the one who
    is not wood!
[16]Therefore the Lord, the Lord of
    hosts,
  will send leanness among his fat
    ones,

---

means are feeding themselves on the misery of the poor. They are guilty of economic cannibalism. Such a society dooms itself and that doom is what the prophet announced to Israel.

In Romans 9:27-28, Paul cites 10:22 to help explain the failure of the early Christian mission to the Jews. The apostle implies that God's promises never included all the people of Israel.

And under his glory there will be a
kindling
like the kindling of fire.
[17]The Light of Israel will become a
fire,
the Holy One, a flame,
That burns and consumes its briers
and its thorns in a single day.
[18]And the glory of its forests and
orchards
will be consumed, soul and body,
and it will be like a sick man
who wastes away.
[19]And the remnant of the trees in
his forest
will be so few,
that any child can record them.
[20]On that day
The remnant of Israel,
the survivors of the house of
Jacob,
will no more lean upon the one
who struck them;
But they will lean upon the LORD,
the Holy One of Israel, in truth.
[21]A remnant will return, the
remnant of Jacob,
to the mighty God.
[22]Though your people, O Israel,
were like the sand of the sea,
Only a remnant of them will return;
their destruction is decreed,
as overflowing justice demands.

[23]For the Lord, the GOD of hosts, is about to carry out the destruction decreed in the midst of the whole land.

[24]Therefore thus says the Lord, the GOD of hosts: My people, who dwell in Zion, do not fear the Assyrian, though he strikes you with a rod, and raises his staff against you as did the Egyptians. [25]For just a brief moment more, and my wrath shall be over, and my anger shall be set for their destruction. [26]Then the LORD of hosts will raise against them a scourge such as struck Midian at the rock of Oreb; and he will raise his staff over the sea as he did in Egypt. [27]On that day,

His burden shall be taken from
your shoulder,
and his yoke shattered from
your neck.

The March of an Enemy Army. He has
come up from Rimmon,
[28]he has reached Aiath, passed
through Migron,
at Michmash he has stored his
supplies.
[29]He has crossed the ravine,
at Geba he has camped for the
night.
Ramah trembles,
Gibeah of Saul has fled.
[30]Cry and shriek, Bath-Gallim!

10:5-34 Assyria—God's instrument of judgment

The great achievement of the prophetic movement was to show the people of Israel that what happened to their two kingdoms fulfilled the purposes of their God. An alternative explanation of events held that the military defeat and political subjection of the Israelite kingdoms were due to the weakness of the Lord compared to the patron deities of the nations. Here the prophet explicitly identifies Assyria as God's instrument of judgment. The fall of the Israelite kingdoms, then, is not due to any failure on the Lord's part but is the result of Israel's failings.

The militarist and expansionist Assyrian Empire will be the means by which Israel and Judah will experience God's judgment on their social

Hearken, Laishah! Answer her,
Anathoth!
³¹Madmenah is in flight,
the inhabitants of Gebim seek
refuge.
³²Even today he will halt at Nob,
he will shake his fist at the
mount of daughter Zion,
the hill of Jerusalem!
³³Now the Lord, the LORD of hosts,
is about to lop off the boughs
with terrible violence;
The tall of stature shall be felled,
and the lofty ones shall be
brought low;
³⁴He shall hack down the forest
thickets with an ax,

and Lebanon in its splendor
shall fall.

11 The Ideal Davidic King. ¹But a shoot ▷
shall sprout from the stump of Jesse,
and from his roots a bud shall
blossom.
²The spirit of the LORD shall rest ▷
upon him:
a spirit of wisdom and of
understanding,
A spirit of counsel and of strength,
a spirit of knowledge and of fear
of the LORD,
³and his delight shall be the fear
of the LORD.
Not by appearance shall he judge,
nor by hearsay shall he decide,

---

and economic systems. While the Assyrians have their own purposes for their conquest of the two Israelite kingdoms, Isaiah believes that these really serve God's purposes. The Assyrians wanted to take Egypt to secure its resources and to control the trade routes that connected Egypt to Mesopotamia. Between Assyria and Egypt lay the two Israelite kingdoms. These had to be taken in order for the Assyrian army to protect its lines of communication. The overwhelming power of Assyria's military and the confidence of its leaders sealed the fate of the two Israelite kingdoms.

The prophet saw the hand of God in the expansionist policies of the Assyrian Empire (10:5-11). The aberrant religious practices of the Israelite kingdoms served to provide religious support for their unjust social systems. The Israelite people came into existence by rejecting the religious systems of the nations in order to serve a God who took the side of slaves over their masters. The prophet decries the current religious practices of the Israelites who have subjected themselves to gods who support the greed of the people of means as they enrich themselves at the expense of the peasants. At God's direction, Assyria will bring an end to the religious folly of both Israel and Judah.

The Assyrians wished to establish a world empire, but the prophet insists that Israel's God has already done that. Though Assyria's expansionism is the means God has chosen to bring judgment on the Israelite kings, God will deal with Assyria for its arrogance. Assyria will face its own day of judgment (10:12). Before that happens, the Assyrian army will devastate the Israelite kingdoms. God's judgment will be like a forest fire that consumes

⁴But he shall judge the poor with
    justice,
    and decide fairly for the land's
        afflicted.
He shall strike the ruthless with the
    rod of his mouth,
    and with the breath of his lips
        he shall slay the wicked.
⁵Justice shall be the band around
    his waist,
    and faithfulness a belt upon his
        hips.
⁶Then the wolf shall be a guest of
    the lamb,
    and the leopard shall lie down
        with the young goat;
The calf and the young lion shall
    browse together,
    with a little child to guide them.

⁷The cow and the bear shall graze,
    together their young shall lie
        down;
    the lion shall eat hay like the ox.
⁸The baby shall play by the viper's
    den,
    and the child lay his hand on
        the adder's lair.
⁹They shall not harm or destroy on
    all my holy mountain;
    for the earth shall be filled with
        knowledge of the LORD,
    as water covers the sea.

Restoration. ¹⁰On that day,
The root of Jesse,
    set up as a signal for the
        peoples—
Him the nations will seek out;

---

almost everything in its path. There will be a few trees left, but these will serve simply to mark the movement of the divine judge through the land.

While the devastation of Israel's resources will be horrific, it will not be total. These few trees that survive the fire of God's judgment stand for "the remnant of Israel" that will survive (10:20). Judgment is never God's last word to Israel, and the remnant will be the means of Israel's survival. The importance of this motif for Isaiah is clear from the name he gave to his eldest son: "A remnant shall return" (7:3). Nonetheless, for the prophet the remnant motif involves a proclamation of judgment on unfaithful Judah: 10:19; 17:5-6; 30:17. Faith and conversion are necessary before the remnant can experience God's salvation. This will lead God to restore the remnant to the land from the nations where they have been exiled (11:11). Most of the occurrences of remnant language in Isaiah reflect political usage in which remnant describes what remained of a people who managed to survive a military campaign that aimed at their total destruction.

There are several texts from the book of Isaiah in which the remnant idea is defined as a miraculously preserved minority (4:3; 10:20; and 38:5). This idea meshes with a principal Isaianic theme: Jerusalem is threatened but ultimately delivered. In Isaiah the remnant motif is part of the prophet's call for repentance and faith. Still, Isaiah says practically nothing about the identity of this remnant. Zephaniah, a Judahite prophet who lived about two hundred years after Isaiah, is not so reticent and identifies the remnant

his dwelling shall be glorious.
¹¹On that day,
The Lord shall again take it in hand
to reclaim the remnant of his
people
that is left from Assyria and
Egypt,
Pathros, Ethiopia, and Elam,
Shinar, Hamath, and the isles of
the sea.
¹²He shall raise a signal to the
nations
and gather the outcasts of Israel;
The dispersed of Judah he shall
assemble
from the four corners of the earth.
¹³The envy of Ephraim shall pass
away,
and those hostile to Judah shall
be cut off;
Ephraim shall not envy Judah,
and Judah shall not be hostile to
Ephraim;
¹⁴But they shall swoop down on the
foothills
of the Philistines to the west,
together they shall plunder the
people of the east;
Edom and Moab shall be their
possessions,
and the Ammonites their
subjects.
¹⁵The LORD shall dry up the tongue
of the Sea of Egypt,
and wave his hand over the
Euphrates with his fierce
wind,

---

with the poor (Zeph 2:3; 3:12-13). They will survive the judgment and be the nucleus of a new people of God.

The poem in verses 28-34 describes with geographical detail the Assyrian advance on Jerusalem from the north. It appears that nothing can stand in the way of the Assyrian invader. Still, God, who is called here "the Lord of hosts" ("host" being a traditional term for "army") prevents the Assyrians from taking Zion. Instead, the Assyrians themselves suffer a great defeat.

11:1-9 The shoot from Jesse

The prophet shifts away from political and military realities back into an idealistic vision of the future. As in 9:2-7, Isaiah gives a central place in that future to an ideal king who will be everything that Judah's actual kings were not.

God's promise regarding Judah's future will find its fulfillment through a descendant of Jesse, the father of David. "The shoot from the stump of Jesse" is an engaging poetic metaphor for an ideal king who will be equipped for his rule by God's spirit. This will insure his success. This savior-king will be known for his judicial wisdom, his ability to translate his decisions into action, his attitude toward the poor, his readiness to deal harshly with evildoers, his devotion to God, and his righteousness (11:25). The rule of this coming king will please both God and God's people.

"Then the wolf shall be the guest of the lamb . . ." (See Isaiah 11:6ff.)

And divide it into seven streamlets,
    so that it can be crossed in
        sandals.
[16]There shall be a highway for the
    remnant of his people
    that is left from Assyria,
As there was for Israel
    when it came up from the land
        of Egypt.

12 **Song of Thanksgiving.** [1]On that day, you will say:
I give you thanks, O LORD;
    though you have been angry
        with me,
    your anger has abated, and you
        have consoled me.
[2]God indeed is my salvation;
    I am confident and unafraid.

The coming of this ideal king will be marked by the taming of wild animals (11:6-8). At present people have to fear for the safety of their domestic animals and their children. The prophet envisions a future when this danger will be removed; however, he is clear that this change will take place only when all people act righteously in accord with the guidance provided by the savior-king (11:9b). The absence of this "knowledge of the LORD" is the reason for alienation from God and the consequent divine judgment (1:3; 5:13; 6:10). The knowledge the prophet speaks of is not information about God but a commitment to God and traditional Israelite moral values.

At the end of his infancy narrative, Matthew states that Joseph settled his family in Nazareth to fulfill the prophetic word that "He shall be called a Nazorean" (Matt 2:23). There is no such text in the Hebrew Bible, though there is a similarity in sound between the Aramaic word for Nazareth and the Hebrew word that the NAB translates as "shoot" in verse 1. Of course, Christian believers have claimed that this prophetic vision of a second David has been fulfilled in Jesus. The expectations of the prophet, however, were not fulfilled in a literal sense but were reinterpreted by people of faith. Religious Jews continue to look for the coming of the king that the prophet describes. Both Jews and Christians together wait for the final revelation of God's power and glory in a completely definitive way.

The redemption that the prophet describes is not directed at the salvation of individual people. The coming of this ideal king will involve the renewal of all creation. Because the world is God's creation, it will not devolve into nothingness, but will be transformed and renewed in the final consummation which both Jew and Christian still await.

11:10-16 Israel and Judah united

Speaking of the rule of the ideal king leads the prophet to speak of the kingdom over which that king will rule. For most of their history, the two Israelite kingdoms were antagonistic to one another with Israel, the more

For the LORD is my strength and
　my might,
　and he has been my salvation.
³With joy you will draw water
　from the fountains of salvation,
⁴And you will say on that day:
　give thanks to the LORD, acclaim
　　his name;
　Among the nations make known
　　his deeds,
proclaim how exalted is his
　name.
⁵Sing praise to the LORD for he has
　done glorious things;
　let this be known throughout all
　　the earth.
⁶Shout with exultation, City of
　Zion,
　for great in your midst
　is the Holy One of Israel!

---

powerful of the two usually taking the upper hand. What the prophet envisions are the two kingdoms united under the rule of a single sovereign from "the root of Jesse," i.e., the Davidic dynasty. Before that vision can find fulfillment, God will first have to gather the remnant of the two kingdoms that have been dispersed through exile. Once this remnant has been assembled, there will be no evidence of the rivalry that had marked the relations between Israel (Ephraim) and Judah. The new united people will enjoy sovereignty over neighboring national states. The prophet compares this future act of deliverance to the exodus from Egypt that transformed the Hebrew slaves into the people of God.

In Romans 15:8-12, Paul cites several texts including verse 10 to emphasize that, while Jesus' being a Jew proves God's fidelity to the promises made to the patriarchs, the salvation promised was for the Gentiles as well.

12:1-6 A hymn of salvation

This is a short hymn of thanksgiving for Jerusalem's deliverance. While Isaiah was certain that Jerusalem was going to experience divine judgment for the failure of its leaders to maintain a just society, he was equally convinced that judgment on Jerusalem was not final. One call to praise and thanksgiving follows another as the prophet exclaims his confidence in Zion's future. One can look beyond judgment to a glorious future for Zion because the Holy One of Israel remains in the midst of the city. While the mission of the prophet was to confront Judah with the consequences of its failure to maintain a just society, there was another aspect to that mission that cannot be ignored. The prophet's mission makes sense only if there is to be a future for Judah. This hymn of salvation expresses the prophet's assurance that divine judgment will not be the end of Judah but the beginning of a new act of salvation.

C. Oracles against the Foreign Nations

13 **Babylon.** ¹An oracle concerning Babylon; a vision of Isaiah, son of Amoz.

²Upon the bare mountains set up a
signal;
cry out to them,
Beckon for them to enter
the gates of the nobles.
³I have commanded my
consecrated ones,
I have summoned my warriors,
eager and bold to carry out my
anger.
⁴Listen! the rumble on the
mountains:
that of an immense throng!
Listen! the noise of kingdoms,
nations assembled!
The LORD of hosts is mustering
an army for battle.
⁵They come from a far-off country,
and from the end of the
heavens,
The LORD and the instruments of
his wrath,
to destroy all the land.
⁶Howl, for the day of the LORD is
near;
as destruction from the
Almighty it comes.
⁷Therefore all hands fall helpless,
every human heart melts,
⁸and they are terrified,

JERUSALEM AND THE NATIONS

Isaiah 13:1–27:13

The prophets addressed their words to a real people, who lived at a real time and in a real place, and who had to deal with real problems. Among the most serious of these problems were the political and military pressures brought to bear upon the Israelite kingdoms by neighboring national states and imperial powers. Economic and political realities usually meant that ancient Israel regarded its neighbors as potential threats to its existence. In speaking about Jerusalem's future, Isaiah could not avoid speaking about the nations. In this second section of the book, the dominant attitude toward the nations is negative since these oracles reflect the experience of Israel and Judah with the nations. For most of their history, the two Israelite kingdoms had to contend with the other national states in the eastern Mediterranean region for control of the region's commercial and agricultural resources. The kingdom of Israel's principal rivals were Aram and Moab, while Judah's were the Philistine city-states and Edom. The two Israelite kingdoms contended with each other as well, with Israel having the most success. But it was the rise of the neo-Assyrian and neo-Babylonian empires with their aggressive and expansionist policies that led to the end of first Israel and then Judah as national states.

Oracles against the nations are a prominent feature in several prophetic books, e.g., Amos 1:2–2:3; Jeremiah 46:1–51:64; and Ezekiel 25–32. Indeed, an

Pangs and sorrows take hold of
them,
like a woman in labor they
writhe;
They look aghast at each other,
their faces aflame.
⁹Indeed, the day of the Lord comes,
cruel, with wrath and burning
anger;
To lay waste the land
and destroy the sinners within
it!
¹⁰The stars of the heavens and their
constellations
will send forth no light;
The sun will be dark at its rising,
and the moon will not give its
light.
¹¹Thus I will punish the world for
its evil

and the wicked for their guilt.
I will put an end to the pride of the
arrogant,
the insolence of tyrants I will
humble.
¹²I will make mortals more rare
than pure gold,
human beings, than the gold of
Ophir.
¹³For this I will make the heavens
tremble
and the earth shall be shaken
from its place,
At the wrath of the Lord of hosts
on the day of his burning anger.
¹⁴Like a hunted gazelle,
or a flock that no one gathers,
They shall turn each to their own
people
and flee each to their own land.

---

oracle against Assyria comprises the whole of the book of Nahum. Since the people of the two Israelite kingdoms experienced other nations as threats to their existence, it is not surprising that they called upon their God to defend them from such threats. The oracles against the nations are an expression of ancient Israel's belief that God would never permit these nations to destroy Israel completely. While God has chosen to use these nations to bring judgment upon the Israelite kingdoms for their failure to maintain a just society, God will move against these nations for their failures as well. God's judgment of the nations will mean salvation for Israel.

Some modern readers find these oracles difficult to read. First, the nations against whom the prophet announces God's judgment are simply geographical names devoid of any emotional content. But the prophet's first audience reacted to names like Assyria, Edom, Philistia, and Babylon the same way that the Irish react to England, the Tibetans to China, the Bosnians to Serbia, and the Koreans to Japan. Second, some of the prophet's modern readers are shocked by the harshness of the prophet's words. While the severity of the judgments pronounced by the prophet reflects rhetorical patterns of his culture, also displays an anger that is genuine. There may be a holdover of this attitude toward the nations when Jesus refers to the Syrophoenician woman and her daughter as "dogs" (Mark 7:27-28). Certainly, the book of Revelation is as harsh toward Rome as any of the Old Testament's oracles against the nations.

45

¹⁵Everyone who is taken shall be
    run through;
  and everyone who is caught
    shall fall by the sword.
¹⁶Their infants shall be dashed to
    pieces in their sight;
  their houses shall be plundered
    and their wives ravished.
¹⁷I am stirring up against them the
    Medes,
  who think nothing of silver
    and take no delight in gold.
¹⁸With their bows they shall shatter
    the young men,
And the fruit of the womb they
    shall not spare,

  nor shall their eye take pity on
    children.
¹⁹And Babylon, the jewel of
    kingdoms,
  the glory and pride of the
    Chaldeans,
Shall become like Sodom and
    Gomorrah,
  overthrown by God.
²⁰It shall never be inhabited,
  nor dwelt in, from age to age;
Arabians shall not pitch their tents
    there,
  nor shepherds rest their flocks
    there.
²¹But desert demons shall rest there
  and owls shall fill the houses;

Like the first section of the book, this one also begins with an oracle of judgment against arrogance and injustice, though here the oracle is addressed to Babylon rather than Judah. Again, as was the case with the previous section, this second section of the book ends on a positive note. The prophet announces salvation for Judah.

13:1–14:23 Against Babylon

First place among the nations under divine judgment is given to Babylon. The events that led to the production of Isaiah as we have it and, indeed, a good part of the Old Testament in its present form were those surrounding the Babylonian conquest of Jerusalem in 587 B.C. and the fall of Babylon less than fifty years later. The fall of this mighty empire and the subsequent restoration of Jerusalem and its temple gave Judah hope for the future. It is fitting, then, that the first of the oracles against the nations has Babylon as its subject. The ascription of this oracle to the eighth-century prophet is appropriate because of his insistence that divine judgment upon Judah, though well deserved, was not God's final word to Jerusalem. While the nations are God's instruments of judgment, they will have to answer for their own excesses, arrogance, and folly.

This poem opens with Babylon's sentinels sounding the alarm as an army of conquest is approaching the city. The marching feet of its immense horde moving toward the city make sounds like the rumble of thunder on a distant mountain as the storm gathers strength and begins its approach. Of course, it is Judah's God who has gathered this mighty force against

There ostriches shall dwell,
and satyrs shall dance.
²²Wild dogs shall dwell in its
castles,
and jackals in its luxurious
palaces.
Its time is near at hand
and its days shall not be
prolonged.

14 **Restoration of Israel.** ¹But the
Lord will take pity on Jacob and
again choose Israel, and will settle them
on their own land; foreigners will join
them and attach themselves to the house
of Jacob. ²The nations will take them and
bring them to their place, and the house
of Israel will possess them as male and
female slaves on the Lord's land; they
will take captive their captors and rule
over their oppressors.

Downfall of the King of Babylon.
³On the day when the Lord gives you
rest from your sorrow and turmoil, from
the hard service with which you served,
⁴you will take up this taunt-song against
the king of Babylon:

How the oppressor has come to an
end!
how the turmoil has ended!

⁵The Lord has broken the rod of the
wicked,
the staff of the tyrants
⁶That struck the peoples in wrath
with relentless blows;
That ruled the nations in anger,
with boundless persecution.
⁷The whole earth rests peacefully,
song breaks forth;
⁸The very cypresses rejoice over
you,
the cedars of Lebanon:
"Now that you are laid to rest,
no one comes to cut us down."
⁹Below, Sheol is all astir
preparing for your coming;
Awakening the shades to greet you,
all the leaders of the earth;
Making all the kings of the nations
rise from their thrones.
¹⁰All of them speak out
and say to you,
"You too have become weak like
us,
you are just like us!
¹¹Down to Sheol your pomp is
brought,
the sound of your harps.
Maggots are the couch beneath
you,
worms your blanket."

Babylon, whose military forces desert as the army assembled by God approaches. The portents in the heavens make it obvious that this is no ordinary military adventure, but one directed by God. The devastation will be complete and Babylon will experience the horrors of war. The Medes, who are God's chosen instruments of judgment, will turn Babylon into a wasteland.

The prophet uses a type of hyperbole that often appears in biblical texts with a high emotional content. The poem is trying to revive the spirit of the Judahite community that was devastated by the fall of Jerusalem, the destruction of its temple, and the exile of a sizeable portion of its population. Many of the exiles accommodated themselves to the new realities. The prophet insists that Babylon has no future and implies that its fall is

¹²How you have fallen from the
heavens,
O Morning Star, son of the
dawn!
How you have been cut down to
the earth,
you who conquered nations!
¹³In your heart you said:
"I will scale the heavens;
Above the stars of God
I will set up my throne;
I will take my seat on the Mount of
Assembly,
on the heights of Zaphon.
¹⁴I will ascend above the tops of the
clouds;
I will be like the Most High!"

¹⁵No! Down to Sheol you will be
brought
to the depths of the pit!
¹⁶When they see you they will stare,
pondering over you:
"Is this the man who made the
earth tremble,
who shook kingdoms?
¹⁷Who made the world a wilderness,
razed its cities,
and gave captives no release?"
¹⁸All the kings of the nations lie in
glory,
each in his own tomb;
¹⁹But you are cast forth without
burial,
like loathsome carrion,

---

a harbinger of a new future for Judah. The fall of Babylon makes Judah's restoration possible. The prophet elaborates on this reversal of fortunes as he taunts Babylon. He asserts that the exile will be reversed: instead of the people of Israel being led off to Babylon as slaves, the Babylonians will be led to the land of Israel to serve the community restored to its native land. Of course, here the prophet is becoming carried away by his own rhetoric.

The oracle in 14:4b-21 begins by proclaiming the fall of the tyrant responsible for the oppression of many nations, all of whom delight in the tyrant's fall. Peace has come again to the world. The trees of Lebanon's lush forests are personified to represent the nations who are relieved to know there will be no one to cut them down again.

Tyrants of the distant past welcome the king of Babylon to their realm in the nether world. He is now one of them, exchanging the accouterments of a regal life style for the worms that devour the corpses of the dead. Babylon's king did not even have the benefit of a decent burial. His corpse is simply trampled underfoot. This terrible fate is due him because of his failures as a king. His sons will also be killed to insure that his name will be forgotten. The oracle against Babylon concludes with a prose statement (14:22-23) in which God affirms the decision to destroy Babylon totally. The book of Revelation adopts Babylon as its code name for Rome, which it perceived as a threat to the existence of the early Christian community.

The New Testament uses the imagery of 13:10 in speaking about the end of the age (Matt 24:29; Mark 13:24-25; Luke 21:25; Rev 6:12-13; 8:12). In 14:12 the prophet calls the king of Babylon the "Morning Star," which

Covered with the slain, with those
struck by the sword,
a trampled corpse,
Going down to the very stones of
the pit.
²⁰You will never be together
with them in the grave,
For you have ruined your land,
you have slain your people!
Let him never be named,
that offshoot of evil!
²¹Make ready to slaughter his sons
for the guilt of their fathers;
Lest they rise and possess the earth,
and fill the breadth of the world
with cities.

²²I will rise up against them, says the
Lord of hosts, and cut off from Babylon
name and remnant, progeny and offspring, says the Lord. ²³I will make it a
haunt of hoot owls and a marshland; I
will sweep it with the broom of destruction, oracle of the Lord of hosts.

God's Plan for Assyria. ²⁴The Lord of
hosts has sworn:
As I have resolved,
so shall it be;
As I have planned,
so shall it stand:
²⁵To break the Assyrian in my land
and trample him on my
mountains;
Then his yoke shall be removed
from them,
and his burden from their
shoulder.
²⁶This is the plan proposed for the
whole earth,
and this the hand outstretched
over all the nations.
²⁷The Lord of hosts has planned;
who can thwart him?

Jerome rendered into Latin as "Lucifer." Patristic and medieval interpreters, influenced by Jerome and connecting Isaiah 14:12 with Luke 10:18,
read this passage as a description of the fall of rebellious angels. Of course,
this interpretation is an example of creative imagination. Still, Lucifer has
passed into popular language as a name for the leader of the fallen angels.

14:24-27 Against Assyria

The aggressively expansionist neo-Assyrian empire made a series of
incursions into the territory of the two Israelite kingdoms during the last
third of the eighth century B.C. This oracle implies that God would destroy
the Assyrian Empire during one of those incursions. While the Assyrian
army was besieging Jerusalem in 701 B.C., civil unrest back in Assyria required the return of the army. Perhaps the oracle refers to the lifting of that
siege (Isa 37:36-37; 2 Kgs 19:35-37). In any case, the Assyrian Empire fell
in 612 B.C. to the Babylonians. Certainly the prophet wanted to insure that
the people of Judah would see the working out of a divine purpose in the
collapse of that empire. Again, the fall of a great empire was a sign of God's
power and determination to rehabilitate Judah and Jerusalem.

His hand is stretched out;
who can turn it back?

Philistia. ²⁸In the year that King Ahaz died, there came this oracle:

²⁹Do not rejoice, Philistia, not one of
you,
that the rod which struck you is
broken;
For out of the serpent's root shall
come an adder,
its offspring shall be a flying
saraph. *Babylon*
³⁰In my pastures the poor shall graze,
and the needy lie down in
safety;
But I will kill your root with famine
that shall slay even your
remnant.
³¹Howl, O gate; cry out, O city!
Philistia, all of you melts away!
For there comes a smoke from the
north,
without a straggler in its ranks.
³²What will one answer the
messengers of the nations?

"The LORD has established Zion,
and in her the afflicted of his
people find refuge."

15 Moab. ¹Oracle on Moab:
Laid waste in a night,
Ar of Moab is destroyed;
Laid waste in a night,
Kir of Moab is destroyed.
²Daughter Dibon has gone up
to the high places to weep;
Over Nebo and over Medeba
Moab is wailing.
Every head is shaved,
every beard sheared off.
³In the streets they wear sackcloth,
and on the rooftops;
In the squares
everyone wails, streaming with
tears.
⁴Heshbon and Elealeh cry out,
they are heard as far as Jahaz.
At this the loins of Moab tremble,
his soul quivers within him;
⁵My heart cries out for Moab,
his fugitives reach Zoar,
Eglath-shelishiyah:

14:28-32 Against Philistia

The prophet had already asserted that God used the Philistines to punish Israel for its infidelity (9:11). Now he warns the Philistines that they, in turn, will face their day of judgment. Like all the peoples who lived along the eastern Mediterranean coast, the Philistines were subjugated by Assyria. Though Assyria has fallen, the Philistines should not be too quick to celebrate. Another serpent whose venom is even stronger than that of the Assyrians will strike them. Of course, Babylon, whom the prophet characterizes as a "flying seraph," is that foe from the north who will bring an end to the Philistine cities that harassed Judah in its weakness. Philistia's trouble is Jerusalem's salvation.

15:1–16:14 Against Moab

Moab too had to deal with the Assyrian incursions into its territory. Unlike the two Israelite kingdoms, Moab was much more compliant. It even assisted the Assyrians in dealing with Arab tribes who resisted Assyrian domination. This collaboration with Assyria may have led the prophet to

The ascent of Luhith
 they ascend weeping;
On the way to Horonaim
 they utter rending cries;
[6]The waters of Nimrim
 have become a waste,
The grass is withered,
 new growth is gone,
 nothing is green.
[7]So now whatever they have
 acquired or stored away
they carry across the Wadi of the
 Poplars.
[8]The cry has gone round
 the territory of Moab;
As far as Eglaim his wailing,
 even at Beer-elim his wailing.
[9]The waters of Dimon are filled
 with blood,
but I will bring still more upon
 Dimon:
Lions for those who are fleeing
 from Moab
and for those who remain in the
 land!
16 [1]Send them forth, hugging the
earth like reptiles,
 from Sela across the desert,
 to the mount of daughter Zion.
[2]Like flushed birds,

like scattered nestlings,
Are the daughters of Moab
 at the fords of the Arnon.
[3]Offer counsel, take their part;
 at high noon make your shade
 like the night;
Hide the outcasts,
 do not betray the fugitives.
[4]Let the outcasts of Moab live with
 you,
 be their shelter from the
 destroyer.
When there is an end to the
 oppressor,
 when destruction has ceased,
 and the marauders have
 vanished from the land,
[5]A throne shall be set up in mercy,
 and on it shall sit in fidelity,
 in David's tent,
A judge upholding right,
 prompt to do justice.
[6]We have heard of the pride of Moab,
 how very proud he is,
Of his haughtiness, pride, and
 arrogance
 that his empty words do not
 match.
[7]Therefore let Moab wail,
 let everyone wail for Moab;

---

include Moab among the nations that were to experience divine judgment. The oracle likely reflects the result of a later Babylonian campaign in the region that ended the existence of Moab as a political entity. It describes the total devastation that affected every major Moabite city as well as the surrounding countryside. The humiliations that come with occupation led the people to ritual mourning whose purpose was to induce the gods to have pity on them, but it had no effect. Moab's ruination continued and its people fled before the invader, but many did not escape.

Some of Moab's refugees will make their way to Zion, where they will seek to escape the Babylonian forces invading their homeland. Though these refugees will find protection, nothing can be done to stop the total devastation of their homeland. What was once a formidable power in the region will barely survive the Babylonian invasion. The Moabites will lament and

For the raisin cakes of Kir-hareseth
    let them sigh, stricken with grief.
⁸The terraced slopes of Heshbon
    languish,
    the vines of Sibmah,
Whose clusters once overpowered
    the lords of nations,
Reaching as far as Jazer
    winding through the wilderness,
Whose branches spread forth,
    crossing over the sea.
⁹Therefore I weep with Jazer
    for the vines of Sibmah;
I drench you with my tears,
    Heshbon and Elealeh;
For on your summer fruits and
    harvests
    the battle cry has fallen.
¹⁰From the orchards are taken away
    joy and gladness,
In the vineyards there is no singing,
    no shout of joy;

In the wine presses no one treads
    grapes,
    the vintage shout is stilled.
¹¹Therefore for Moab
    my heart moans like a lyre,
    my inmost being for Kir-hareseth.
¹²When Moab wears himself out on
    the high places,
    and enters his sanctuary to pray,
    it shall avail him nothing.

¹³That is the word the LORD spoke against Moab in times past. ¹⁴But now the LORD speaks: In three years, like the years of a hired laborer, the glory of Moab shall be empty despite all its great multitude; and the remnant shall be very small and weak.

17 **Damascus.** ¹Oracle on Damascus:
    See, Damascus shall cease to be a
    city
    and become a pile of ruins;

---

pray but without effect. Nothing can stop what will happen to their country. The prophet assures his readers that Moab will indeed experience God's judgment. There will only be a small and weak remnant left of what was once a significant regional power. Of course, the remnant of Judah will be the instrument that God will use to restore Jerusalem.

17:1-6 Against Damascus

Damascus was the capital of Aram (Syria), a one-time rival of the kingdom of Israel and then its ally against the encroachments of the Assyrians. When Ahaz, the king of Judah, refused to join their anti-Assyrian coalition, Aram and Israel were preparing to invade Judah to depose Ahaz and replace him with a more cooperative monarch. Isaiah was certain that these plans would fail (7:1–8:4). The prophet knew the ferocity of the Assyrian military machine. He was sure that the Assyrians would give those arrayed against them no quarter. Hardly anything will be left of Aram and Israel once the Assyrians move against them. The inevitable Assyrian response will cause terrible devastation to cities and villages throughout both Aram and Israel. The destructive forces of the Assyrian army would leave as little behind as do harvesters in a wheat field or on an olive tree.

²Her cities shall be forever
  abandoned,
  for flocks to lie in undisturbed.
³The fortress shall vanish from
  Ephraim
  and dominion from Damascus;
The remnant of Aram shall become
  like the glory
  of the Israelites—
  oracle of the LORD of hosts.
⁴On that day
The glory of Jacob shall fade,
  and his full body shall grow
  thin.
⁵Like the reaper's mere armful of
  stalks,
  when he gathers the standing
  grain;
Or as when one gleans the ears
  in the Valley of Rephaim.
⁶Only gleanings shall be left in it,
  as when an olive tree has been
  beaten—
Two or three olives at the very top,
  four or five on its most fruitful
  branches—
  oracle of the LORD, the God of
  Israel.

⁷On that day people shall turn to
  their maker,
  their eyes shall look to the Holy
  One of Israel.
⁸They shall not turn to the altars,
  the work of their hands,
  nor shall they look to what their
  fingers have made:
  the asherahs or the incense
  stands.
⁹On that day his strong cities shall be
  like those abandoned by the
  Hivites and Amorites
When faced with the Israelites;
  and there shall be desolation.
¹⁰Truly, you have forgotten the God
  who saves you,
  the Rock, your refuge, you have
  not remembered.
Therefore, though you plant plants
  for the Pleasant One,
  and set out cuttings for a foreign
  one,
¹¹Though you make them grow the
  day you plant them
  and make them blossom the
  morning you set them
  out,

17:7-11 Against the worship of other gods

The metaphor comparing the Assyrian army to harvesters led the prophet to inveigh against the worship of other gods, which was so offensive to someone who believed in the holiness of Judah's God and in the exclusive claims that God had on Judah. What the people of Judah expected from their God was fertility for the land and protection from enemies. They sought these not only from the Lord, their patron deity, but from other gods as well. Here the prophet mentions the trappings of non-Yahwistic worship as a cause of shame for the people of Judah. The "alien god" of verse 10 is likely Tammuz, a god connected with grain production. The prophet asserts that those who sought to secure a good harvest through rituals associated with Tammuz (see also Ezek 8:14-15) will find that all their activity was in vain and they will enjoy no harvest at all.

The judgment against Israel and Aram will lead Judah to recognize the claims that its national God makes upon it. Judah will see the folly of

The harvest shall disappear on a
day of sickness
and incurable pain.
[12]Ah! the roaring of many peoples—
a roar like the roar of the seas!
The thundering of nations—
thunder like the thundering of
mighty waters!
[13]But God shall rebuke them,
and they shall flee far away,
Driven like chaff on the mountains
before a wind,
like tumbleweed before a storm.
[14]At evening, there is terror,
but before morning, they are
gone!

Such is the portion of those who
despoil us,
the lot of those who plunder us.

18 **Ethiopia.** [1]Ah! Land of buzzing
insects,
beyond the rivers of Ethiopia,
[2]Sending ambassadors by sea,
in papyrus boats on the waters!
Go, swift messengers,
to a nation tall and bronzed,
To a people dreaded near and far,
a nation strong and conquering,
whose land is washed by rivers.
[3]All you who inhabit the world,
who dwell on earth,

---

serving other gods. They will reject all forms of non-Yahwistic religion. Those people who do not will lose their claim to the land just as their ancestors dispossessed earlier inhabitants of the land.

17:12-14 Against the nations

To summarize the oracles against the two great Mesopotamian empires and three local powers, the prophet composed a short poem on the power of God. He used an old metaphor from the ancient Near Eastern religious tradition: the power of God as manifested in the control of the unruly and potentially chaotic sea. The peoples of the ancient Near East believed the greatest manifestation of divine power was keeping the power of the sea in check. The story of creation begins with the "spirit of God" moving over the sea and bringing order and life to what was void and without form (Gen 1:2).

The prophet asserts that God can bring order out of the chaos unleashed by the greed and ferocity of the nations. Though these nations look strong and appear ready to overwhelm Judah, they will not succeed. Their threats will disappear as quickly and suddenly as they appeared. The prophet believes that God will protect Jerusalem (see also Pss 46, 48)—a belief that gave shape to his ministry.

The gospels use this same metaphor centuries later when they testify to Christian belief in the divinity of Jesus. Jesus calms the Sea of Galilee and his disciples marvel at his power asking, "What sort of man is this, whom even the winds and the sea obey?" (Matt 8:27).

When the signal is raised on the
    mountain, look!
When the trumpet blows, listen!
⁴For thus says the LORD to me:
I will be quiet, looking on from
    where I dwell,
Like the shimmering heat in
    sunshine,
    like a cloud of dew at harvest
      time.
⁵Before the vintage, when the
    flowering has ended,
and the blooms are succeeded
    by ripening grapes,
Then comes the cutting of branches
    with pruning hooks,
and the discarding of the
    lopped-off shoots.
⁶They shall all be left to the
    mountain vultures
and to the beasts of the earth;
The vultures shall summer on them,
    all the beasts of the earth shall
      winter on them.

⁷Then will gifts be brought to the
LORD of hosts—to the place of the name
of the LORD of hosts, Mount Zion—from
a people tall and bronzed, from a people
dreaded near and far, a nation strong
and conquering, whose land is washed
by rivers.

19 **Egypt.** ¹Oracle on Egypt:
See, the LORD is riding on a swift
    cloud
    on his way to Egypt;
The idols of Egypt tremble before
    him,
    the hearts of the Egyptians melt
      within them.

²I will stir up Egypt against Egypt:
    brother will war against brother,
Neighbor against neighbor,
    city against city, kingdom
      against kingdom.
³The courage of the Egyptians shall
    ebb away within them,
    and I will bring their counsel to
      nought;
They shall consult idols and
    charmers, ghosts and
      clairvoyants.
⁴I will deliver Egypt
    into the power of a cruel master,
A harsh king who shall rule over
    them—
    oracle of the Lord, the LORD of
      hosts.
⁵The waters shall be drained from
    the sea,
    the river shall parch and dry up;
⁶Its streams shall become foul,
    and the canals of Egypt shall
      dwindle and parch.
Reeds and rushes shall wither away,
    ⁷and bulrushes on the bank of
      the Nile;
All the sown land along the Nile
    shall dry up and blow away,
      and be no more.
⁸The fishermen shall mourn and
    lament,
    all who cast hook in the Nile;
Those who spread their nets in the
    water
    shall pine away.
⁹The linen-workers shall be
    disappointed,
    the combers and weavers shall
      turn pale;

18:1–19:25 Against Egypt

The two Israelite kingdoms were sandwiched between Egypt and the Mesopotamian Empires. The goal of the latter was the conquest of Egypt, command of its resources, and control over the trade routes between Egypt

¹⁰The spinners shall be crushed,
    all the hired laborers shall be
        despondent.
¹¹Utter fools are the princes of Zoan!
    the wisest of Pharaoh's advisers
        give stupid counsel.
How can you say to Pharaoh,
    "I am a descendant of wise men,
        of ancient kings"?
¹²Where then are your wise men?
    Let them tell you and make
        known
What the LORD of hosts has
        planned
    against Egypt.
¹³The princes of Zoan have become
        fools,
    the princes of Memphis have
        been deceived.
The chiefs of its tribes
    have led Egypt astray.
¹⁴The LORD has prepared among
        them
    a spirit of dizziness,
And they have made Egypt stagger
    in whatever she does,
        as a drunkard staggers in his
            vomit.
¹⁵Egypt shall accomplish nothing—
    neither head nor tail, palm
        branch nor reed, shall
            accomplish anything.

¹⁶On that day the Egyptians shall be like women, trembling with fear, because of the LORD of hosts shaking his fist at them. ¹⁷And the land of Judah shall be a terror to the Egyptians. Every time they think of Judah, they shall stand in dread because of the plan the LORD of hosts has in mind for them.

¹⁸On that day there shall be five cities in the land of Egypt that speak the language of Canaan and swear by the LORD of hosts; one shall be called "City of the Sun."

¹⁹On that day there shall be an altar to the LORD at the center of Egypt, and a sacred pillar to the LORD near its boundary. ²⁰This will be a sign and witness to the LORD of hosts in the land of Egypt, so that when they cry out to the LORD because of their oppressors, he will send them a savior to defend and deliver them. ²¹The LORD shall make himself known to Egypt, and the Egyptians shall know the LORD in that day; they shall offer sacrifices and oblations, make vows to the LORD and fulfill them. ²²Although the LORD shall smite Egypt severely, he shall heal them; they shall turn to the LORD and he shall be moved by their entreaty and heal them.

---

and Mesopotamia. Egypt, of course, resisted, and the Israelite kingdoms were caught in the crossfire. There was a particularly destructive escalation of this crossfire in 714 B.C. The Assyrians were poised on the border of Egypt, ready to invade. Egypt wanted a buffer between it and the Assyrian army so it encouraged several Assyrian vassal states in the eastern Mediterranean region to revolt and reassert their independence. What the prophet suggests is that Judah keep away from any such activity.

The prophet was certain that Judah could maintain its political independence if it learned to trust God rather than to engage in futile political and military machinations. It was an open secret that Egypt and Ethiopia were conspiring against the aggression of Assyria. The prophet believed

²³On that day there shall be a highway from Egypt to Assyria; the Assyrians shall enter Egypt, and the Egyptians enter Assyria, and the Egyptians shall worship with the Assyrians.

²⁴On that day Israel shall be a third party with Egypt and Assyria, a blessing in the midst of the earth, ²⁵when the LORD of hosts gives this blessing: "Blessed be my people Egypt, and the

that God determines the course of events—the plans that people make are worthless. God will bring about an end to the Assyrian Empire, but it will come when God chooses. What Judah must do is wait for a sign that God will begin to move against the Assyrians. The victory that God will effect will lead the conspirators to Jerusalem to bring tribute to Judah's God. What Judah must do is wait.

The prophet then becomes specific as he describes some of the signs of God's dominion over Egypt. The first of these are the internal divisions in Egypt that make possible the rise of a new pharaoh (the "cruel master" and "harsh king" of 19:4). The new king that the prophet speaks of is likely Piankhi, the founder of the twenty-fifth dynasty. This Nubian monarch took the throne of Egypt around 714 B.C. and united Egypt, Nubia, and Ethiopia under his rule. An even more serious manifestation of divine power will come when the Nile dries up. The Egyptian economy will collapse because of this disaster. Of course, Egypt's political and economic problems make it an unreliable ally.

Despite these internal difficulties, the pharaoh's advisors urged him to become involved in international politics. Isaiah had little use for the counselors who advised the king of Judah (5:18-25), and he had no respect for the sages of Egypt, even though these sages had a reputation for wisdom. Their advice is necessarily flawed because they do not take into account the judgment of Judah's God on their country. Egypt's political and military leaders will be making decisions based on flawed advice, and these decisions will have disastrous consequences for Egypt and for its allies.

One goal of the Assyrian Empire was to bring Egypt and its wealth under Assyrian control. The two Israelite kingdoms were merely stepping-stones on the way to the real prize. Here the prophet transforms that grand strategy by making Israel the linchpin that will join Egypt and Assyria. These two bitter rivals will find themselves allied in the worship of Israel's God. Again, the prophet is carried away by his own rhetoric and describes a vision that has never been realized.

20:1-6 A dramatic gesture

The prophets tried to persuade people not only with their eloquence but also with their actions. The dramatic gesture became an important part

work of my hands Assyria, and my heritage, Israel."

20 **Isaiah's Warning Against Trust in Egypt and Ethiopia.** ¹In the year the general sent by Sargon, king of Assyria, came to Ashdod, fought against it, and captured it—²at that time the LORD had spoken through Isaiah, the son of Amoz: Go and take off the sackcloth from your waist, and remove the sandals from your feet. This he did, walking naked and barefoot. ³Then the LORD said: Just as my servant Isaiah has gone naked and barefoot for three years as a sign and portent against Egypt and Ethiopia, ⁴so shall the king of Assyria lead away captives from Egypt, and exiles from Ethiopia, young and old, naked and barefoot, with buttocks uncovered, the shame of Egypt.

⁵They shall be dismayed and ashamed because of Ethiopia, their hope, and because of Egypt, their boast. ⁶The inhabitants of this coastland shall say on that day, "See what has happened to those we hoped in, to whom we fled for help and deliverance from the king of Assyria! What escape is there for us now?"

21 **Fall of Babylon.** ¹Oracle on the wastelands by the sea:
Like whirlwinds sweeping through the Negeb,
it comes from the desert,
from the fearful land.
²A harsh vision has been announced to me:
"The traitor betrays,
the despoiler spoils.
Go up, O Elam; besiege, O Media;
put an end to all its groaning!"

---

of the prophetic repertoire. Hosea married a prostitute (Hos 1–3). Jeremiah purchased land during the Babylonian siege of Jerusalem (32:1-44). Ezekiel kept silence for seven and one-half years (Ezek 3:26; 24:26-27; 33:21-22). Eclipsing them all was Isaiah's three-year period of nudity. The purpose of this gesture was to dramatize the futility of the anti-Assyrian machinations encouraged by Egypt. The prophet wanted everyone to see what would happen to the Egyptians when Assyria moved against them: they will be carried off into slavery without any clothes to cover their shame.

The Egyptians encouraged the Philistine city-state of Ashdod, which was located on the Mediterranean coast twenty-nine miles south of Jaffa, to rebel against the Assyrians. The territory of Ashdod became incorporated into the Assyrian provincial system in 734 B.C. When Sargon II came to put down the rebellion with overwhelming force, the Egyptians thought the better of challenging him and simply abandoned Ashdod to its fate. The city fell to the Assyrian army in 713 B.C. While Isaiah's advice to Judah was sound, Assyria never conquered Egypt.

21:1-10 Against Babylon

This second oracle against Babylon repeats the message of 13:1–14:22. The title of this oracle is enigmatic. The Greek suggests that the title should read: "An oracle roaring like whirlwinds in the Negev. . . ." The prophet

³Therefore my loins are filled with
   anguish,
   pangs have seized me like those
      of a woman in labor;
I am too bewildered to hear,
   too dismayed to look.
⁴My mind reels,
   shuddering assails me;
The twilight I yearned for
   he has turned into dread.
⁵They set the table,
   spread out the rugs;
   they eat, they drink.
Rise up, O princes,
   oil the shield!
⁶For thus my Lord said to me:
   Go, station a watchman,
   let him tell what he sees.
⁷If he sees a chariot,
   a pair of horses,
Someone riding a donkey,
   someone riding a camel,
Then let him pay heed,
   very close heed.

⁸Then the watchman cried,
"On the watchtower, my Lord,
   I stand constantly by day;
And I stay at my post
   through all the watches of the
      night.
⁹Here he comes—
   a single chariot,
   a pair of horses—
He calls out and says,
   'Fallen, fallen is Babylon!
All the images of her gods
   are smashed to the ground!'"
¹⁰To you, who have been threshed,
   beaten on my threshing floor,
What I have heard
   from the LORD of hosts,
The God of Israel,
   I have announced to you.

Dumah. ¹¹Oracle on Dumah:
   They call to me from Seir,
   "Watchman, how much longer
      the night?

describes the fall of Babylon. Elam and Media to the east of Babylon are preparing to engulf the ancient Near East in a new wave on conquest. The conqueror will itself be conquered. Everything is in place. The great battle is about to begin. In verses 6-10, the scene shifts. The prophet, like a sentry, is scanning the horizon for a messenger bringing news of Babylon's defeat. Finally the messenger comes: "Fallen, fallen is Babylon." The prophet's words are confirmed by events. The implication is that the reader can have confidence in Judah's prophets.

John of Revelation cites the cry to the messenger who proclaims the fall of Babylon to the prophet (21:9; Rev 14:8; 18:2) to assert his faith in the triumph of Christ and the church over Rome and its emperor.

21:11-12 Against Edom

The prophet returns to the anti-Assyrian revolt encouraged by Egypt and led by Ashdod. Edom was an active participant in that revolt. "Dumah" may be a poetic name for Edom, which came to be known as Idumea in the Greek and Roman periods. This short oracle implies that there will be some respite from Assyrian pressure ("morning comes"), but that it will be followed by a new round of oppression ("also the night").

Watchman, how much longer
the night?"
¹²The watchman replies,
"Morning has come, and again
night.
If you will ask, ask; come back
again."

In the Steppe. ¹³Oracle: in the steppe:
In the thicket in the steppe you will
spend the night,
caravans of Dedanites.
¹⁴Meet the thirsty, bring them water,
inhabitants of the land of Tema,
greet the fugitives with bread.
¹⁵For they have fled from the sword,
from the drawn sword;
From the taut bow,
from the thick of battle.

¹⁶For thus the Lord has said to me: In another year, like the years of a hired laborer, all the glory of Kedar shall come to an end. ¹⁷Few of Kedar's stalwart archers shall remain, for the LORD, the God of Israel, has spoken.

22 **The Valley of Vision.** ¹Oracle on the Valley of Vision:
What is the matter with you now,
that you have gone up,
all of you, to the housetops,
²You who were full of noise,
tumultuous city,
exultant town?
Your slain are not slain with the
sword,
nor killed in battle.
³All your leaders fled away
together,
they were captured without use
of bow;
All who were found were captured
together,
though they had fled afar off.

21:13-17 Against Arabia

After speaking about Edom's future, the prophet turns his attention to Kedar, an association of Arabian tribes living to the east of Edom. That the prophet singles Kedar out for words of judgment shows they were a significant military force, as is confirmed by Assyrian and Babylonian sources. Isaiah announces an end of Kedar's "glory." The prophet wants to impress the people of Judah with the futility of military adventures. This was an important message for the first readers of the book of Isaiah, since Judah had no military power at all. From the prophet's perspective, this did not matter. It was Judah's commitment to justice that was decisive. It was not the Judahite state that would secure Jerusalem's future but a community founded on a just social and economic order.

22:1-14 Against Jerusalem

The prophet was not finished with his comments on the fallout from the failed revolt against Assyria led by Ashdod. Judah did not join the conspirators, so when Sargon II led his army from Assyria to Ashdod, he bypassed Jerusalem. The city's people celebrated. Isaiah regarded their response to be inappropriate since God's "beloved people" still faced divine judgment. Indeed, judgment was coming because the people of means were guilty of

⁴That is why I say: Turn away from
   me,
   let me weep bitterly;
Do not try to comfort me
   for the ruin of the daughter of
      my people.
⁵It is a day of panic, rout and
      confusion,
   from the Lord, the GOD of hosts,
      in the Valley of Vision
Walls crash;
   a cry for help to the mountains.
⁶Elam takes up the quiver,
   Aram mounts the horses
   and Kir uncovers the shields.
⁷Your choice valleys are filled with
      chariots,
   horses are posted at the gates—
⁸and shelter over Judah is
   removed.

On that day you looked to the weapons in the House of the Forest; ⁹you saw that the breaches in the City of David were many; you collected the water of the lower pool. ¹⁰You numbered the houses of Jerusalem, tearing some down to strengthen the wall; ¹¹you made a reservoir between the two walls for the water of the old pool. But you did not look to the city's Maker, nor consider the one who fashioned it long ago.

¹²On that day the Lord,
   the GOD of hosts, called
For weeping and mourning,
   for shaving the head and
      wearing sackcloth.
¹³But look! instead, there was
   celebration and joy,
   slaughtering cattle and
      butchering sheep,
Eating meat and drinking wine:
   "Eat and drink, for tomorrow
      we die!"

¹⁴This message was revealed in my
   hearing from the LORD of
      hosts:
   This iniquity will not be for-
      given you until you die,
   says the Lord, the GOD of hosts.

Shebna and Eliakim. ¹⁵Thus says the
   Lord, the GOD of hosts:
   Up, go to that official,
   Shebna, master of the palace,

conspicuous consumption—seemingly unmoved by the prophet's warnings. Mercenaries from Elam and Kir will turn the city's "choicest valleys" into highways for an invasion. Though the city will prepare itself for this invasion, these efforts will provide no real security because God is the one planning the city's judgment while its foolish citizens are celebrating their apparent deliverance. Jerusalem, however, will not escape judgment because it has not responded to the prophet's call for justice.

Paul quotes the words of the people of Jerusalem in verse 13 when writing about the significance of the resurrection from the dead. The apostle asserts that without belief in the resurrection, people would think only of their pleasure (1 Cor 15:32).

22:15-25 Against Shebna and Eliakim

The prophet lays the blame for Jerusalem's folly on its leaders for the most part. Here he singles out two royal counselors for particular criticism.

¹⁶"What have you here? Whom
have you here,
that you have hewn for yourself
a tomb here,
Hewing a tomb on high,
carving a resting place in the
rock?"
¹⁷The LORD shall hurl you down
headlong, mortal man!
He shall grip you firmly,
¹⁸And roll you up and toss you like
a ball
into a broad land.
There you will die, there with the
chariots you glory in,
you disgrace to your master's
house!
¹⁹I will thrust you from your office
and pull you down from your
station.
²⁰On that day I will summon my
servant
Eliakim, son of Hilkiah;
²¹I will clothe him with your robe,
gird him with your sash,
confer on him your authority.
He shall be a father to the inhabitants of Jerusalem,
and to the house of Judah.
²²I will place the key of the House
of David on his shoulder;
what he opens, no one will shut,
what he shuts, no one will open.
²³I will fix him as a peg in a firm
place,

a seat of honor for his ancestral
house;
²⁴On him shall hang all the glory of
his ancestral house:
descendants and offspring,
all the little dishes, from bowls
to jugs.

²⁵On that day, says the LORD of hosts,
the peg fixed in a firm place shall give
way, break off and fall, and the weight
that hung on it shall be done away with;
for the LORD has spoken.

23 **Tyre and Sidon.** ¹Oracle on Tyre:
Wail, ships of Tarshish,
for your port is destroyed;
From the land of the Kittim
the news reaches them.
²Silence! you who dwell on the
coast,
you merchants of Sidon,
Whose messengers crossed the sea
³over the deep waters,
Whose revenue was the grain of
Shihor, the harvest of the
Nile,
you who were the merchant
among the nations.
⁴Be ashamed, Sidon, fortress on the
sea,
for the sea has spoken,
"I have not been in labor, nor given
birth,
nor raised young men,
nor reared young women."

Shebna was King Hezekiah's chief of staff. Isaiah saw the impressive tomb
that Shebna was preparing for himself. This prompted the prophet to speak
about Shebna's certain fall from power. He likely advised Hezekiah to become involved in the anti-Assyrian revolt led by Ashdod. Fortunately for
Judah, Hezekiah did not take Shebna's advice and demoted him (36:3). His
place as chief of staff was taken by Eliakim. Isaiah expected great things
from Eliakim though he too proved to be a disappointment (22:25). Those
in a position to bring significant change to Judahite society did nothing
to disrupt the economic status quo. They believed that their political and

⁵When the report reaches Egypt
  they shall be in anguish at the
    report about Tyre.
⁶Pass over to Tarshish,
  wail, you who dwell on the
    coast!
⁷Is this your exultant city,
  whose origin is from old,
Whose feet have taken her
  to dwell in distant lands?
⁸Who has planned such a thing
  against Tyre, the bestower of
    crowns,
Whose merchants are princes,
  whose traders are the earth's
    honored men?
⁹The LORD of hosts has planned it,
  to disgrace the height of all
    beauty,
  to degrade all the honored of
    the earth.
¹⁰Cross to your own land,
  ship of Tarshish;
  the harbor is no more.
¹¹His hand he stretches out over the
    sea,
  he shakes kingdoms;
The LORD commanded the
    destruction

of Canaan's strongholds:
¹²Crushed, you shall exult no more,
  virgin daughter Sidon.
Arise, pass over to the Kittim,
  even there you shall find no rest.
¹³Look at the land of the Chaldeans,
  the people that has ceased to be.
Assyria founded it for ships,
  raised its towers,
Only to tear down its palaces,
  and turn it into a ruin.
¹⁴Lament, ships of Tarshish,
  for your stronghold is destroyed.

¹⁵On that day, Tyre shall be forgotten
for seventy years, the lifetime of one king.
At the end of seventy years, the song
about the prostitute will be Tyre's song:

¹⁶Take a harp, go about the city,
  forgotten prostitute;
Pluck the strings skillfully, sing
    many songs,
  that you may be remembered.

¹⁷At the end of the seventy years the
LORD shall visit Tyre. She shall return to
her hire and serve as prostitute with all
the world's kingdoms on the face of the
earth. ¹⁸But her merchandise and her hire

---

military maneuvering would provide Judah with security. One goal of the prophet's mission was to convince Judah of just the opposite. Only a society based on justice—one that seeks the welfare of the poor—would survive.

The book of Revelation uses the imagery of verse 22 in speaking about Christ to the church of Philadelphia (Rev 3:7).

23:1-18 Against Tyre and Sidon

Tyre and Sidon were commercial centers located on the seacoast north of ancient Israel. Their merchant ships plied the Mediterranean Sea, going as far as Tarshish, located in what is now Spain. By being efficient conduits for international trade, these cities enriched themselves. Their economic resources made them attractive prey for the aggressive Assyrian Empire. The oracles against these cities are intertwined, as was their ultimate fate. The oracle against Sidon (23:1-4, 12-14) asserts that this city would no longer

shall be sacred to the LORD. It shall not be stored up or laid away; instead, her merchandise shall belong to those who dwell before the LORD, to eat their fill and clothe themselves in choice attire.

D. Apocalypse of Isaiah

24 Judgment upon the World and the Lord's Enthronement on Mount Zion. ¹See! The LORD is about to empty the earth and lay it waste;
he will twist its surface,
and scatter its inhabitants:
²People and priest shall fare alike:
servant and master,
Maid and mistress,
buyer and seller,
Lender and borrower,
creditor and debtor.
³The earth shall be utterly laid waste, utterly stripped,
for the LORD has decreed this word.

⁴The earth mourns and fades,
the world languishes and fades;
both heaven and earth languish.
⁵The earth is polluted because of its inhabitants,
for they have transgressed laws, violated statutes,
broken the ancient covenant.
⁶Therefore a curse devours the earth,
and its inhabitants pay for their guilt;
Therefore they who dwell on earth have dwindled,
and only a few are left.
⁷The new wine mourns, the vine languishes,
all the merry-hearted groan.
⁸Stilled are the cheerful timbrels,
ended the shouts of the jubilant,
stilled the cheerful harp.
⁹They no longer drink wine and sing;
strong brew is bitter to those who drink it.

---

profit from the grain it transported from Egypt to the rest of the ancient Near East. The prophet also proclaims that Tyre will experience divine judgment but for a limited period. Tyre will rise again, but its wealth will be dedicated to the Lord, so that it might support "those who dwell before the LORD." This flight of prophetic fancy is consistent with Isaiah's view of wealth: it is to be shared with those in need rather than being hoarded by the wealthy.

When Jesus condemns the cities of Capernaum, Bethsaida, and Chorazin for their failure to respond to his preaching, he says that the judgment on Tyre and Sidon will be easier than the judgment on them. It is likely that the evangelists were thinking of this oracle against the two Phoenician cities (Matt 11:21-22; Luke 10:13-14).

24:1-23 Judgment upon the whole earth

The oracles of judgment that the prophet utters against the nations of the ancient Near East—including Judah—provide the setting for more general prophecies of a universal judgment that follow in chapters 24–27. In these chapters, the prophet is far less specific and far more pessimistic than in chapters 13–23. Still, the prophet's pessimism is not total. While

¹⁰Broken down is the city of chaos,
    every house is shut against
      entry.
¹¹In the streets they cry out for lack
    of wine;
    all joy has grown dim,
    cheer is exiled from the land.
¹²In the city nothing remains but
    desolation,
    gates battered into ruins.
¹³For thus it shall be in the midst of
    the earth,
    among the peoples,
As when an olive tree has been
    beaten,
    as with a gleaning when the
      vintage is done.
¹⁴These shall lift up their voice,
    they shall sing for joy in the maj-
      esty of the LORD,
    they shall shout from the west-
      ern sea:
¹⁵"Therefore, in the east
    give glory to the LORD!
In the coastlands of the sea,
    to the name of the LORD, the
      God of Israel!"
¹⁶From the end of the earth we hear
    songs:
    "Splendor to the Just One!"
But I said, "I am wasted, wasted
    away.
    Woe is me! The traitors betray;
    with treachery have the traitors
      betrayed!

¹⁷Terror, pit, and trap
    for you, inhabitant of the earth!
¹⁸One who flees at the sound of
    terror
    will fall into the pit;
One who climbs out of the pit
    will be caught in the trap.
For the windows on high are open
    and the foundations of the earth
      shake.
¹⁹The earth will burst asunder,
    the earth will be shaken apart,
    the earth will be convulsed.
²⁰The earth will reel like a
    drunkard,
    sway like a hut;
Its rebellion will weigh it down;
    it will fall, never to rise again."
²¹On that day the LORD will punish
    the host of the heavens in the
      heavens,
    and the kings of the earth on the
      earth.
²²They will be gathered together
    like prisoners into a pit;
They will be shut up in a dungeon,
    and after many days they will
      be punished.
²³Then the moon will blush
    and the sun be ashamed,
For the LORD of hosts will reign
    on Mount Zion and in
      Jerusalem,
    glorious in the sight of the
      elders.

---

he speaks about the desolation that comes with divine judgment upon a world without justice, he does hope for a decisive manifestation of divine power that will remake the world into a place where justice triumphs. Readers will be tempted to find precise referents for the nonspecific images that these chapters contain. For example, is the city that the prophet mentions Babylon, Nineveh, Jerusalem, or Samaria? The most plausible answer is that the city is any city and every city founded on injustice and oppression. The nonspecific character of the prophet's words disengages them from a particular time and place and makes their appropriation by

25 Praise for God's Deliverance and the Celebration in Zion.

¹O LORD, you are my God,
  I extol you, I praise your name;
For you have carried out your won-
      derful plans of old,
    faithful and true.
²For you have made the city a heap,
    the fortified city a ruin,
The castle of the insolent, a city no
      more,
    not ever to be rebuilt.

³Therefore a strong people will
      honor you,
  ruthless nations will fear you.
⁴For you have been a refuge to the
      poor,
  a refuge to the needy in their
      distress;
Shelter from the rain,
  shade from the heat.
When the blast of the ruthless was
      like a winter rain,
⁵the roar of strangers like heat in
      the desert,

---

readers today easier. On the other hand, the vague generalities of these chapters challenge the reader's attention as the prophet tries to draw a picture of what lies ahead not simply for Babylon, Jerusalem, and Egypt but for the whole world.

Chapters 24–27 have been sometimes called the "Isaiah Apocalypse." They do contain images and motifs that later apocalyptic texts develop. While chapters 24–27 are not full-blown apocalypses, they do share with later apocalyptic texts such as Daniel 7–12 and Revelation the absolute conviction of God's sovereign rule over all creation. They look forward to its coming and await God's final triumph over the power of evil.

The first oracle (24:1-6) envisions the devastation of the earth. All people will be caught up in the destruction that will take place. Those of high social and economic status will find that their wealth will not save them, and those of a lower class will not be exempt from the evil that will come upon all. The prophet gives no specific reason for this universal judgment except for universal disobedience. Only a few people will survive.

This universal judgment will make it impossible for wine to gladden people's hearts—so terrible will be the earth's fate. Carefree hilarity will be replaced by cries of desperation. Still, when judgment comes people will be moved to praise God's righteousness (24:14-16). The theme of universal judgment is picked up again in verses 16b-23. Isaiah sees earthquakes, storms, and astronomical events as the means of divine judgment. Some early Jewish interpreters understood "the host of heaven" to refer to rebellious angels, though this is not explicit here. Most people in the ancient world thought that heavenly bodies were manifestations of deities (see Zeph 1:5; Jer 19:13), so personifying them as "the host of the heavens" (24:21) is something to be expected. The judgment, when it comes, will reveal the power of Judah's God, who will reign in Jerusalem. Human beings are

You subdued the heat with the
 shade of a cloud,
  the rain of the tyrants was van-
   quished.
⁶On this mountain the LORD of
  hosts
 will provide for all peoples
A feast of rich food and choice
 wines,
  juicy, rich food and pure, choice
   wines.
⁷On this mountain he will destroy
  the veil that veils all peoples,
The web that is woven over all
 nations.
  ⁸He will destroy death forever.
The Lord GOD will wipe away
 the tears from all faces;

The reproach of his people he will
  remove
 from the whole earth; for the
  LORD has spoken.
⁹On that day it will be said:
"Indeed, this is our God; we looked
 to him, and he saved us!
This is the LORD to whom we
 looked;
  let us rejoice and be glad that he
   has saved us!"

Judgment on Moab. ¹⁰For the hand
 of the LORD will rest on this
  mountain,
but Moab will be trodden down
 as straw is trodden down in the
  mire.

---

responsible for the coming judgment, but the ultimate purpose of that judgment is not vindictiveness. Its ultimate purpose is to reveal to all the world the justice of God. The prophet envisions the end of the age with God reigning in Jerusalem "in the sight of the elders" (24:23). The book of Revelation sees God's throne sounded by those "twenty-four elders" (Rev 4:4).

25:1-5 A prayer of thanksgiving

This hymn thanks God for a victory over a powerful but unnamed enemy. This victory is another instance of God's marvelous acts on Israel's behalf—acts that stretch back to the distant past. The enemy's capital has been destroyed, leading that "strong people" to recognize the power of Israel's God—a power that was unleashed to protect a helpless Israel. The enemy came upon Israel as an east wind off the desert whose withering heat brings crop failure, famine, and starvation in its wake. God's presence was like a cloud that protected people from the terrible heat of the terrible east wind.

Those protected by God are the "poor" and the "needy." Apocalyptic texts usually address people who consider themselves to be victims of political, social, or economic oppression. It gives their struggles meaning by assuring them that God will take their side against their oppressors. This prayer thanks God for doing just that.

25:6-10a The Lord's feast

Eating sparingly with little variation in diet was the rule for most people in the ancient world. Little wonder then that a lavish banquet became a

11He will spread out his hands in its midst,
as a swimmer spreads out his hands to swim;
His pride will be brought low despite his strokes.
12The high-walled fortress he will raze,
bringing it low, leveling it to the ground, to the very dust.

26 **Judah's Praise and Prayer for Deliverance.** 1On that day this song shall be sung in the land of Judah:

"A strong city have we;

he sets up victory as our walls and ramparts.
2Open up the gates that a righteous nation may enter,
one that keeps faith.
3With firm purpose you maintain peace;
in peace, because of our trust in you."
4Trust in the LORD forever!
For the LORD is an eternal Rock.
5He humbles those who dwell on high,
the lofty city he brings down,

---

potent symbol of the restoration of God's rule on the earth (see also Joel 2:24-26; 4:18; Ezra 3:13; Matt 22:1-10; Luke 14:15-24). What is significant about this passage is its assertion that "all nations" will share in that banquet since God will lift the veil that obscures the vision of the nations, bringing an end to that which keeps Israel and the nations apart. They will recognize Israel as God's people. It will be as if death itself were overcome. Here the prophet's words have a double meaning that escapes most readers today. The Canaanite god of the underworld was Mot, whose name is the Hebrew word for "death." Mot was locked in a continuous battle with Baal, the god of fertility. When the prophet asserts that the Lord will destroy death forever, he implies that in the new age there will be no lack of fertility. Hunger will no longer be a threat. People will not have to eat sparingly. This text does not imply that the dead will rise. What it does suggest is that God will make life worth living. Israel will be able to acclaim its God as savior since it is only by the power of God that all this has happened. It is God's doing.

When Paul proclaims God's victory over the power of death (1 Cor 15:54-55), he sees this victory as the fulfillment of Scripture. Though his citations are free and not ascribed to a specific book, it is likely that Paul had verse 8 in mind. The book of Revelation also finds inspiration in the prophet's assertion that God "will wipe away the tears from all faces" (25:8; Rev 7:17).

25:10b-12 Against Moab

The reader's attention is drawn back to the motif of verses 1-5: God's victory over the powerful. Here Moab is the symbol of Israel's powerful enemies. God will frustrate its designs on Israel and it will experience a devastating

Brings it down to the ground,
   levels it to the dust.
⁶The feet of the needy trample on
   it—
   the feet of the poor.
⁷The way of the just is smooth;
   the path of the just you make
   level.
⁸The course of your judgments,
   LORD, we await;
   your name and your memory
   are the desire of our
   souls.
⁹My soul yearns for you at night,
   yes, my spirit within me seeks
   you at dawn;
When your judgment comes upon
   the earth,
the world's inhabitants learn
   justice.
¹⁰The wicked, when spared, do not
   learn justice;
   in an upright land they act per-
   versely,
   and do not see the majesty of
   the LORD.
¹¹LORD, your hand is raised high,
   but they do not perceive it;
Let them be put to shame when
   they see your zeal for your
   people:
   let the fire prepared for your
   enemies consume them.
¹²LORD, you will decree peace for us,
   for you have accomplished all
   we have done.

---

defeat. This short oracle clashes with what just preceded. In 25:6-8, God will invite all nations to the feast. Once again Israel's attitude toward other people is shaped less by its vision of the future and more by its experience.

26:1-6 The song of the redeemed

When the prophet dreams about the future, his dreams are cast in patterns that try to reestablish Israel in the service of the God who takes the side of the poor against the powerful. This is precisely the imagery behind the prophet's "song of the redeemed." The vision celebrated in this song foresees a future in which the fortunes of the present will be reversed: the mighty will be brought low. The prophet looks toward a time when all Judah will sing a song of victory to God. That song will celebrate Jerusalem—its walls and gates that have withstood the enemy but which welcome and enclose the faithful. The key to the victory was the people's trust in God on whom Judah must always depend. It will be those least able who will seal Judah's victories. Victory will come to the lowly, who will enter the city as victors who have been made such by the power of God alone. The poor and the lowly have no power in the present age, but the future will bring these people total victory over their oppressors.

26:7-19 A psalm celebrating victory

For the prophet, the key to Judah's future was its confidence in its God. The prophet keeps returning to that theme. Military and political realities, of course, made any other source of hope a delusion. The prayer begins

¹³LORD, our God, lords other than
    you have ruled us;
  only because of you can we call
    upon your name.
¹⁴Dead they are, they cannot live,
  shades that cannot rise;
Indeed, you have punished and
    destroyed them,
  and wiped out all memory of
    them.
¹⁵You have increased the nation,
  LORD,
  you have increased the nation,
    have added to your glory,
  you have extended far all the
    boundaries of the land.
¹⁶LORD, oppressed by your
  punishment,

we cried out in anguish under
  your discipline.
¹⁷As a woman about to give birth
  writhes and cries out in pain,
  so were we before you, LORD.
¹⁸We conceived and writhed in pain,
  giving birth only to wind;
Salvation we have not achieved for
    the earth,
  no inhabitants for the world
    were born.
¹⁹But your dead shall live, their
    corpses shall rise!
  Awake and sing, you who lie in
    the dust!
For your dew is a dew of light,
  and you cause the land of
    shades to give birth.

---

by lifting up God's justice and affirms that the righteous may have confidence in it. The wicked, however, never grasp the significance of God's action in the world. The prophet prays that one day they might recognize the meaning of what God will accomplish for Judah. God will bring peace and security for Judah, but its enemies will face destruction. The letter to the Hebrews quotes verse 11 to assure its readers that judgment is coming on those who do not persevere in the faith (Heb 10:27).

Because the promised peace has not come, the just turn to God in their distress. God's people face a very difficult time. It is like the agony of a woman in labor, but at the end of that agony, there is life. The prophet prays that there will be life for Judah. His vision of the future and the ultimate redemption of Judah shapes his attitude toward the present difficulties that the just face. That vision helps the just make sense out of the apparent contradictions of their lives. In his confidence, the prophet prays that Judah's dead also share in God's victory. Is the prophet getting carried away with his rhetoric again, or is verse 19 an expression of faith in the resurrection of the dead? It is difficult to say, but, at the very least, this text provided support for those who held that belief in years to come.

26:20–27:1 The coming judgment

Though the prophet is confident about Judah's future, his attention is drawn to the dire military and political circumstances that it faced. There is death all around, but soon God will reverse Judah's fortunes by destroying those nations allied against it. Giving advice reminiscent of the story of the

The Lord's Response. ²⁰Go, my people,
  enter your chambers,
    and close the doors behind you;
  Hide yourselves for a brief moment,
    until the wrath is past.
²¹See, the LORD goes forth from his
    place,
    to punish the wickedness of the
      earth's inhabitants;
  The earth will reveal the blood shed
    upon it,
    and no longer conceal the slain.

27 **The Judgment and Deliverance of
  Israel.** ¹On that day,
The LORD will punish with his
    sword
    that is cruel, great, and strong,
  Leviathan the fleeing serpent,
    Leviathan the coiled serpent;
    he will slay the dragon in the
      sea.

  ²On that day—

The pleasant vineyard, sing about it!
  ³I, the LORD, am its keeper,
    I water it every moment;
  Lest anyone harm it,
    night and day I guard it.
⁴I am not angry.
  But if I were to find briers and
      thorns,
  In battle I would march against it;
    I would burn it all.
⁵But if it holds fast to my refuge,
    it shall have peace with me;
    it shall have peace with me.

⁶In days to come Jacob shall take
      root,
  Israel shall sprout and blossom,
  covering all the world with
      fruit.
⁷Was he smitten as his smiter was
      smitten?
  Was he slain as his slayer was
      slain?

---

first Passover (Exod 12), the prophet warns his readers to shut their door until death passes them by.

To express his confidence in God's victory over every evil power, the prophet uses imagery that was ancient but never loses its power to move people. The Canaanites envisioned the creation of the world as following the defeat of a great sea monster that the prophet calls Leviathan. While the Canaanites believed that the decisive defeat of Leviathan took place in the past, leading to the creation of this world, the prophet asserts that this battle has yet to take place. However, he is certain that God will be victorious. Hundreds of years later, the book of Revelation uses similar imagery of a monster from the sea to speak of God's final victory over the power of evil (Rev 13:1).

27:2-6 The Lord's vineyard

The vision of God's final victory over the power of evil leads to another prayer of confidence. The prophet takes up the imagery of 5:1-7 to speak not about God's judgment on the unproductive vineyard that is Israel but about the productivity of that vineyard that is under God's protection. The fruit from the Lord's vineyard will fill "the whole world." Thus the prophet again sounds a note of universalism that will be an important dimension in section four of the book.

⁸Driving out and expelling, he
    struggled against it,
carrying it off with his cruel
    wind on a day of storm.
⁹This, then, shall be the expiation of
    Jacob's guilt,
this the result of removing his sin:
He shall pulverize all the stones of
    the altars
like pieces of chalk;
no asherahs or incense altars
    shall stand.
¹⁰For the fortified city shall be
    desolate,
an abandoned pasture, a
    forsaken wilderness;
There calves shall graze, there they
    shall lie down,
and consume its branches.
¹¹When its boughs wither, they shall
    be broken off;
and women shall come to kindle
    fires with them.

For this is not an understanding
    people;
therefore their maker shall not
    spare them;
their creator shall not be
    gracious to them.
¹²On that day,
The LORD shall beat out grain
    from the channel of the
        Euphrates to the Wadi
    of Egypt,
and you shall be gleaned one by
    one, children of Israel.
¹³On that day,
A great trumpet shall blow,
    and the lost in the land of
        Assyria
    and the outcasts in the land of
        Egypt
Shall come and worship the LORD
    on the holy mountain, in
        Jerusalem.

27:7-11 The end of idolatry

Israel's salvation will take place because Israel will finally leave the worship of other gods behind. It will recognize that it is the Lord who gives the land its fertility and that it makes no sense to worship other deities. Finally, Israel is faithful to its God alone because God has removed every trace of false worship just as the withering east wind dries up every blade of grass that it touches. Once God delivers Israel, now freed from serving other gods, its enemies will face defeat and destruction.

27:12-13 Israel's restoration

God will pass in judgment one final time over the land of Israel promised to Abraham (see Gen 15:18). The Lord will traverse the full extent of that land from north to south, separating the wicked from the faithful as threshers separate grain from chaff. When that has taken place, the restoration will begin. A trumpet will sound to gather Israel, as happens for every solemn assembly (see Num 10:2-10). This time Israel in exile will assemble to worship God in Jerusalem. Thus the second section of the book of Isaiah ends like the first—with the people of Israel worshiping the Lord, their ancestral God, in Jerusalem.

E. The Lord Alone, Israel's and Judah's Salvation

28

The Fate of Samaria. ¹Ah! majestic garland
of the drunkards of Ephraim,
Fading blooms of his glorious
beauty,
at the head of the fertile valley,
upon those stupified with
wine.
²See, the LORD has a strong one, a
mighty one,
who, like an onslaught of hail, a
destructive storm,

Like a flood of water, great and
overflowing,
levels to the ground with
violence;
³With feet that will trample
the majestic garland of the
drunkards of Ephraim.
⁴The fading blooms of his glorious
beauty
at the head of the fertile valley
Will be like an early fig before
summer:
whoever sees it,
swallows it as soon as it is in
hand.

JERUSALEM'S JUDGMENT AND SALVATION

Isaiah 28:1–39:8

The third section of the book of Isaiah is a series of literary diptychs, one side of which describes divine judgment on the two Israelite kingdoms in general and the city of Jerusalem in particular. The second side of the diptych assures the people of Jerusalem that there is a future beyond judgment. Sometimes this assurance takes the form of an oracle against one of Judah's enemies; other times the prophet proclaims an oracle of salvation for Jerusalem. The final four chapters of this section (Isa 36–39) are narratives taken almost verbatim from 2 Kings 18:13–20:19. But even they replicate this alternation between judgment and salvation. Jerusalem is threatened by the Assyrians and then miraculously saved from their power. Similarly, Hezekiah faces imminent death, but at the last moment his life is spared. But this section ends with the ominous words of the prophet Isaiah, who tells Hezekiah that Babylon will bring an end to Judah's dynasty and state.

28:1-4 The proud crown

As was the case with the two previous sections of the book, this third section begins with an oracle of judgment. This time it is directed at the arrogance of the northern kingdom of Israel. The prophet uses several metaphors in announcing divine judgment on the northern kingdom—here called Ephraim after one of its principal regions. The northern kingdom was blessed with natural beauty and agriculturally valuable land. Isaiah proclaims that its excesses have finally caught up with Ephraim. Its capital, Samaria, was a beautiful city perched on the top of a mountain. The prophet

73

⁵On that day the LORD of hosts
　　will be a glorious crown
And a brilliant diadem
　　for the remnant of his people,
⁶A spirit of judgment
　　for the one who sits in judgment,
And strength for those
　　who turn back the battle at the
　　　gate.

Against Judah. ⁷But these also stagger
　　from wine
　and stumble from strong drink:
Priest and prophet stagger from
　　strong drink,
　overpowered by wine;
They are confused by strong drink,
　they stagger in their visions,

they totter when giving
　　judgment.
⁸Yes, all the tables
　　are covered with vomit,
　with filth, and no place left clean.
⁹"To whom would he impart
　　knowledge?
To whom would he convey the
　　message?
To those just weaned from milk,
　those weaned from the breast?
¹⁰For he says,
'Command on command,
　　command on command,
　rule on rule, rule on rule,
　here a little, there a little!'"
¹¹Yes, with stammering lips and in a
　　strange language

---

is certain that it is going to fall to its enemies. The prophet compares the city to the wilting blossoms on the crown of a merrymaker after a night of drinking. Like that garland, the city has outlived its usefulness. A storm is coming that will overwhelm it. Assyrian kings on military expeditions often compared themselves to the fury of a storm that would destroy all that stood in its path. Finally, the prophet speaks of Samaria as an early ripening fig, especially attractive to passers-by since late summer is the usual time for figs. The reason for Ephraim's predicament is the extravagance of the wealthy. They enjoy lavish meals while those who actually produced the food were living on the subsistence level with barely enough to eat. Isaiah believes that Assyria, God's chosen instrument of judgment, will make short work of Samaria and its proud crown.

28:5-6 A glorious crown

The word of judgment is followed by a word of hope that takes up the image of the crown from the previous unit. The proud crown that is Samaria is contrasted with the "glorious crown" that is the Lord. The former is facing judgment; the latter brings salvation for the remnant that will survive God's judgment on Israel. The remnant is composed of those who believe that there is a future in Zion despite the disasters that threaten.

28:7-13 Against priest and prophet

The prophet indicts the priests and prophets of his day. They fail in their appointed tasks because they are usually drunk. Here the prophet links

> he will speak to this people,
> ¹²to whom he said:
> "This is the resting place,
>   give rest to the weary;
> And this is the place of repose"—
>   but they refused to hear.
> ¹³So for them the word of the LORD
>   shall be:
>   "Command on command,
>   command on command,
> Rule on rule, rule on rule,
>   here a little, there a little!"
> So that when they walk, they shall
>   stumble backward,
>   broken, ensnared, and captured.
> ¹⁴Therefore, hear the word of the
>   LORD, you scoffers,
> who rule this people in
>   Jerusalem:
> ¹⁵You have declared, "We have
>   made a covenant with death,
> with Sheol we have made a pact;
> When the raging flood passes
>   through,
>   it will not reach us;

> For we have made lies our refuge,
>   and in falsehood we have found
>   a hiding place,"—
> ¹⁶Therefore, thus says the Lord
>   GOD:
>   See, I am laying a stone in Zion,
>   a stone that has been tested,
> A precious cornerstone as a sure
>   foundation;
>   whoever puts faith in it will not
>   waver.
> ¹⁷I will make judgment a measuring
>   line,
>   and justice a level.—
> Hail shall sweep away the refuge of
>   lies,
>   and waters shall flood the
>   hiding place.
> ¹⁸Your covenant with death shall be
>   canceled
>   and your pact with Sheol shall
>   not stand.
> When the raging flood passes
>   through,
>   you shall be beaten down by it.

his specific criticism with the more general indictment in 28:1. Leviticus 10:8-11 forbids priests on duty to drink. In their drunken state, Israel's religious leaders babble like infants. The quotation of the advice given by Israel's inebriated priests (28:10b) is a succession of nonsense syllables in Hebrew, though the NABRE obscures this. Similarly for those who have rejected Isaiah's indictment of their infidelity, the word of God has become a succession of nonsense syllables. What awaits them is a tragic end. Paul certainly thought of this passage when he was speaking about "the gift of tongues." He freely cites verses 11-12 in 1 Corinthians 14:21-22, although he incorrectly states that the text is from the torah.

28:14-22 Against Jerusalem's political leaders

The actions of Jerusalem's leaders to forestall the inevitable are nothing but a pact with death. Again, the prophet is playing on the name of a Canaanite deity, Mot, the god of the netherworld, whose name means death and whose activity endangers the fertility of the land (see 25:8). Jerusalem's political leaders believe that their leadership will safeguard their city's future, but actually they are only hastening its fall—its death.

¹⁹Whenever it passes, it shall seize
   you;
   morning after morning it shall
      pass,
   by day and by night.
Sheer terror
   to impart the message!
²⁰For the bed shall be too short to
      stretch out in,
   and the cover too narrow to
      wrap in.
²¹For the LORD shall rise up as on
      Mount Perazim,
   bestir himself as in the Valley of
      Gibeon,

To carry out his work—strange his
   work!
   to perform his deed—alien his
      deed!
²²Now, cease scoffing,
   lest your bonds be tightened,
For I have heard a decree of de-
      struction
   from the Lord, the GOD of hosts,
   for the whole land.

The Parable of the Farmer. ²³Give ear
   and hear my voice,
   pay attention and hear my
      word:

The only way that Jerusalem can have any future is if it establishes a just economic system. Trying to protect the city through alliances amounts to little more than suicide. A violent rainstorm that undermined hastily built fortifications around the city gave the prophet the occasion to speak about the solid foundation that God was preparing for the city's future. This foundation is justice. While it is true that Jerusalem was dependent on God's presence in the city, God's presence was, in turn, dependent on the behavior of the city's people—in particular Jerusalem's political leaders. They, however, have not fostered justice—quite the opposite. This has left God no choice but to begin an "urban renewal project" in the city. The project had to begin with demolition so that the city could be built on the solid foundation of a just economic system.

Jerusalem's leaders believed that strong fortifications would provide all the security the city needed. Isaiah sees devastation ahead since the city will be without the effective protection that justice provides. The prophet stipulates that in the past God fought for Israel against its enemies, the Canaanites (see Josh 10:7-14) and the Philistines (see 2 Sam 5:17-25). But in the coming conflict with Assyria, God will fight against Judah and Jerusalem, something Isaiah characterizes as a "strange deed." There is time to forestall this disaster if the city changes its attitude toward the prophet's message.

At the conclusion of the parable of the Vineyard (Matt 21:33-46), Jesus makes a statement made up of several Old Testament verses strung together to explain the negative reaction to his ministry as a divine necessity. Among those verses is 28:16.

²⁴Is the plowman forever plowing
    in order to sow,
  always loosening and
    harrowing the field?
²⁵When he has leveled the surface,
    does he not scatter caraway and
    sow cumin,
Put in wheat and barley,
  with spelt as its border?
²⁶His God has taught him this rule,
  he has instructed him.
²⁷For caraway is not threshed with a
    sledge,
  nor does a cartwheel roll over
    cumin.
But caraway is beaten out with a
    staff,
  and cumin with a rod.
²⁸Grain is crushed for bread, but not
    forever;
  though he thresh it thoroughly,
  and drive his cartwheel and
    horses over it,
  he does not pulverize it.
²⁹This too comes from the LORD of
    hosts;

wonderful is his counsel and
  great his wisdom.

29 Judgment and Deliverance of Jerusalem.

¹Ah! Ariel, Ariel,
  city where David encamped!
Let year follow year,
  and feast follow feast,
²But I will bring distress upon Ariel,
  and there will be mourning and
    moaning.
You shall be to me like Ariel:
  ³I will encamp like David
    against you;
I will circle you with outposts
  and set up siege works against
    you.
⁴You shall speak from beneath the
    earth,
  and from the dust below, your
    words shall come.
Your voice shall be that of a ghost
    from the earth,
  and your words shall whisper
    from the dust.
⁵The horde of your arrogant shall
    be like fine dust,

28:23-29 A parable on judgment

Here the prophet uses a succession of rhetorical questions to underscore his message. The judgment that Jerusalem is facing will happen because God acts at the right time for the right purpose. Plowing and planting take place during specific and limited periods according to a plan. Similarly, activities connected with the harvest follow a pattern. The message is clear: all that will happen to Jerusalem will happen at God's discretion for a good reason. Another implication of the parable is that the farmer's various activities, while necessary, have a limited duration so Jerusalem's judgment will be of limited duration as well. While divine judgment is coming, it is not God's final word to Jerusalem.

29:1-8 Jerusalem's judgment and salvation

Isaiah addresses Jerusalem as "Ariel," a name whose significance is unclear. This Hebrew word simply does not occur often enough in the Bible to be sure about its meaning. Ezekiel uses this word to speak of the place of sacrifice, the "altar hearth" where offerings are burnt (Ezek 43:15).

a horde of tyrants like flying
chaff.
Then suddenly, in an instant,
⁶you shall be visited by the
Lᴏʀᴅ of hosts,
With thunder, earthquake, and
great noise,
whirlwind, storm, and the flame
of consuming fire.
⁷Then like a dream,
a vision of the night,
Shall be the horde of all the nations
who make war against Ariel:
All the outposts, the siege works
against it,
all who distress it.
⁸As when a hungry man dreams he
is eating
and awakens with an empty
stomach,
Or when a thirsty man dreams he is
drinking
and awakens faint, his throat
parched,

So shall the horde of all the nations
be,
who make war against Mount
Zion.

Blindness and Perversity. ⁹Stupefy
yourselves and stay stupid;
blind yourselves and stay blind!
You who are drunk, but not from
wine,
who stagger, but not from
strong drink!
¹⁰For the Lᴏʀᴅ has poured out on
you
a spirit of deep sleep.
He has shut your eyes (the prophets)
and covered your heads (the
seers).

¹¹For you the vision of all this has be- ▸
come like the words of a sealed scroll.
When it is handed to one who can read,
with the request, "Read this," the reply
is, "I cannot, because it is sealed." ¹²When

If Isaiah understands Ariel in the same way, the prophet may intend this
word to imply that Jerusalem will be the setting for the forthcoming sacrifice
of Judah's leaders and people. The literal meaning of Ariel is "the lion of
God," but the significance of that meaning in this context is also not obvious.

The opening verse of the oracle suggests that the New Year's celebration provided the prophet with an opportunity to speak about what lay
ahead for the city. Isaiah declares that a hostile army will surround the city.
This siege will lead the people to raise a great lamentation, which will fail
to move God since God is intent on making a sacrifice of the city. But the
nations chosen to place Jerusalem on the altar of sacrifice will not escape
divine judgment. This will not save Jerusalem, but the nations arrayed
against it will be judged for their failures as well. Still, the judgment of
these nations is a sign of Jerusalem's restoration. Jesus' lament over Jerusalem uses the language and imagery of the prophet's oracle against Ariel
(29:3; Luke 19:43).

29:9-16 Against the sages

The prophet, who has already criticized some of Israel's leadership
(28:7-22), turns his attention to Jerusalem's sages. He probably has in mind

the scroll is handed to one who cannot
read, with the request, "Read this," the
reply is, "I cannot read."

> [13] The Lord said:
> Since this people draws near with
> words only
> and honors me with their lips
> alone,
> though their hearts are far from
> me,
> And fear of me has become
> mere precept of human
> teaching,
> [14] Therefore I will again deal with
> this people
> in surprising and wondrous
> fashion:
> The wisdom of the wise shall
> perish,
> the prudence of the prudent
> shall vanish.
> [15] Ah! You who would hide a plan
> too deep for the LORD!
> Who work in the dark, saying,

> "Who sees us, who knows us?"
> [16] Your perversity is as though the
> potter
> were taken to be the clay:
> As though what is made should say
> of its maker,
> "He did not make me!"
> Or the vessel should say of the
> potter,
> "He does not understand."

> **Redemption.** [17] Surely, in a very little
> while,
> Lebanon shall be changed into
> an orchard,
> and the orchard be considered a
> forest!
> [18] On that day the deaf shall hear
> the words of a scroll;
> And out of gloom and darkness,
> the eyes of the blind shall see.
> [19] The lowly shall again find joy in
> the LORD,
> the poorest rejoice in the Holy
> One of Israel.

the royal counselors rather than the wise and prudent elders that people
sought out for their advice. Like the rest of Jerusalem's leadership, the
sages are not fulfilling their responsibilities. The contribution to Judah is
as effective as that of a drunk, but they were not drunk with wine like the
priests and prophet. They are unable to provide sound advice because
God has made it impossible for them to see Jerusalem's true status before
God. It is as if all their skill has left them. The prophet blames this on the
people of Jerusalem who are content with merely going through the mo-
tions during worship. Worst of all, the sages approach the crisis Jerusalem
was facing as if it should be handled by diplomatic maneuvering. They
do not recognize that the city's future is in God's hands—not theirs. Jesus
quotes verse 13 when he criticizes the religious observance of some of his
contemporaries (Matt 15:8; Mark 7:6-7). Paul cites verse 16 to affirm the
justice of God (Rom 9:21).

29:17-24 A reversal of fortunes

The prophet looks forward to a time when Israel will have the kind of
spiritual sensitivity that should mark the people of God. Unfortunately,

²⁰For the tyrant shall be no more,
　the scoffer shall cease to be;
All who are ready for evil shall be
　cut off,
²¹those who condemn with a
　mere word,
Who ensnare the defender at the
　gate,
　and leave the just with an empty
　claim.
²²Therefore thus says the LORD,
　the God of the house of Jacob,
　who redeemed Abraham:
No longer shall Jacob be ashamed,
　no longer shall his face grow pale.

²³For when his children see
　the work of my hands in his
　midst,
They shall sanctify my name;
　they shall sanctify the Holy One
　of Jacob,
　be in awe of the God of Israel.
²⁴Those who err in spirit shall
　acquire understanding,
　those who find fault shall
　receive instruction.

30 **Oracle on the Futility of an Alliance with Egypt.** ¹Ah! Rebellious children,
oracle of the LORD,

---

this is still lacking. There are the devout who tried to live in accord with the Divine Will (the "lowly" and "poorest" of 29:19). Then there are those who led a life that was best described as godless (the "arrogant" of 29:20). Finally, there is a large percentage of "Jacob's children" who are simply ignorant of God's will and promises for Israel (the "blind" and the "deaf" of 29:18). The prophet envisions a time when the latter will be healed, but he appears to intimate that the arrogant are beyond hope. For the prophet a sure sign of God's final act in favor of Israel will be the conversion and incorporation of those who are spiritually insensitive within the community of those already committed to justice.

The social and economic disparity between the poor and the arrogant was serious and it could not go on for much longer. The prophet believed that a reversal of fortunes was coming. God was about to act on behalf of those who were being oppressed. The lowly and poor will find joy, while the arrogant will have gone. When the devout see God's actions on their behalf, their faith will be confirmed and they will be led to an ever greater fidelity to God, for they will stand in awe of God's holiness. The most significant outcome of God's action on behalf of the poor will be the effect it will have on those who "err in spirit" and "find fault." Those people who drag down the spirit of Israel will be transformed and will be firmly convinced that the future belongs to the God of Israel.

30:1-17 Against a compact with Egypt

Conventional wisdom for a small state like Judah caught between two superpowers like Egypt and Assyria was to play off the superpowers against each other. Judah does just that by considering an alliance with

Who carry out a plan that is not
mine,
who make an alliance I did not
inspire,
thus adding sin upon sin;
²They go down to Egypt,
without asking my counsel,
To seek strength in Pharaoh's
protection
and take refuge in Egypt's
shadow.
³Pharaoh's protection shall become
your shame,
refuge in Egypt's shadow your
disgrace.
⁴When his princes are at Zoan
and his messengers reach Hanes,
⁵All shall be ashamed
of a people that gain them
nothing,
Neither help nor benefit,
but only shame and reproach.
⁶Oracle on the Beasts of the
Negeb.
Through the distressed and
troubled land
of the lioness and roaring lion,
of the viper and flying saraph,
They carry their riches on the backs
of donkeys

and their treasures on the
humps of camels
To a people good for nothing,
⁷to Egypt whose help is futile
and vain.
Therefore I call her
"Rahab Sit-still."
⁸Now come, write it on a tablet they
can keep,
inscribe it on a scroll;
That in time to come it may be
an eternal witness.
⁹For this is a rebellious people,
deceitful children,
Children who refuse
to listen to the instruction of the
LORD;
¹⁰Who say to the seers, "Do not
see";
to the prophets, "Do not
prophesy truth for us;
speak smooth things to us, see
visions that deceive!
¹¹Turn aside from the way! Get out
of the path!
Let us hear no more
of the Holy One of Israel!"
¹²Therefore, thus says the Holy One
of Israel:
Because you reject this word,

Egypt to insure that the Assyrian threat would be neutralized. The prophet consistently advises against this conventional wisdom. Isaiah characterizes Egypt as "Rahab quelled." Rahab is another name for the sea monster that represents the forces of chaos, which God has already defeated (see Job 26:12). The prophet believed that by aligning itself with Egypt, Judah was setting itself up for more severe treatment from Assyria than if it simply submitted. The prophet's strategy in dealing with the Assyrian threat was for Judah to remain passive, making no overt attempts at opposing the unstoppable Assyrian army. He is convinced that the people of Judah will not escape foreign domination because God has chosen Assyria as the instrument of judgment upon Jerusalem.

Isaiah's words reflect his frustration with Judah's political leaders. They look for prophets whose words support their fatally flawed foreign policy.

And put your trust in oppression
and deceit,
and depend on them,
¹³This iniquity of yours shall be
like a descending rift
Bulging out in a high wall
whose crash comes suddenly, in
an instant,
¹⁴Crashing like a potter's jar
smashed beyond rescue,
And among its fragments cannot be
found
a sherd to scoop fire from the
hearth
or dip water from the cistern.
¹⁵For thus said the Lord God,
the Holy One of Israel:
By waiting and by calm you shall
be saved,
in quiet and in trust shall be
your strength.
But this you did not will.
¹⁶"No," you said,
"Upon horses we will flee."
Very well, you shall flee!
"Upon swift steeds we will ride."

Very well, swift shall be your
pursuers!
¹⁷A thousand shall tremble at the
threat of one—
if five threaten, you shall flee.
You will then be left like a flagstaff
on a mountaintop,
like a flag on a hill.

Zion's Future Deliverance. ¹⁸Truly, the
Lord is waiting to be
gracious to you,
truly, he shall rise to show you
mercy;
For the Lord is a God of justice:
happy are all who wait for him!
¹⁹Yes, people of Zion, dwelling in
Jerusalem,
you shall no longer weep;
He will be most gracious to you
when you cry out;
as soon as he hears he will
answer you.
²⁰The Lord will give you bread in
adversity
and water in affliction.

But Isaiah believes that God did not speak through those prophets. Judah has rejected Isaiah's message, which counseled trust in God alone—without relying on alliances, national pride, or armed resistance. The prophet, of course, has made it clear that Judah will not evade divine judgment because of the injustice in Judahite society. But he asserts that submission to Assyria will prevent the total destruction of Judah. The country's leaders, however, labored under the illusion that they could escape judgment. This was their great mistake.

30:18-26 Jerusalem's future

The prophet can envision a glorious future for Jerusalem because he believes that the city's future is not determined by its infidelity but by God's fidelity. After the city experiences God's judgment, there will come deliverance. This oracle begins by identifying the Lord as a "God of justice." The key then to the glorious future that awaits Jerusalem is a just social and economic order—not the city's supposed status as God's dwelling place on earth.

No longer will your Teacher hide
> himself,
> but with your own eyes you
>> shall see your Teacher,
21And your ears shall hear a word
> behind you:
> "This is the way; walk in it,"
> when you would turn to the
>> right or the left.
22You shall defile your silver-plated
>> idols
> and your gold-covered images;
You shall throw them away like
> filthy rags,
> you shall say, "Get out!"
23He will give rain for the seed
> you sow in the ground,
And the bread that the soil produces
> will be rich and abundant.
On that day your cattle will graze

in broad meadows;
24The oxen and the donkeys that till
> the ground
> will eat silage tossed to them
> with shovel and pitchfork.
25Upon every high mountain and
> lofty hill
> there will be streams of running
> water.
On the day of the great slaughter,
> when the towers fall,
26The light of the moon will be like
> the light of the sun,
> and the light of the sun will be
> seven times greater,
like the light of seven days,
On the day the LORD binds up the
> wounds of his people
> and heals the bruises left by his
> blows.

The intensity of Jerusalem's distress at the prospect of Assyrian domination should not lead it to despair but to confident assurance in the coming redemption. God will give to the people all that they need for their life and will insure that the people of Jerusalem have the kind of instruction which, when heard and applied, will keep them from deviating in any way from a life that is in accord with God's will, thus insuring the permanence of the city's deliverance.

The consequence of this new obedience will go beyond the moral order and affect nature; the land will enjoy unparalleled fertility. The contemporary concern for the wise use of natural resources can easily resonate with the prophet's vision which posits a connection between human righteousness and the fruitfulness of the land.

The prophet concludes by using apocalyptic imagery in speaking of Jerusalem's restoration. The light of the sun and the moon will be so increased that night will be indistinguishable from day and the daylight will be seven times more intense than in the present. When will this happen? The answer is on the day of the "great slaughter" when God will rise up against the enemies of the just and bring down the towers of their strength. In order that the faithful be not afraid of that day, the prophet concludes by describing it as a time when God will heal the wounds of the past that were endured by the just.

funeral pyre

Divine Judgment on Assyria. [27]See, the
name of the LORD is coming from
afar,
    burning with anger, heavy with
threat,
His lips filled with fury,
    tongue like a consuming fire,
[28]Breath like an overflowing torrent
    that reaches up to the neck!
He will winnow the nations with a
destructive winnowing
    and bridle the jaws of the peoples
to send them astray.
[29]For you, there will be singing
    as on a night when a feast is
observed,
And joy of heart
    as when one marches along with
a flute
Going to the mountain of the LORD,
    to the Rock of Israel.
[30]The LORD will make his glorious
voice heard,
    and reveal his arm coming down
In raging fury and flame of
consuming fire,
    in tempest, and rainstorm, and
hail.

[31]For at the voice of the LORD,
    Assyria will be shattered,
as he strikes with the rod;
[32]And every sweep of the rod of his
punishment,
    which the LORD will bring down
on him,
Will be accompanied by timbrels
and lyres,
    while he wages war against
him.
[33]For his tophet has long been ready,
    truly it is prepared for the king;
His firepit made both deep and
wide,
    with fire and firewood in
abundance,
And the breath of the LORD, like a
stream of sulfur,
    setting it afire.

31 Against the Egyptian Alliance. [1]Ah!
Those who go down to Egypt for
help,
    who rely on horses;
Who put their trust in chariots
    because of their number,
and in horsemen because of
their combined power,

30:27-33 Against Assyria

For Jerusalem to live in peace, Assyria will have to fall. Here the prophet
asserts that one day this mighty empire will be no more. While Isaiah teaches
that God is using the militaristic and expansionist Assyrian Empire as a
means to bring down Judah and its unjust social and economic system, the
prophet does not endorse the policies of Assyria. Again he makes it clear
that Assyria will have to answer for its own crimes. God will descend upon
Assyria like a violent winter storm. Assyria will not be able to resist this
divine judgment. Of course, Judah will rejoice at Assyria's fall, which is
certain to come since God's judgment comes upon injustice and oppression
wherever it is found.

31:1-3 Against Egypt

The prophet returns to his attempts to discourage Judah from making
an alliance with Egypt against Assyria. An alliance with Egypt appeared

But look not to the Holy One of
Israel
    nor seek the LORD!
²Yet he too is wise and will bring
disaster;
    he will not turn from his threats.
He will rise up against the house of
the wicked
    and against those who help
    evildoers.
³The Egyptians are human beings,
not God,
    their horses flesh, not spirit;
When the LORD stretches forth his
hand,
    the helper shall stumble, the one
    helped shall fall,
and both of them shall perish
together.
⁴For thus says the LORD to me:

As a lion or its young
    growling over the prey,
With a band of shepherds
    assembled against it,
Is neither dismayed by their shouts
    nor cowed by their noise,
So shall the LORD of hosts come
down
    to wage war upon Mount Zion,
    upon its height.
⁵Like hovering birds, so the LORD of
hosts
    shall shield Jerusalem,
To shield and deliver,
    to spare and rescue.

⁶Return, O Israelites, to him whom you
have utterly deserted. ⁷On that day each
one of you shall reject his idols of silver
and gold, which your hands have made.

---

to be the right move since Egypt could supply a formidable chariot force
which could aid Judah in resisting the Assyrian invaders. Actually, Egypt's
chariots would have been of limited use since most of Judah's important
cities were in the central highlands where chariots were not maneuverable.

The prophet reasserts the advice he consistently gives to Judah under
threat from Assyria: trust in God. God's purposes will be achieved no matter
what alliances Judah may make. After all, the Egyptians are human beings
and their horses are mere flesh. They could not possibly thwart the plan of
God, who has determined to bring an end of Judah's political, religious, and
economic institutions because of the injustice that they foster. No chariot
army will be able to stop this plan.

31:4-7 God protects Jerusalem

The prophet uses two metaphors to speak of Jerusalem's deliverance.
The first is clear enough. God is like a lion which will not surrender its
prey though shepherds will try to frighten it off (31:4). The second is more
obscure (31:5). The phrasing in the NABRE suggests that God is like birds
circling overhead, protecting the city. The Hebrew is not as clear though
the parallel with verse 4 suggests that the goal of this imagery is to suggest that God will not abandon Jerusalem. Still, the image of birds circling
overhead suggests desolation rather than protection. Of course, this must
be seen against the wider backdrop of the Isaianic tradition that affirms

⁸Assyria shall fall by a sword, not
wielded by human being,
no mortal sword shall devour
him;
He shall flee before the sword,
and his young men shall be
impressed as laborers.
⁹He shall rush past his crag in
panic,
and his princes desert the
standard in terror,
Says the LORD who has a fire in
Zion
and a furnace in Jerusalem.

32 **The Kingdom of Justice.** ¹See, a
king will reign justly
and princes will rule rightly.
²Each of them will be like a shelter
from the wind,
a refuge from the rain.
They will be like streams of water
in a dry country,
like the shade of a great rock in
a parched land.
³The eyes of those who see will not
be closed;
the ears of those who hear will
be attentive.

that Jerusalem must expect divine judgment because of its oppressive and unjust economic system. Still, the city has a future beyond judgment. What this passage affirms is that God's protection will not allow Jerusalem's total destruction at the hands of its enemies. God's deliverance of the city will finally persuade its people to recognize the claims that God has on their exclusive loyalty. The people will finally stop looking for security by serving gods other than the Lord.

31:8-9 Against Assyria

God's deliverance of Jerusalem can come only at the expense of the Assyrians. Again, the prophet affirms that the time of Assyrian power is limited. When the Assyrian Empire falls, it will be God's doing. The prophet is trying to persuade his readers that their future and the future of their city are in God's hands so they can look toward that future with confidence and assurance. Those who read these words, after the book of Isaiah achieved the shape it now has, lived many years after the Assyrian Empire had fallen to the Babylonian Empire, which, in turn, fell to the Persian Empire. The prophet's audience, however, was still looking for the complete restoration of Jerusalem. Certainly these words were meant to keep their hopes from flagging. After all, Assyria did fall as the prophet said it would. One could have confidence in the prophetic word.

32:1-8 New leadership for Jerusalem

To put a positive spin on his vision of Jerusalem's future, the prophet speaks about leadership. He assures his readers that there will come a time when the current perverse social and economic order will be set aright. Those who have the responsibility for maintaining a just social order will fulfill their responsibilities. In the prophet's day, justice was perverted.

⁴The hasty of heart shall take
thought to know,
and tongues of stutterers shall
speak readily and clearly.
⁵No more will the fool be called
noble,
nor the deceiver be considered
honorable.
⁶For the fool speaks folly,
his heart plans evil:
Godless actions,
perverse speech against the LORD,
Letting the hungry go empty
and the thirsty without drink.
⁷The deceits of the deceiver are evil,
he plans devious schemes:
To ruin the poor with lies,
and the needy when they plead
their case.
⁸But the noble plan noble deeds,
and in noble deeds they persist.

The Women of Jerusalem. ⁹You
women so complacent, rise up and
hear my voice,
daughters so confident, give
heed to my words.
¹⁰In a little more than a year
your confidence will be shaken;
For the vintage will fail,
no fruit harvest will come in.
¹¹Tremble, you who are so
complacent!
Shudder, you who are so
confident!
Strip yourselves bare,
with only a loincloth for cover.
¹²Beat your breasts
for the pleasant fields,
for the fruitful vine;
¹³For the soil of my people,
overgrown with thorns and
briers;

People called evil good and fools wise. The poor deserve to have justice done when they are in the right, and apparently there is no one to take their side. But it is not only the poor that suffer. Society itself is transformed into something it should not be. The prophet looks for the day when competent and just political leadership will guide the community. Note there is no hint that this political leadership will come from the Davidic dynasty.

32:9-14 Judgment on Jerusalem

The prophet again shifts his mood abruptly. After describing his vision of a just city led by competent rulers, he moves back to the harsh reality that he has experienced. He speaks to a city under judgment. He turns his attention to the women of the upper classes as he did in 3:16–4:1, because these women were good symbols of the excesses of the wealthy. The prophet warns them that their lives of ease will come to an unexpected end very soon. They ought to be worried. A most appropriate response would be for them to adopt the attitude of mourners with the hope of engaging God's sympathy for their plight. Soon the wealthy will be mourning because their lives of extravagance will end. The soil will lose its fecundity and the cities of Judah will be deserted. The land will revert to the state before human habitation transformed it.

87

For all the joyful houses,
the exultant city.
[14]The castle will be forsaken,
the noisy city deserted;
Citadel and tower will become
wasteland forever,
the joy of wild donkeys, the
pasture of flocks;
[15]Until the spirit from on high
is poured out on us.
And the wilderness becomes a
garden land
and the garden land seems as
common as forest.
[16]Then judgment will dwell in the
wilderness
and justice abide in the garden
land.
[17]The work of justice will be peace;

the effect of justice, calm and
security forever.
[18]My people will live in peaceful
country,
in secure dwellings and quiet
resting places.
[19]And the forest will come down
completely,
the city will be utterly laid low.
[20]Happy are you who sow beside
every stream,
and let the ox and the donkey
go freely!

33 **Overthrow of Assyria.** [1]Ah! You destroyer never destroyed,
betrayer never betrayed!
When you have finished
destroying, you will be
destroyed;

32:15-20 An idyllic future

As quickly as the prophet moved from vision to reality, he shifts back to a vision of an idyllic future. He is convinced that the oracle of judgment he conveyed to the women of the upper classes is not God's final word to Judah. God will send the spirit to make the earth fruitful once again. Human society will be marked by justice. Justice will make it possible for all people to have what they need to lead happy lives. The imagery that the prophet uses here appears to suggest he believes that in the future the people of Judah would be living in small villages. Again, the prophet allows his rhetoric to get the best of him. He expects Jerusalem to be restored. It will be purged of the injustices that have made it the object of divine judgment. The prophet, then, was not one who rejected city life as somehow incompatible to the ideals of traditional Israelite morality. What is essential to the prophet's vision of Judah's future is that justice will lead to peace.

33:1-16 God's justice

This chapter begins with a woe oracle against an unnamed enemy who has threatened Jerusalem—a conventional way of speaking about the city's importance for the future of God's people. The unnamed enemy is the Assyrian Empire, whose demise the prophet announces yet again. The destruction of its enemy means the glorification of Jerusalem, which occupies the prophet's attention in this oracle. That glorification comes

when you have stopped
 betraying, you will be
 betrayed.
²LORD, be gracious to us; for you we
 wait.
 Be our strength every morning,
 our salvation in time of trouble!
³At the roaring sound, peoples flee;
 when you rise in your majesty,
 nations are scattered.
⁴Spoil is gathered up as caterpillars
 gather,
 an onrush like the rush of
 locusts.
⁵The LORD is exalted, enthroned on
 high;
 he fills Zion with right and
 justice.
⁶That which makes her seasons
 certain,
 her wealth, salvation, wisdom,
 and knowledge,
 is the fear of the LORD, her
 treasure.
⁷See, the men of Ariel cry out in the
 streets,
 the messengers of Shalem weep
 bitterly.
⁸The highways are desolate,
 travelers have quit the paths,
Covenants are broken, witnesses
 spurned;
 yet no one gives it a thought.

⁹The country languishes in
 mourning,
 Lebanon withers with shame;
Sharon is like the Arabah,
 Bashan and Carmel are stripped
 bare.
¹⁰Now I will rise up, says the LORD,
 now exalt myself,
 now lift myself up.
¹¹You conceive dry grass, bring
 forth stubble;
 my spirit shall consume you like
 fire.
¹²The peoples shall be burned to
 lime,
 thorns cut down to burn in fire.
¹³Hear, you who are far off, what I
 have done;
 you who are near, acknowledge
 my might.
¹⁴In Zion sinners are in dread,
 trembling grips the impious:
"Who of us can live with
 consuming fire?
 who of us can live with
 everlasting flames?"
¹⁵Whoever walks righteously and
 speaks honestly,
 who spurns what is gained by
 oppression,
Who waves off contact with a bribe,
 who stops his ears so as not to
 hear of bloodshed,

because God will rule Jerusalem. God's rule will insure that Zion will be filled with justice and righteousness. These, of course, are prophetic code words for a just social order in which the poor find protection against the greed and arrogance of the rich. Verses 14-16 show how the prophet adapted the question-and-answer pattern of entrance liturgies (e.g., Pss 15, 24) to underscore the importance of justice in the lives of those who would be part of a restored Jerusalem.

33:17-24 A new Jerusalem

The prophet describes Jerusalem after God has removed the Assyrian threat to the city and established justice for the city's poor and oppressed.

who closes his eyes so as not to
look on evil—
[16]That one shall dwell on the
heights,
with fortresses of rock for
stronghold,
food and drink in steady supply.
[17]Your eyes will see a king in his
splendor,
they will look upon a vast land.
[18]Your mind will dwell on the
terror:
"Where is the one who counted,
where the one who
weighed?
Where the one who counted the
towers?"
[19]You shall no longer see a defiant
people,
a people of speech too obscure
to comprehend,
stammering in a tongue not
understood.
[20]Look to Zion, the city of our
festivals;
your eyes shall see Jerusalem
as a quiet abode, a tent not to be
struck,
Whose pegs will never be pulled
up,

nor any of its ropes severed.
[21]Indeed the LORD in majesty will
be there for us
a place of rivers and wide
streams
on which no galley may go,
where no majestic ship may
pass.
[22]For the LORD is our judge,
the LORD is our lawgiver,
the LORD is our king;
he it is who will save us.
[23]The rigging hangs slack;
it cannot hold the mast in place,
nor keep the sail spread out.
Then the blind will divide great
spoils
and the lame will carry off the
loot.
[24]No one who dwells there will say,
"I am sick";
the people who live there will be
forgiven their guilt.

F. The Lord, Zion's Avenger

34 **Judgment upon Edom.** [1]Come near,
nations, and listen;
be attentive, you peoples!
Let the earth and what fills it listen,
the world and all it produces.

The prophet uses conventional imagery to speak about God's rule from
Zion. The worship of Judah's God will take place without interruption.
God's law will guide the city's government, but the prophet allows himself
a little poetic license as he speaks of God's dwelling in Zion protected by
"broad rivers and streams." There are no rivers or streams in the vicinity
of Jerusalem. Finally, sickness and sin will be only a memory. The prophet
uses this imagery to move the people to see their future as the work of God
rather than the result of political maneuvering.

34:1-17 Against Edom

The prophet turns his attention to the nations again. He does not specify
the crimes that the nations have committed, but he promises that God's
judgment will be severe and complete. Edom is singled out for harsh judg-

²The LORD is angry with all the
  nations,
   enraged against all their host;
He has placed them under the ban,
   given them up to slaughter.
³Their slain shall be cast out,
   their corpses shall send up a
    stench;
   the mountains shall run with
    their blood,
⁴All the host of heaven shall rot;
   the heavens shall be rolled up
    like a scroll.
All their host shall wither away,
   as the leaf wilts on the vine,
   or as the fig withers on the tree.
⁵When my sword has drunk its fill
   in the heavens,
   it shall come down upon Edom
    for judgment,
   upon a people under my ban.
⁶The LORD has a sword sated with
    blood,
   greasy with fat,
With the blood of lambs and goats,
   with the fat of rams' kidneys;
For the LORD has a sacrifice in
    Bozrah,
   a great slaughter in the land of
    Edom.
⁷Wild oxen shall be struck down
   with fatlings,
   and bullocks with bulls;
Their land shall be soaked with
    blood,
   and their soil greasy with fat.
⁸For the LORD has a day of
    vengeance,
   a year of requital for the cause
    of Zion.
⁹Edom's streams shall be changed
   into pitch,
   its soil into sulfur,
   and its land shall become
    burning pitch;
¹⁰Night and day it shall not be
    quenched,
   its smoke shall rise forever.
From generation to generation it
   shall lie waste,
   never again shall anyone pass
    through it.
¹¹But the desert owl and hoot owl
   shall possess it,
   the screech owl and raven shall
    dwell in it.

---

ment because of its proximity to Judah and its behavior when Jerusalem was militarily and politically impotent.

The prophet promises the territory of Edom will become a region without human habitation. Its land will be a haunt for wild creatures once again. Edom will sink into chaos and will be little more than a bad memory for Judah. Its destruction will be as complete as that of Sodom and Gomorrah (Gen 19:24). Nothing can save Edom from its judgment.

Modern readers find the language of this oracle particularly repellant. The prophet's harshness reflects his conviction that the conflict he was describing was not simply between Judah and the nations but a conflict between God and the powers of evil that attempt to frustrate God's rule. It is not just that Assyria or Edom suffers military defeat. The heavens and their host are the opponents that God defeats. In a battle with the powers of evil, God can give no quarter. What happens to the nations is simply

The LORD will stretch over it the
    measuring line of chaos,
    the plumb line of confusion.
[12]Its nobles shall be no more,
    nor shall kings be proclaimed
       there;
    all its princes are gone.
[13]Its castles shall be overgrown with
    thorns,
    its fortresses with thistles and
       briers.
It shall become an abode for jackals,
    a haunt for ostriches.
[14]Wildcats shall meet with desert
    beasts,
    satyrs shall call to one another;
There shall the lilith repose,
    and find for herself a place to
       rest.
[15]There the hoot owl shall nest and
    lay eggs,
    hatch them out and gather them
       in her shadow;
There shall the kites assemble,
    each with its mate.

[16]Search through the book of the
    LORD and read:
    not one of these shall be lacking,
For the mouth of the LORD has
    ordered it,
    and his spirit gathers them
       there.
[17]It is he who casts the lot for them;
    his hand measures off their
       portions;
They shall possess it forever,
    and dwell in it from generation
       to generation.

35 **Israel's Deliverance.** [1]The wilderness and the parched land will
    exult;
    the Arabah will rejoice and
       bloom;
[2]Like the crocus it shall bloom
    abundantly,
    and rejoice with joyful song.
The glory of Lebanon will be given
    to it,
    the splendor of Carmel and
       Sharon;

---

the terrible consequence of the conflict that went on in the heavens. The focus on Edom, of course, reflects the pressure that Edom was exerting on Judah. The exaggeration so clearly evident in the oracle is a matter of rhetorical convention and also a genuine ill will that gripped the people of Judah toward Edom.

35:1-10 Zion's joy

The contrast between this passage and the preceding oracle against Edom could not be any stronger. In the previous oracle, nature serves as the means of divine judgment with Edom's territory reverting to a wild state. Here nature is transformed to make the restoration of Jerusalem possible. In both instances, God's power accomplishes the deed. Both the judgment of Edom and the salvation of Jerusalem bring glory to God.

This imagery and the thrust of this oracle are similar to that found in the fourth section of the book, chapters 40–55. The motif of the desert's transformation in verses 1-2 recurs in 40:3; that of God's coming to save in verse 4 in 40:9-10; the healing of the blind in verse 5 and of lame in verse 6 in 40:5

"The wilderness and the parched land will exult . . . Like the crocus it shall bloom abundantly." (See Isaiah 35:1-2.)

They will see the glory of the LORD,
  the splendor of our God.
³Strengthen hands that are feeble,
  make firm knees that are weak,
⁴Say to the fearful of heart:
  Be strong, do not fear!
Here is your God,
  he comes with vindication;
With divine recompense
  he comes to save you.
⁵Then the eyes of the blind shall
    see,
  and the ears of the deaf be
    opened;
⁶Then the lame shall leap like a
    stag,
  and the mute tongue sing for joy.
For waters will burst forth in the
    wilderness,
  and streams in the Arabah.
⁷The burning sands will become
    pools,

and the thirsty ground, springs
    of water;
The abode where jackals crouch
  will be a marsh for the reed and
    papyrus.
⁸A highway will be there,
  called the holy way;
No one unclean may pass over it,
  but it will be for his people;
no traveler, not even fools, shall
    go astray on it.
⁹No lion shall be there,
  nor any beast of prey approach,
  nor be found.
But there the redeemed shall
    walk,
¹⁰And the ransomed of the LORD
    shall return,
  and enter Zion singing,
  crowned with everlasting joy;
They meet with joy and gladness,
  sorrow and mourning flee away.

---

and 42:7; the miraculous highway of verse 8 in 40:3; and the disappearance of sorrow in verse 10 in 51:11. Clearly, this chapter was meant to serve as a bridge to the next section of the book. But why is this chapter placed here, before the chapters (36–39) that end the third section of the book with a historical review of the Assyrian and Babylonian crises? One possibility is that the prophet wished to emphasize that God's plans for Zion transcend history. They are not dependent upon what people do but on the sovereign act of a God who is determined to restore Jerusalem.

The transformation of the desert from an arid, life-threatening place to a fertile, life-supporting place is a common biblical image of salvation. Israel is not blessed with a river system like those in Egypt and Mesopotamia. The threat of drought followed by crop failure, famine, and starvation was always a serious threat. Speaking of God's movement in Israel's life as eliminating that threat was natural for ancient Israel's poets and theologians. The text affirms that the desert and parched lands will become like Lebanon where rains are plentiful, the Carmel range that guards the fertile Jezreel Valley, and Sharon that was a well-watered plain along the coast.

These new circumstances ought to encourage those people who were unable to see any future for themselves as God's people. Similarly, God's movement in their lives will be as miraculous as the opening of blind eyes

G. Historical Appendix

36 **Invasion of Sennacherib.** [1]In the fourteenth year of King Hezekiah, Sennacherib, king of Assyria, went up against all the fortified cities of Judah and captured them. [2]From Lachish the king of Assyria sent his commander with a great army to King Hezekiah in Jerusalem. When he stopped at the conduit of the upper pool, on the highway of the fuller's field, [3]there came out to him the master of the palace, Eliakim, son of Hilkiah, and Shebna the scribe, and the chancellor, Joah, son of Asaph.

[4]The commander said to them, "Tell Hezekiah: Thus says the great king, the king of Assyria: On what do you base this trust of yours? [5]Do you think mere words substitute for strategy and might in war? In whom, then, do you place your trust, that you rebel against me? [6]Do you trust in Egypt, that broken reed of a staff which pierces the hand of anyone who leans on it? That is what Pharaoh, king of Egypt, is to all who trust in him. [7]Or do you say to me: It is in the LORD, our God, we trust? Is it not he whose high places and altars Hezekiah

---

and the loosing of a mute's tongue. Returning to the metaphor of the transformed desert in verse 7, the prophet asserts that the wilderness will no longer be a dangerous place, the haunt of lions and jackals. There will be a highway there, allowing the people of Judah to return to Jerusalem with joy. The death of Judah's political and religious institutions and the exile of its leading citizens threatened the people's very existence, but God will come with vindication and salvation.

There are at least six allusions to this text in the New Testament: 35:3 (Heb 12:12); verses 5-6 (Matt 11:5; Mark 7:37; Luke 7:22; Acts 26:18); and verse 10 (Rev 21:4). The most striking is the citing of this text by the people who witnessed Jesus' healing of a man with impaired hearing and speaking (Mark 7:37). Though the prophet composed this text to encourage Jews to hold on to their ancestral faith, the New Testament reinterprets this text to proclaim its faith in Jesus.

36:1–37:9a Jerusalem threatened

The third section of the book of Isaiah closes with a prose account of the Assyrian siege of Jerusalem that took place during the reign of Hezekiah (715–698 B.C.). The account is taken from 2 Kings 18:13–20:19 with some notable differences.

The Assyrians, led by their king Sennacherib, began their campaign in Judah by taking forty-six fortified cities. From Lachish, the last of these, Sennacherib sends his Rabshakeh (chief of staff) to Jerusalem, demanding surrender. Meeting with his Judahite counterparts, the Rabshakeh underscores the futility of resistance to the Assyrian forces arrayed against Jerusalem.

has removed, commanding Judah and Jerusalem, 'Worship before this altar'?

⁸"Now, make a wager with my lord, the king of Assyria: I will give you two thousand horses, if you are able to put riders on them. ⁹How then can you turn back even a captain, one of the least servants of my lord, trusting, as you do, in Egypt for chariots and horses? ¹⁰Did I come up to destroy this land without the Lord? The Lord himself said to me, Go up and destroy that land!"

¹¹Then Eliakim and Shebna and Joah said to the commander, "Please speak to your servants in Aramaic; we understand it. Do not speak to us in the language of Judah within earshot of the people who are on the wall."

¹²But the commander replied, "Was it to your lord and to you that my lord sent me to speak these words? Was it not rather to those sitting on the wall, who, with you, will have to eat their own excrement and drink their own urine?" ¹³Then the commander stepped forward and cried out in a loud voice in the language of Judah, "Listen to the words of the great king, the king of Assyria. ¹⁴Thus says the king: Do not let Hezekiah deceive you, for he cannot rescue you. ¹⁵And do not let Hezekiah induce you to trust in the Lord, saying, 'The Lord will surely rescue us, and this city will not be

handed over to the king of Assyria.' ¹⁶Do not listen to Hezekiah, for thus says the king of Assyria:

> Make peace with me
>   and surrender to me!
> Eat, each of you, from your vine,
>   each from your own fig tree.
> Drink water, each from your own
>   well,
>   ¹⁷until I arrive and take you
>   to a land like your own,
> A land of grain and wine,
>   a land of bread and vineyards.

¹⁸Do not let Hezekiah seduce you by saying, 'The Lord will rescue us.' Has any of the gods of the nations rescued his land from the power of the king of Assyria? ¹⁹Where are the gods of Hamath and Arpad? Where are the gods of Sepharvaim? Where are the gods of Samaria? Have they saved Samaria from my power? ²⁰Who among all the gods of these lands ever rescued their land from my power, that the Lord should save Jerusalem from my power?" ²¹But they remained silent and did not answer at all, for the king's command was, "Do not answer him."

²²Then the master of the palace, Eliakim, son of Hilkiah, Shebna the scribe, and the chancellor Joah, son of Asaph, came to Hezekiah with their garments

---

He asserts that Egypt is an unreliable ally, that Hezekiah's centralization of worship in Jerusalem undermined any religious support he may have enjoyed, and that Jerusalem's fighting forces have been seriously depleted. Finally, the Assyrian asserts that he is following the command of Jerusalem's own God by attacking the city.

The Judahite negotiators are afraid that the Rabshakeh's confident assertions will undermine the morale of Jerusalem's defenders so they ask the Assyrian to speak Aramaic rather than Hebrew, in order to keep the nego-

torn, and reported to him the words of the commander.

37 ¹When King Hezekiah heard this, he tore his garments, covered himself with sackcloth, and went into the house of the LORD. ²He sent Eliakim, the master of the palace, and Shebna the scribe, and the elders of the priests, covered with sackcloth, to tell the prophet Isaiah, son of Amoz,

³"Thus says Hezekiah:
A day of distress and rebuke,
    a day of disgrace is this day!
Children are due to come forth,
    but the strength to give birth is
        lacking.

⁴Perhaps the LORD, your God, will hear the words of the commander, whom his lord, the king of Assyria, sent to taunt the living God, and will rebuke him for the words which the LORD, your God, has heard. So lift up a prayer for the remnant that is here."

⁵When the servants of King Hezekiah had come to Isaiah, ⁶he said to them: "Tell this to your lord: Thus says the LORD: Do not be frightened by the words you have heard, by which the deputies of the king of Assyria have blasphemed me.

⁷I am putting in him such a spirit
    that when he hears a report
    he will return to his land.
I will make him fall by the
    sword in his land."

⁸When the commander, on his return, heard that the king of Assyria had withdrawn from Lachish, he found him

---

tiations secret from the people of Jerusalem. This, of course, the Assyrian negotiator refused to do. In fact, he spoke directly to the city's defenders, who had to face the shortages that are inevitable in any siege. The Assyrian demanded the surrender of the city, but he promised to provide an ample supply of food if the people gave up their resistance. He reminded the people of Jerusalem that the gods of many nations proved unable to save their peoples from the Assyrian onslaught, so the likelihood of the Lord saving Judah is remote. The Judahite negotiators were clearly shaken as they made their report to Hezekiah.

When the Judahite negotiators consult Isaiah, he says that Sennacherib will break off the siege, return to Assyria, and be killed there. The prophet asserts that Hezekiah has nothing to fear from the Assyrian threat. When the Rabshakeh returned to Lachish, he found out that Sennacherib had left that city because he heard of Egyptian plans to move against Assyria.

One detail that this account omits from that of 2 Kings 18 is Hezekiah's submission to Sennacherib and the subsequent payment of a heavy indemnity to the Assyrian king (see 2 Kgs 18:14-16). Such action clashes with the advice the prophet gives in verses 6-7. What the Isaianic account underscores is the hopelessness of Jerusalem's situation and Isaiah's confidence in the city's eventual deliverance.

besieging Libnah. ⁹The king of Assyria heard a report: "Tirhakah, king of Ethiopia, has come out to fight against you." Again he sent messengers to Hezekiah to say: ¹⁰"Thus shall you say to Hezekiah, king of Judah: Do not let your God in whom you trust deceive you by saying, 'Jerusalem will not be handed over to the king of Assyria.' ¹¹You, certainly, have heard what the kings of Assyria have done to all the lands: they put them under the ban! And are you to be delivered? ¹²Did the gods of the nations whom my fathers destroyed deliver them—Gozan, Haran, Rezeph, and the Edenites in Telassar? ¹³Where are the king of Hamath, the king of Arpad, or a king of the cities Sepharvaim, Hena or Ivvah?"

¹⁴Hezekiah took the letter from the hand of the messengers and read it; then he went up to the house of the LORD, and spreading it out before the LORD, ¹⁵Hezekiah prayed to the LORD:

¹⁶"LORD of hosts, God of Israel,
  enthroned on the cherubim!
You alone are God
  over all the kingdoms of the
    earth.
It is you who made
  the heavens and the earth.
¹⁷Incline your ear, LORD, and listen!
  open your eyes, LORD, and see!
Hear all the words Sennacherib has
    sent
  to taunt the living God.
¹⁸Truly, O LORD,
  the kings of Assyria have laid
    waste
  the nations and their lands.
¹⁹They gave their gods to the fire
  —they were not gods at all,
  but the work of human hands—
Wood and stone, they destroyed
    them.

37:9b-36 Jerusalem saved

In what appears to be a parallel account of the Assyrian siege of Jerusalem, Isaiah's role is much more prominent. After receiving a letter from Sennacherib calling for the surrender of Jerusalem, Hezekiah prays that the Lord will do what the gods of the nations could not: halt the Assyrian juggernaut. The prophet responds in poetic form that Sennacherib's plans will fail because the Assyrian king has insulted the Lord. God promises that, despite Sennacherib's earlier conquests, his attempt to take Jerusalem will fail. The prophet also asserts that before Jerusalem's deliverance, it will have to suffer because the normal cultivation of crops will not take place, inducing a famine that will be relieved only after two years. Also, only a remnant of Jerusalem's population will survive this disaster.

The prose accounts end with the prophet's prediction that Sennacherib would never even invade Jerusalem because God will protect it for the sake of David. But the Assyrians did besiege the city, though they did end it and return to Assyria. The narrative underscores the miraculous nature of Jerusalem's deliverance by asserting that an "angel of the Lord" annihilated the Assyrian army in its camp. What actually led to the end of the siege is not

20Therefore, LORD, our God,
  save us from this man's power,
That all the kingdoms of the earth
    may know
  that you alone, LORD, are God."

21Then Isaiah, son of Amoz, sent this message to Hezekiah: "Thus says the LORD, the God of Israel, to whom you have prayed concerning Sennacherib, king of Assyria: I have listened! 22This is the word the LORD has spoken concerning him:

She despises you, laughs you to
    scorn,
  the virgin daughter Zion;
Behind you she wags her head,
  daughter Jerusalem.
23Whom have you insulted and
    blasphemed,
  at whom have you raised your
      voice
And lifted up your eyes on high?
  At the Holy One of Israel!
24Through the mouths of your
    messengers
  you have insulted the Lord
    when you said:
'With my many chariots I went up

to the tops of the peaks,
  to the recesses of Lebanon,
To cut down its lofty cedars,
  its choice cypresses;
I reached the farthest shelter,
  the forest ranges.
25I myself dug wells
  and drank foreign water;
Drying up all the rivers of Egypt
  beneath the soles of my feet.'
26Have you not heard?
  A long time ago I prepared it,
  from days of old I planned it,
Now I have brought it about:
  You are here to reduce
  fortified cities to heaps of ruins,
27Their people powerless,
  dismayed and distraught,
They are plants of the field,
  green growth,
  thatch on the rooftops,
Grain scorched by the east wind.
28I know when you stand or sit,
  when you come or go,
  and how you rage against me.
29Because you rage against me
  and your smugness has reached
    my ears,
I will put my hook in your nose
  and my bit in your mouth,

---

known for certain. Most likely Hezekiah paid a heavy price for protection (2 Kgs 18:15-16) and agreed to vassal status. This allowed Sennacherib to break off the siege and return to Assyria so that he could deal with internal unrest, which eventually ended with his assassination.

Over time, the precise circumstances of Jerusalem's deliverance were forgotten. Of course, the city's narrow escape came to support a belief that Jerusalem would never fall because of divine protection. One of Isaiah's contemporaries, Micah, however, announced the city's eventual fall (Mic 3:9-12). Still, most people began to consider it a matter of divine honor for the Lord to keep Jerusalem from all harm. About one hundred years later, Jeremiah was nearly executed for daring to suggest that God would allow Jerusalem to fall (see Jer 26:1-19).

And make you leave by the way
    you came.
³⁰This shall be a sign for you:
This year you shall eat the
    aftergrowth,
    next year, what grows of itself;
But in the third year, sow and reap,
    plant vineyards and eat their
      fruit!
³¹The remaining survivors of the
    house of Judah
    shall again strike root below
    and bear fruit above.
³²For out of Jerusalem shall come a
    remnant,
    and from Mount Zion, survivors.
The zeal of the Lord of hosts shall
    do this.

³³Therefore, thus says the Lord
    about the king of Assyria:
He shall not come as far as this city,
    nor shoot there an arrow,
    nor confront it with a shield,
Nor cast up a siege-work against it.
³⁴By the way he came he shall leave,
    never coming as far as this city,
    oracle of the Lord.
³⁵I will shield and save this city
    for my own sake and the sake of
      David my servant."

³⁶Then the angel of the Lord went forth and struck down one hundred and eighty-five thousand in the Assyrian camp. Early the next morning, there they were, all those corpses, dead! ³⁷So Sennacherib, the king of Assyria, broke camp, departed, returned home, and stayed in Nineveh.

³⁸When he was worshiping in the temple of his god Nisroch, his sons Adrammelech and Sharezer struck him down with the sword and fled into the land of Ararat. His son Esarhaddon reigned in his place.

38 **Sickness and Recovery of Hezekiah.** ▶ ¹In those days, when Hezekiah was mortally ill, the prophet Isaiah, son of Amoz, came and said to him: "Thus says the Lord: Put your house in order, for you are about to die; you shall not recover." ²Hezekiah turned his face to the wall and prayed to the Lord:

³"Ah, Lord, remember how faithfully and wholeheartedly I conducted myself in your presence, doing what was good in your sight!" And Hezekiah wept bitterly.

⁴Then the word of the Lord came to Isaiah: ⁵Go, tell Hezekiah: Thus says the Lord, the God of your father David: I have heard your prayer; I have seen your tears. Now I will add fifteen years to your life. ⁶I will rescue you and this city from the hand of the king of Assyria; I will be a shield to this city.

⁷This will be the sign for you from the Lord that the Lord will carry out the word he has spoken: ⁸See, I will make the shadow cast by the sun on the stairway

---

38:1-8 Hezekiah's illness

The experience of Judah is duplicated in the experience of its king. Hezekiah faces certain death but then is spared to live for fifteen more years. The imagery of verse 38 that recounts the reversal of the sun's movement suggests that deliverance will follow upon the crisis facing both Hezekiah and Jerusalem. Of course, this deliverance is only temporary. Hezekiah will die and Jerusalem will fall.

to the terrace of Ahaz go back the ten steps it has advanced. So the sun came back the ten steps it had advanced.

Hezekiah's Hymn of Thanksgiving.
⁹The song of Hezekiah, king of Judah, after he had been sick and had recovered from his illness:

¹⁰In the noontime of life I said,
  I must depart!
To the gates of Sheol I have been
  consigned
  for the rest of my years.
¹¹I said, I shall see the LORD no more
  in the land of the living.
Nor look on any mortals
  among those who dwell in the
    world.
¹²My dwelling, like a shepherd's
  tent,
  is struck down and borne away
    from me;
You have folded up my life, like a
  weaver
  who severs me from the last
    thread.
From morning to night you make
  an end of me;
¹³I cry out even until the dawn.
Like a lion he breaks all my bones;
  from morning to night you
    make an end of me.

¹⁴Like a swallow I chirp;
  I moan like a dove.
My eyes grow weary looking
  heavenward:
Lord, I am overwhelmed; go
  security for me!
¹⁵What am I to say or tell him?
  He is the one who has done it!
All my sleep has fled,
  because of the bitterness of my
    soul.
¹⁶Those live whom the LORD
  protects;
  yours is the life of my spirit.
You have given me health and
  restored my life!
¹⁷Peace in place of bitterness!
You have preserved my life
  from the pit of destruction;
Behind your back
  you cast all my sins.
¹⁸For it is not Sheol that gives you
  thanks,
  nor death that praises you;
Neither do those who go down into
  the pit
  await your kindness.
¹⁹The living, the living give you
  thanks,
  as I do today.
Parents declare to their children,
  O God, your faithfulness.
²⁰The LORD is there to save us.

38:9-20 Hezekiah's prayer of thanksgiving

Hezekiah offers a prayer that follows the pattern of other biblical prayers that thank God for deliverance in time of personal peril, e.g., Psalms 6, 13, 22. The prayer begins with words expressing resignation. Death is coming. Though Hezekiah cries for help, he expects his end to be imminent. Still, he cries for help. He wants to live. The king realizes that his illness was a message from God that was not designed to punish but to save him. He thanks God for being rescued from sin and death. The king dedicates his life to the praise of God who saved him from death. If only Jerusalem would have responded to its deliverance in a similar fashion.

We shall play our music
In the house of the LORD
   all the days of our life.

²¹Then Isaiah said, "Bring a poultice of figs and apply it to the boil for his recovery." ²²Hezekiah asked, "What is the sign that I shall go up to the house of the LORD?"

39 **Embassy from Merodach-baladan.** ¹At that time Merodach-baladan, son of Baladan, king of Babylon, sent letters and gifts to Hezekiah, when he heard that he had been sick and had recovered. ²Hezekiah was pleased at their coming, and then showed the messengers his treasury, the silver and gold, the spices and perfumed oil, his whole armory, and everything in his storerooms; there was nothing in his house or in all his realm that Hezekiah did not show them.

³Then Isaiah the prophet came to King Hezekiah and asked him, "What did these men say to you? Where did they come from?" Hezekiah replied, "They came to me from a distant land, from Babylon." ⁴He asked, "What did they see in your house?" Hezekiah answered, "They saw everything in my house. There is nothing in my storerooms that I did not show them." ⁵Then Isaiah said to Hezekiah, "Hear the word of the LORD of hosts: ⁶The time is coming when all that is in your house, everything that your ancestors have stored up until this day, shall be carried off to Babylon; nothing shall be left, says the LORD. ⁷Some of your own descendants, your progeny, shall be taken and made attendants in the palace of the king of Babylon." ⁸Hezekiah replied to Isaiah,

---

39:1-4 The embassy from Babylon

The Babylonians wanted to topple the Assyrians from the position of dominance, so they sent an ambassador to enlist Hezekiah's cooperation in an anti-Assyrian coalition. But Judah had few resources to offer to the enterprise. Hezekiah shows his treasury to the Babylonian ambassador to make it clear how much the Assyrians required in tribute. Isaiah comes to the king to make certain he did not join the coalition, but Hezekiah assured him that all he did was show the Babylonians how little he had to offer.

39:5-8 The exile to Babylon

Of course, the prophet wants to make it clear that Judah's future does not lie with Babylon—no matter how attractive an alliance with it may appear to be. He warns the king that the Babylonians were going to strip the royal family of the little wealth it has remaining and, after doing so, lead the royals into exile where they would be servants of Babylon's kings. The king agrees with the prophet's assessment of the future but is confident that his reign will end before disaster comes upon Judah.

The book of Isaiah does not describe Jerusalem's fall to the Babylonians, though the next section (chapters 40–55) envisions Judah's restoration following the Babylonian conquest of Jerusalem, the destruction of its temple,

"The word of the LORD which you have spoken is good." For he thought, "There will be peace and stability in my lifetime."

II. Isaiah 40–55

A. The Lord's Glory in Israel's Liberation

40 **Promise of Salvation.** ¹Comfort, give comfort to my people, says your God.

²Speak to the heart of Jerusalem,
    and proclaim to her
that her service has ended,
that her guilt is expiated,
That she has received from the
    hand of the LORD
double for all her sins.

³A voice proclaims:
In the wilderness prepare the way
    of the LORD!
Make straight in the wasteland a
    highway for our God!

and the exile of its leading citizens. The prophet's words to Hezekiah about the eventual fall of the city are needed to effect the transition to the next section of the book.

JERUSALEM'S LIBERATION

Isaiah 40:1–55:13

Here begins a thoroughly new message for Jerusalem. Unlike earlier prophets, the author of these words did not ask the people to recognize their failure and confess their infidelity. Before the exile, the prophets had to overcome the people's self-delusion fueled by the existence of the national state, the economic prosperity enjoyed by the powerful, and the active national cult in Jerusalem. The fall of that city made continued denials impossible. Judah's religious, political, and social institutions were no more. The Davidic dynasty was no more, the temple was in ruins and its priesthood scattered, the national state ceased to exist, and Judah's powerful and influential citizens were in exile. Cheap promises and vain expectations were no longer persuasive.

Chapter 40 begins a unique response to the disasters that came upon Jerusalem and its people. Unlike the book of Lamentations, the book of Isaiah does not give voice to the grief of the exiles. Unlike the Deuteronomistic History, this book is explicit about its hope for a new and glorious future for Jerusalem. Of course, the prophet believed that the fall of Jerusalem was an act of divine judgment on the unfaithful city, but he also was certain that the city's glorious and miraculous restoration was imminent. The prophet saw a dramatic upheaval stirring on the political horizon. A new vigorous and powerful ruler was about to bring an end to the vaunted Babylonian

⁴Every valley shall be lifted up,
   every mountain and hill made
      low;
The rugged land shall be a plain,
   the rough country, a broad
      valley.
⁵Then the glory of the LORD shall be
   revealed,
   and all flesh shall see it together;
   for the mouth of the LORD has
      spoken.

⁶A voice says, "Proclaim!"
   I answer, "What shall I
      proclaim?"
"All flesh is grass,
   and all their loyalty like the
      flower of the field.
⁷The grass withers, the flower wilts,
   when the breath of the LORD
      blows upon it."
"Yes, the people is grass!
⁸The grass withers, the flower
   wilts,
   but the word of our God stands
      forever."

⁹Go up onto a high mountain,
   Zion, herald of good news!
Cry out at the top of your voice,
   Jerusalem, herald of good news!
Cry out, do not fear!

Empire. He believed that this was happening for one purpose: God was about to restore Jerusalem.

The prophet uses two metaphors to speak about his beliefs concerning Jerusalem's future: one masculine and the other feminine. The masculine servant metaphor (42:1-4; 49:1-6; 50:4-11; and 52:13–53:12) is the more familiar because of the use the New Testament makes of these passages to express faith in Jesus Christ. Like a king, the servant establishes justice (42:4). He is a "sharp-edged sword" and a "sharpened arrow" (49:2) whose suffering will benefit many (53:4-5) and who will be vindicated and then will divide out the spoils of war (53:12). The female figure of Jerusalem/Zion is the second linchpin of the prophet's hopes for the future. Beginning in chapter 49 and extending to chapter 66, the reader hears the story of a woman's life from her abandonment by her husband and consequent childlessness to their reconciliation and the birth of many children. The two images parallel one another. For example, in chapter 49 both express doubts about God's presence and power in their lives: the servant in verse 4 and Zion in verse 14. Both the servant and Zion are humiliated and afflicted. Eventually both will experience vindication through their children: the servant in 53:10 and Zion in 66:7-9. The prophet does not tell the story of the servant or of Zion as a continuous narrative but will keep returning to these metaphors in the course of his prophecy.

40:1-11 Jerusalem the herald

The prophet stands as a mute witness as the members of the Divine Council are about to implement God's decision to begin the process of Jerusalem's rehabilitation. The prophet hears a series of commands in

Say to the cities of Judah:
Here is your God!
¹⁰Here comes with power
the Lord GOD,
who rules by his strong arm;
Here is his reward with him,
his recompense before him.
¹¹Like a shepherd he feeds his flock;
in his arms he gathers the
lambs,
Carrying them in his bosom,
leading the ewes with care.

Power of God and the Vanity of Idols.
¹²Who has measured with his palm
the waters,
marked off the heavens with a
span,
held in his fingers the dust of
the earth,
weighed the mountains in scales
and the hills in a balance?
¹³Who has directed the spirit of the
LORD,
or instructed him as his
counselor?
¹⁴Whom did he consult to gain
knowledge?
Who taught him the path of
judgment,
or showed him the way of
understanding?

---

the second person plural: "comfort . . . Speak to the heart of . . . proclaim. . . ." He wishes his readers to envision one member of the Divine Council ordering others to take the actions that will mean a new day for Jerusalem. This new day will begin with the news that the city's suffering is about to end. In fact, the order implies that Jerusalem's punishment has been more than its infidelity deserved. Next, the prophet hears one member of the council commanding that another begin preparing the way for God's grand triumphal procession that will bring about the exiles' return and Jerusalem's restoration. The death-dealing nature of the desert must teem with life. The high mountains and deep valleys that would hinder the return of the exiles to Jerusalem must become a level highway.

Jerusalem was not to remain a passive recipient of the good news. The city itself was to become a prophet announcing liberation to the other cities of Judah, which shared its fate during the Babylonian crisis. They too lost many people to exile. Zion is to proclaim the great reversal that God is about to accomplish. God is returning to Judah at the head of a great throng of exiles, who were coming home where they could live in freedom as God promised their ancestors. In fulfilling its prophetic mission, Jerusalem uses two metaphors to remove the doubts of those who believed that God had no concern for Judah. In verse 10, the city-turned-prophet presents God as a victorious general who is returning home with the exiles—the prize won by defeating the Babylonians. The image in verse 11 is the perfect counterpoint, for it depicts God as a gentle shepherd who takes care of newborn lambs, leading them back to their mothers. Just so God will lead back the exiles of Judah to their mothers—the cities of their homeland. The juxtaposition of

¹⁵See, the nations count as a drop in the bucket,
as a wisp of cloud on the scales;
the coastlands weigh no more than a speck.
¹⁶Lebanon would not suffice for fuel,
nor its animals be enough for burnt offerings.
¹⁷Before him all the nations are as nought,
as nothing and void he counts them.

¹⁸To whom can you liken God?

With what likeness can you confront him?
¹⁹An idol? An artisan casts it,
the smith plates it with gold,
fits it with silver chains.
²⁰Is mulberry wood the offering?
A skilled artisan picks out a wood that will not rot,
Seeks to set up for himself an idol that will not totter.

²¹Do you not know? Have you not heard?
Was it not told you from the beginning?

---

these two metaphors affirms that God has the power to change the course of history but is still concerned about the exiles as individuals. The exiles needed to hear what both metaphors implied, since their primary experience of God had been the experience of God's absence. This led them to draw all the wrong conclusions about their future. Jerusalem proclaims that God has the power to end the exile and the love to begin the restoration.

Chapter 40:1-11 sums up the prophet's message in just eleven verses. This text makes the astonishing announcement that God has forgiven Jerusalem and its people. It is Jerusalem's task to proclaim this message to all the cities of Judah. The remainder of chapters 40–55 is simply an elaboration of that message.

Each of the evangelists cites 40:3, applying it to John the Baptist (Matt 3:3; Mark 1:2; Luke 3:4; John 1:23). Of course, this involves a reinterpretation of the prophet's words. No longer do they refer simply to the restoration of Jerusalem but to the redemption of all Israel and all nations. The evangelists wish to portray the Baptist as the herald of this new and universal act of salvation. James alludes to verses 6-7 to speak of the transitory nature of wealth (Jas 1:10) and Peter quotes these verses to underscore the eternal character of God's word (1 Pet 1:24-25).

40:12-31 The Lord, the Creator

To arouse the exiles to believe in a future for Jerusalem, the prophet begins with correcting and expanding their notion of deity. The Lord was not simply a God from the desert who chose to make a nation out of the Hebrew slaves. The Lord is not simply the patron of the two former Israelite kingdoms. By asking a series of rhetorical questions in verses 12-14, the prophet leads the

Have you not understood from
the founding of the earth?
²²The one who is enthroned above
the vault of the earth,
its inhabitants like grasshoppers,
Who stretches out the heavens like
a veil
and spreads them out like a tent
to dwell in,
²³Who brings princes to nought
and makes the rulers of the
earth as nothing.
²⁴Scarcely are they planted, scarcely
sown,
scarcely their stem rooted in the
earth,
When he breathes upon them and
they wither,
and the stormwind carries them
away like straw.

²⁵To whom can you liken me as an
equal?
says the Holy One.
²⁶Lift up your eyes on high
and see who created these:
He leads out their army and
numbers them,
calling them all by name.
By his great might and the strength
of his power
not one of them is missing!
²⁷Why, O Jacob, do you say,
and declare, O Israel,
"My way is hidden from the LORD,
and my right is disregarded by
my God"?
²⁸Do you not know?
Have you not heard?
The LORD is God from of old,
creator of the ends of the earth.

---

exiles to the conclusion that the Lord is the Creator of the universe. As such, Jerusalem's God controls the destinies of all nations. Of course, the Lord has the power to end the exile and return the people of Jerusalem to their home.

By way of contrast, the gods of the nations are nothing. A second series of rhetorical questions in verses 18-20 parodies the religious beliefs of the nations. The prophet compares the God of Israel, the Creator of the universe, with the gods of the nations who were manufactured by wood and metal workers. Of course, the people of the ancient Near East had a more nuanced view of the relationship between a god and its image than the prophet implies. Still, the prophet's purpose is not to discuss the merits of religions that use images. His purpose is to stimulate his people to believe in their future, a future made possible by the Creator of the universe, who controls the fate of all nations.

The prophet undercuts belief in astral deities by having Israel's God claim credit for the creation of the stars. It is the Lord who maintains the order of the heavens, and every heavenly body is subject to the God who is about to redeem Jerusalem. The profound and distressing experience of God's absence that led the exiles to question the power of the Lord and the relevance of their faith will dissipate in the face of the stirring events that will shortly and dramatically demonstrate the presence and power of the Lord: the fall of Babylon and the restoration of Jerusalem. These events will

He does not faint or grow weary,
and his knowledge is beyond
scrutiny.
²⁹He gives power to the faint,
abundant strength to the weak.
³⁰Though young men faint and
grow weary,
and youths stagger and fall,
³¹They that hope in the LORD will
renew their strength,
they will soar on eagles' wings;
They will run and not grow weary,
walk and not grow faint.

41 **The Liberator of Israel.** ¹Keep
silence before me, O coastlands;
let the nations renew their
strength.
Let them draw near and speak;
let us come together for
judgment.

²Who has stirred up from the East
the champion of justice,
and summoned him to be his
attendant?
To him he delivers nations
and subdues kings;
With his sword he reduces them to
dust,
with his bow, to driven straw.
³He pursues them, passing on
without loss,
by a path his feet scarcely touch.
⁴Who has performed these deeds?
Who has called forth the
generations from the
beginning?
I, the LORD, am the first,
and at the last I am he.
⁵The coastlands see, and fear;
the ends of the earth tremble:

---

quicken the spirits of the exiles and prevent Judah from disappearing into the pages of history. The people of God will find new strength as they await their return to the land that God promised to their ancestors.

Paul quotes verse 13 in his hymn to God's mercy and wisdom in Romans 11:34-35. He also cites this text again in 1 Corinthians 2:16 to celebrate the revelation of God's will through Jesus Christ.

41:1–42:9 The nations on trial

A typical prophetic strategy to underscore the sovereignty of God is to describe a trial in which God serves as prosecutor and judge. Here the prophet describes two such scenes in which the nations are on trial. The prophet wants to present the restoration of Judah to its land against a wider backdrop. He calls the nations to hear his message for they too will feel the effects of God's new movement, whose ultimate goal is the redemption of God's people.

The evidence of God's control of events that will lead to Jerusalem's liberation is the rise of the person whom the prophet characterizes as "the champion of justice." He comes not from Judah but from the East (41:2). Cyrus the Persian was on the march, winning victories over the Medes and the Greeks. The prophet was certain that Babylon was about to fall to him as well. This string of victories must mean something. The prophet sees them as a sign of God's movement to save Judah and restore it to its

they approach, they come on.

⁶Each one helps his neighbor,
    one says to the other,
        "Courage!"
⁷The woodworker encourages the
    goldsmith,
    the one who beats with the
        hammer, him who strikes
            on the anvil,
Saying of the soldering, "It is good!"
    then fastening it with nails so it
        will not totter.

⁸But you, Israel, my servant,
    Jacob, whom I have chosen,
        offspring of Abraham my
            friend—
⁹You whom I have taken from the
    ends of the earth
    and summoned from its far-off
        places,
To whom I have said, You are my
    servant;
    I chose you, I have not rejected
        you—
¹⁰Do not fear: I am with you;
    do not be anxious: I am your
        God.
I will strengthen you, I will help
    you,

land. It is Judah's God who is transforming the political map of the ancient Near East—all for the sake of Jerusalem. This is certainly evidence of the power of the Lord.

The imminent fall of Babylon is not the end of the first trial scene. The scene ends with a dramatic reassurance for the exiles. The prophet speaks to the exiles in God's name. They have nothing to fear from the military and political upheavals that they are witnessing. On the contrary, all is happening for their sake. God has chosen Israel and has not revoked that choice. The prophet calls the exiles the "offspring of Abraham" because he wishes to underscore the continuing significance of Israel's ancestral religious traditions (41:8). With God's help, Judah will be victorious over all those forces that threaten its existence.

Judah's political impotence will have no bearing on its future. God will be with Judah to insure that it will emerge victorious. It is important to note that the book's favorite term for God, "the Holy One of Israel," is used here with the word "redeemer" (41:14). This will happen several other times in this fourth section of Isaiah (see also 43:14; 47:3-4; 48:17). The book of Isaiah refers to God as "redeemer" more than any other book of the Old Testament. Israel's redeemer will transform it into a power that will overcome those that will try to prevent its restoration. It will emerge with unprecedented power over its enemies. Judah will be able to crush them like a new threshing sledge cuts through the newly harvested shafts of wheat.

God's movement on behalf of the oppressed of Judah will be a miraculous manifestation of God's power. It will be akin to the transformation of the desert into a well-watered garden graced with every beautiful tree and shrub. No one who will witness Judah's restoration will fail to understand

I will uphold you with my
    victorious right hand.

[11]Yes, all shall be put to shame and
    disgrace
    who vent their anger against you;
Those shall be as nothing and
    perish
    who offer resistance.
[12]You shall seek but not find
    those who strive against you;
They shall be as nothing at all
    who do battle with you.

[13]For I am the LORD, your God,
    who grasp your right hand;
It is I who say to you, Do not fear,
    I will help you.
[14]Do not fear, you worm Jacob,
    you maggot Israel;

I will help you—oracle of the LORD;
    the Holy One of Israel is your
      redeemer.
[15]I will make of you a threshing
    sledge,
    sharp, new, full of teeth,
To thresh the mountains and crush
    them,
    to make the hills like chaff.
[16]When you winnow them, the
    wind shall carry them off,
    the storm shall scatter them.
But you shall rejoice in the LORD;
    in the Holy One of Israel you
      shall glory.

[17]The afflicted and the needy seek
    water in vain,
    their tongues are parched with
      thirst.

---

who accomplished this miracle—the Holy One of Israel. The results of the trial of the nations will be the restoration of Jerusalem and the universal recognition of its God.

There is a summons to a second trial in 41:21. The prophet begins offering evidence in the next verse. That evidence consists of the rise of Cyrus, the fall of Babylon, and the restoration of Jerusalem. People had recourse to their gods to divine the future. The prophet ridicules the supposed ability of the gods to inform their worshipers about the future. Who would have predicted that Judah would be restored to its land? But that is precisely what is about to take place. The events that are to occur in a short time will shame the so-called gods of the nations. None of their diviners could have foreseen what God has in store for Jerusalem. Events are unfolding. Cyrus is coming to bring an end to Judah's exile. Jerusalem will no longer be a forlorn, abandoned city. It is to be the herald announcing freedom to the exiles. Clearly, the gods of the nations are nothing.

The trial ends with a reaffirmation of the election of Israel as God's people. God's choice of Israel is a fundamental datum of its faith. But this belief was called into question by the fall of the two Israelite kingdoms. The prophet's message implies that Israel's election is not tied to the political status of the two former kingdoms. Judah in exile is still God's servant. It has a destiny to fulfill that cannot be frustrated by political turmoil and military defeat. God will restore Judah to its land so that it can become a model of justice for

I, the LORD, will answer them;
    I, the God of Israel, will not
        forsake them.
¹⁸I will open up rivers on the bare
        heights,
    and fountains in the broad
        valleys;
I will turn the wilderness into a
        marshland,
    and the dry ground into springs
        of water.
¹⁹In the wilderness I will plant the
        cedar,
    acacia, myrtle, and olive;
In the wasteland I will set the
        cypress,
    together with the plane tree and
        the pine,
²⁰That all may see and know,
    observe and understand,
That the hand of the LORD has done
        this,

the Holy One of Israel has
        created it.

²¹Present your case, says the LORD;
    bring forward your arguments,
        says the King of Jacob.
²²Let them draw near and foretell to
        us
    what it is that shall happen!
What are the things of long ago?
    Tell us, that we may reflect on
        them
    and know their outcome;
Or declare to us the things to come,
    ²³tell what is to be in the future,
    that we may know that you are
        gods!
Do something, good or evil,
    that will put us in awe and in fear.
²⁴Why, you are nothing
    and your work is nought;
    to choose you is an abomination!

---

the nations. The Israelite kingdoms fell precisely because of the failure of the monarchy to maintain a just social and economic system. Judah's mission to establish justice is repeated three times (42:1, 4, 6).

Note that the prophet does not imply that the monarchy will be restored. The establishment and maintenance of a just society were the principal responsibilities of Israel's kings. The book of Isaiah very clearly notes the failure of the monarchy to do this. In fact, Israel's political leadership actually facilitated the oppression of the poor (e.g., 1:21-23; 3:1-12; 28:14-22; 29:14-15). Here the responsibilities of the monarchy fall upon the people as a whole. It will be the responsibility of all the people of Judah to insure "the victory of justice." The trial of the nations ends with an affirmation of God's uniqueness. Only the Lord has announced the liberation of Jerusalem's exiles—something everyone, including those exiles, thought impossible. This shows that the Lord alone is God.

Chapter 42:1-4 is the first of four passages from the book of Isaiah that have become known as the "Servant Songs" (see also 49:1-6; 50:4-11; and 52:13–53:12). While there is some value in isolating these passages, here they will be treated simply as elements in the broader and unified message about Jerusalem's liberation that comprises the fourth section of the book of Isaiah. There has been some controversy about the propriety of

²⁵I have stirred up one from the
north, and he comes;
from the east I summon him by
name;
He shall trample the rulers down
like mud,
like a potter treading clay.
²⁶Who announced this from the
beginning, that we might
know;
beforehand, that we might say,
"True"?
Not one of you foretold it, not one
spoke;
not one heard you say,
²⁷"The first news for Zion: here they
come,"
or, "I will give Jerusalem a
herald of good news."
²⁸When I look, there is not one,
not one of them to give counsel,
to make an answer when I
question them.
²⁹Ah, all of them are nothing,
their works are nought,
their idols, empty wind!

42 **The Servant of the Lord.** ¹Here is
my servant whom I uphold,
my chosen one with whom I am
pleased.
Upon him I have put my spirit;
he shall bring forth justice to the
nations.
²He will not cry out, nor shout,
nor make his voice heard in the
street.
³A bruised reed he will not break,
and a dimly burning wick he
will not quench.
He will faithfully bring forth
justice.

---

isolating these texts from their literary and theological context, and there
are several possibilities about the identity of the "servant." Understood in
the light of the total argument made in this fourth section, it is most likely
that the servant is Judah fulfilling its destiny to be the light to the nations,
bringing about the victory of justice. Of course, this is an idealized picture
of the potential of the restored community, but the whole of this fourth
section of Isaiah is a powerfully constructed and expressed argument by
the prophet, who is trying to persuade a thoroughly demoralized people
that their God is about to do something wondrous for them and that they
have a decisive role in their own restoration.

Matthew has John the Baptist allude to 41:16 to persuade people that
God is about to do something decisive through Jesus (Matt 3:12). The evangelist also cites 42:1-4 to show that Jesus' healing ministry fulfilled the
words of the prophet and, therefore, show Jesus to be the "servant" about
whom the prophet was speaking (Matt 12:15-21). Simeon's canticle in Luke
2:29-32 is a combination of texts taken from the fourth section of the book
of Isaiah: 42:6; 46:13; 49:6; 52:10.

42:10-17 The Lord, the Victor

The prophet sings a hymn of praise to the Lord who is about to liberate the exiles of Jerusalem. This, in turn, will lead all nations to acclaim

⁴He will not grow dim or be bruised
  until he establishes justice on
    the earth;
  the coastlands will wait for his
    teaching.

⁵Thus says God, the LORD,
  who created the heavens and
    stretched them out,
  who spread out the earth and its
    produce,
Who gives breath to its people
  and spirit to those who walk on
    it:

⁶I, the LORD, have called you for
    justice,
  I have grasped you by the hand;
I formed you, and set you
  as a covenant for the people,
  a light for the nations,
⁷To open the eyes of the blind,
  to bring out prisoners from
    confinement,
  and from the dungeon, those
    who live in darkness.
⁸I am the LORD, LORD is my name;
  my glory I give to no other,
  nor my praise to idols.

---

the Lord as God. The hymn is reminiscent of several similar compositions found in the Psalter (Pss 93, 96, 149). The hymn begins with a call to praise that includes all regions of earth and sea—even remote and isolated places like Kedar and Sela. The call goes out to join in praising the Lord because Israel's God has finally chosen to emerge from self-imposed inactivity. God will now deal with God's enemies. Those who serve other gods will recognize their folly.

Two features of this hymn call for comment because both cause problems for some modern readers of Isaiah. The first is the hymn's military imagery. The people who first heard or read this book felt much more at ease with this imagery than do people today. After all, the origins of Israel were associated with battles that God fought and won: the victory over the Egyptian army at the Red Sea, the victories over the Canaanites during the time of Joshua and the judges, and the victories over the Philistines during the time of David. Judah was in exile because apparently God stopped taking its side against its enemies. This metaphor affirms that God's purposes are fulfilled—even in the wars that people fight over land and resources. It is important to remember that the Lord, the warrior, was not the only way that ancient Israel spoke of its God. The Lord was also the shepherd, who gathers the lambs, carries them gently, and feeds them abundantly (see Isa 40:11). While the New Testament speaks about Jesus as the "good shepherd" (John 10), it also remembers that Jesus said that he came to bring fire on the earth and could not wait until the blaze begins (see Luke 12:49).

A second metaphor in this passage compares the Lord to "a woman in labor" (42:14). Though most of the images that the Bible uses for God are masculine, the book of Isaiah does make use of feminine imagery to speak

⁹See, the earlier things have come to
pass,
new ones I now declare;
Before they spring forth
I announce them to you.

The Lord's Purpose for Israel. ¹⁰Sing
to the LORD a new song,
his praise from the ends of the
earth:
Let the sea and what fills it
resound,
the coastlands, and those who
dwell in them.
¹¹Let the wilderness and its cities
cry out,
the villages where Kedar dwells;
Let the inhabitants of Sela exult,
and shout from the top of the
mountains.
¹²Let them give glory to the LORD,
and utter his praise in the
coastlands.

¹³The LORD goes forth like a
warrior,
like a man of war he stirs up his
fury;
He shouts out his battle cry,
against his enemies he shows
his might:

¹⁴For a long time I have kept silent,
I have said nothing, holding
myself back;
Now I cry out like a woman in
labor,
gasping and panting.
¹⁵I will lay waste mountains and
hills,
all their undergrowth I will dry
up;
I will turn the rivers into marshes,
and the marshes I will dry up.
¹⁶I will lead the blind on a way they
do not know;
by paths they do not know I will
guide them.
I will turn darkness into light
before them,
and make crooked ways
straight.
These are my promises:
I made them, I will not forsake
them.

¹⁷They shall be turned back in utter
shame
who trust in idols;
Who say to molten images,
"You are our gods."
¹⁸You deaf ones, listen,
you blind ones, look and see!

---

of the God of Israel (see also 49:15). The prophet did not hesitate to use feminine metaphors to speak of the God of Israel despite the patriarchal bent of his culture.

42:18–43:8 Judah's disabilities

The prophet recognizes to whom he is speaking. His audience is made up of people in shock, people still coping with the loss of the political, social, economic, and religious institutions that gave them identity and purpose. What is worse is that these people fail to recognize that they are responsible for this loss. The prophet calls the people of Judah blind and deaf. These handicaps prevent them from recognizing their true standing before God. They are unable to recognize God's hand in their plight. They fail to see that the loss of their state, national dynasty, temple, and land was

[19]Who is blind but my servant,
or deaf like the messenger I send?
Who is blind like the one I restore,
blind like the servant of the
LORD?
[20]You see many things but do not
observe;
ears open, but do not hear.
[21]It was the LORD's will for the sake
of his justice
to make his teaching great and
glorious.

[22]This is a people plundered and
despoiled,
all of them trapped in holes,
hidden away in prisons.
They are taken as plunder, with no
one to rescue them,
as spoil, with no one to say,
"Give back!"

[23]Who among you will give ear to
this,
listen and pay attention from
now on?
[24]Who was it that gave Jacob to
be despoiled,
Israel to the plunderers?
Was it not the LORD, against whom
we have sinned?
In his ways they refused to
walk,
his teaching they would not
heed.
[25]So he poured out wrath upon
them,
his anger, and the fury of battle;
It blazed all around them, yet they
did not realize,
it burned them, but they did not
take it to heart.

---

due to their refusal to "walk in God's ways," i.e., maintain a society built on justice. They fail to hear the message of the prophets who announced God's judgment on their society and its values.

Still, the prophet believes that Judah's future is not dependent upon its ability to overcome its blindness and deafness. God will save Judah from its own sin. The prophet affirms that God will allow Cyrus to take Egypt and Ethiopia as the price for Judah's freedom. Here the prophet's word reflects the scandal of election: God favors one people over all others. The only explanation that the prophet gives is that God loves the people of Israel and will do anything to save Israel from itself. God assures Judah that the exiles will gather from wherever they have been scattered, even though they still suffer from handicaps.The prophet affirms that God is willing to allow the conquest of nations like Egypt and Ethiopia in exchange for Jerusalem's liberation. How does this relate to the prophet's contention that God's chosen servant is to be a "light to the nations"? The significance of the prophet's concept of Israel's election is one of the principal problems in interpreting this book. Even the New Testament's more consistent inclusiveness does not solve the problem. There God does not give up Egypt, Ethiopia, or any nation for Israel's salvation. But God does not spare Jesus so that all people might be saved. Why was it necessary for Jesus to die in order for the New Israel to be saved from the power of sin? Here we see this important issue in Christian theology presaged in the book of Isaiah.

43 **Promises of Redemption and Restoration.** ¹But now, thus says the LORD,
who created you, Jacob, and
formed you, Israel:
Do not fear, for I have redeemed
you;
I have called you by name: you
are mine.
²When you pass through waters, I
will be with you;
through rivers, you shall not be
swept away.
When you walk through fire, you
shall not be burned,
nor will flames consume you.
³For I, the LORD, am your God,
the Holy One of Israel, your
savior.
I give Egypt as ransom for you,
Ethiopia and Seba in exchange
for you.
⁴Because you are precious in my eyes
and honored, and I love you,
I give people in return for you
and nations in exchange for
your life.
⁵Fear not, for I am with you;
from the east I will bring back
your offspring,
from the west I will gather you.
⁶I will say to the north: Give them
up!
and to the south: Do not hold
them!
Bring back my sons from afar,

and my daughters from the
ends of the earth:
⁷All who are called by my name
I created for my glory;
I formed them, made them.

⁸Lead out the people, blind though
they have eyes,
deaf though they have ears.

⁹Let all the nations gather together,
let the peoples assemble!
Who among them could have
declared this,
or announced to us the earlier
things?
Let them produce witnesses to
prove themselves right,
that one may hear and say, "It is
true!"
¹⁰You are my witnesses—oracle of
the LORD—
my servant whom I have chosen
To know and believe in me
and understand that I am he.
Before me no god was formed,
and after me there shall be none.
¹¹I, I am the LORD;
there is no savior but me.
¹²It is I who declared, who saved,
who announced, not some
strange god among you;
You are my witnesses—oracle of
the LORD.
I am God,
¹³yes, from eternity I am he;

43:9-15 Judah—God's witness

The prophet returns to the metaphor of a trial. The issue at hand is the Lord's claim to be God. How could people take this claim seriously when Judah was in exile? Of what value is a God who cannot protect or save? The liberation of Jerusalem will change people's views, so it is important that the exiles enthusiastically respond to the prophet's message of their imminent redemption. Of course, no one could have foreseen the circumstances that led to Judah's freedom. The prophet has consistently asserted that

There is none who can deliver from
my hand:
I act and who can cancel it?

¹⁴Thus says the Lord, your redeemer,
the Holy One of Israel:
For your sake I send to Babylon;
I will bring down all her
defenses,
and the Chaldeans shall cry out
in lamentation.
¹⁵I am the Lord, your Holy One,
the creator of Israel, your King.
¹⁶Thus says the Lord,
who opens a way in the sea,
a path in the mighty waters,
¹⁷Who leads out chariots and
horsemen,
a powerful army,
Till they lie prostrate together,
never to rise,
snuffed out, quenched like a
wick.
¹⁸Remember not the events of the
past,

the things of long ago consider
not;
¹⁹See, I am doing something new!
Now it springs forth, do you not
perceive it?
In the wilderness I make a way,
in the wasteland, rivers.
²⁰Wild beasts honor me,
jackals and ostriches,
For I put water in the wilderness
and rivers in the wasteland
for my chosen people to drink,
²¹The people whom I formed for
myself,
that they might recount my
praise.

²²Yet you did not call upon me,
Jacob,
for you grew weary of me,
Israel.
²³You did not bring me sheep for
your burnt offerings,
nor honor me with your
sacrifices.

---

judgment was not God's last word to Jerusalem. He described a restored Zion and now his words are about to be fulfilled. The exiles are to put flesh and bone on those words and thereby become God's witnesses.

Judah's witnessing does not consist of providing rational proofs for God's existence. What Judah will show is God's power to save. When Judah had a king, the king's successes manifested God's power. But now the miraculous return of the exiles to Jerusalem will show the nations that Israel's God is God alone. The restoration of Jerusalem will be an irrefutable proof of the Lord's power to save. The fact of the exile appears to have undercut the credibility of Israel's witness. How could Israel's God claim any status given the fall of Jerusalem and the exile of its people? But the exile itself is a testament to God's sovereignty, since it was God who sent Israel to Babylon, but now that tragic episode in Israel's life is about to end. The Babylonians, on the other hand, will lament the fall of their city.

43:16–44:5 Something new

God's victory over the powers of nature during the exodus from Egypt has already shown God's might (Exod 7:8–11:10; 14:21), but these wondrous

I did not exact from you the service
of offerings,
nor weary you for frankincense.
²⁴You did not buy me sweet cane,
nor did you fill me with the fat
of your sacrifices;
Instead, you burdened me with
your sins,
wearied me with your crimes.
²⁵It is I, I, who wipe out,
for my own sake, your
offenses;
your sins I remember no more.
²⁶Would you have me remember,
have us come to trial?
Speak up, prove your
innocence!
²⁷Your first father sinned;
your spokesmen rebelled
against me
²⁸Till I repudiated the holy princes,
put Jacob under the ban,
exposed Israel to scorn.

44 ¹Hear then, Jacob, my servant,
Israel, whom I have chosen.
²Thus says the LORD who made you,
your help, who formed you
from the womb:
Do not fear, Jacob, my servant,
Jeshurun, whom I have chosen.
³I will pour out water upon the
thirsty ground,
streams upon the dry land;
I will pour out my spirit upon your
offspring,
my blessing upon your
descendants.
⁴They shall spring forth amid grass
like poplars beside flowing
waters.
⁵One shall say, "I am the LORD's,"
another shall be named after
Jacob,
And this one shall write on his
hand, "The LORD's,"
and receive the name Israel.

---

deeds are not simply memories. God will again act for Israel's sake. For the prophet, the exodus became a prototype of the restoration. Though the two events were separated from each other by hundreds of years, he was certain that the former illuminated the latter. God will free the exiles, lead them through the wilderness again, and bring them back to Jerusalem, where their praise of God's glory will be an effective witness to the one God. This new act of deliverance will be so spectacular that people will no longer remember the exodus but will recall with wonder and praise this new act of God's saving power. Just as the prophet reinterpreted the exodus story in terms of the exiles' experience, so did the New Testament reinterpret that same story as a way to speak of the significance of Jesus. The hymns of the African-American Christian community followed the same pattern, as does the liberation theology of the Americas. The prophet has shown many generations of believers how the exodus can always be something new.

Unfortunately, God's liberation of the Hebrew slaves from Egypt did not produce a grateful people. They constantly murmured in the wilderness on the way to the promised land, and they rebelled against Moses. This pattern continued once Israel arrived in Canaan. Instead of gratitude, Israel burdened God with its sins. At first, God chose to ignore Israel's sins,

The True God and False Gods. ⁶Thus
 says the LORD, Israel's king,
  its redeemer, the LORD of hosts:
 I am the first, I am the last;
  there is no God but me.
⁷Who is like me? Let him stand up
 and declare,
  make it evident, and confront
  me with it.
Who of old announced future
 events?
  Let them foretell to us the things
  to come.
⁸Do not fear or be troubled.
Did I not announce it to you long
 ago?
  I declared it, and you are my
  witnesses.
Is there any God but me?
 There is no other Rock, I know
 of none!

⁹Those who fashion idols are all
 nothing;
  their precious works are of no
  avail.
They are their witnesses:
 they see nothing, know nothing,
 and so they are put to shame.

¹⁰Who would fashion a god or cast
 an idol,
  that is of no use?
¹¹Look, all its company will be
 shamed;
  they are artisans, mere human
  beings!
They all assemble and stand there,
 only to cower in shame.
¹²The ironsmith fashions a likeness,
 he works it over the coals,
Shaping it with hammers,
 working it with his strong arm.
With hunger his strength wanes,
 without water, he grows faint.
¹³The woodworker stretches a line,
 and marks out a shape with a
 stylus.
He shapes it with scraping tools,
 with a compass measures it off,
Making it the copy of a man,
 human display, enthroned in a
 shrine.
¹⁴He goes out to cut down cedars,
 takes a holm tree or an oak.
He picks out for himself trees of the
 forest,
 plants a fir, and the rain makes
 it grow.

---

but its constant rebellion led God to remember the sins of all Israel—from those of Jacob to those of the present generation. God had no other choice but to abandon Israel. Still, the prophet suggests that Judah not focus on the past but on what God will do in the future. God has taken the initiative in empowering Israel as a witness. God will transform Israel and make it an effective witness though the outpouring of God's spirit into the dispirited exilic community. This community is God's *Jeshurun* (44:2; a Hebrew term translated as "darling" in the earlier NAB). The verbs of verses 4-5 point to some sort of an outward witness, not an inward transformation alone but something that people can see.

44:6-23 A parody on idol worship

The claims of the Lord's sovereignty seemed inflated to many people. After all, the Lord appeared unable to protect Judah from Babylon. At

¹⁵It is used for fuel:
  with some of the wood he
    warms himself,
  makes a fire and bakes bread.
Yet he makes a god and worships
  it,
  turns it into an idol and adores
    it!
¹⁶Half of it he burns in the fire,
  on its embers he roasts meat;
  he eats the roast and is full.
He warms himself and says, "Ah!
  I am warm! I see the flames!"
¹⁷The rest of it he makes into a god,
  an image to worship and adore.
He prays to it and says,
  "Help me! You are my god!"
¹⁸They do not know, do not
  understand;
  their eyes are too clouded to see,
  their minds, to perceive.
¹⁹He does not think clearly;
  he lacks the wit and knowledge
    to say,
"Half the wood I burned in the fire,
  on its embers I baked bread,
  I roasted meat and ate.

Shall I turn the rest into an
  abomination?
  Shall I worship a block of wood?"
²⁰He is chasing ashes!
A deluded mind has led him astray;
  He cannot save himself,
  does not say, "This thing in my
    right hand—is it not a
    fraud?"
²¹Remember these things, Jacob,
  Israel, for you are my servant!
I formed you, a servant to me;
  Israel, you shall never be
    forgotten by me:
²²I have brushed away your
    offenses like a cloud,
  your sins like a mist;
  return to me, for I have
    redeemed you.

²³Raise a glad cry, you heavens—the
  LORD has acted!
  Shout, you depths of the earth.
Break forth, mountains, into song,
  forest, with all your trees.
For the LORD has redeemed Jacob,
  shows his glory through Israel.

---

the very least, this must have led most of the prophet's contemporaries to view Israel's God as a second-rate deity. Certainly Marduk, Babylon's god, proved to be more powerful. Flying in the face of these attitudes, the prophet compares the Lord with other gods. The prophet begins by reminding people that the word of the Lord was spoken through the prophets who predicted the restoration of Jerusalem. That restoration is about to happen. This miracle will make the exiles God's witnesses before all peoples.

The prophet's comparison of Israel's God with the nations' gods continues with a parody on idol worship. The religion of ancient Israel was unique among the religions of the ancient Near East because it did not depict its patron deity in plastic form. Archaeologists have uncovered virtually no representations of male gods from the ancient Israelite period, though figurines depicting female deities have been found in surprising numbers. The torah prohibits the use of images of God several times: Exodus 20:4-5, 23; 34:17; Deuteronomy 4:15-18; 5:8; 27:15. The prophet plays on this special feature of Israelite religion to underscore the uniqueness of the Lord.

Cyrus, Anointed of the Lord, Agent of Israel's Liberation. ²⁴Thus says the
LORD, your redeemer,
who formed you from the
womb:
I am the LORD, who made all
things,
who alone stretched out the
heavens,
I spread out the earth by myself.

²⁵I bring to nought the omens of
babblers,
make fools of diviners,
Turn back the wise
and make their knowledge
foolish.
²⁶I confirm the words of my servant,
carry out the plan my
messengers announce.
I say to Jerusalem, Be inhabited!

The prophet's basic point is that the gods of the nations are obviously unable to save because they are merely wooden or metal objects made by human beings. To make his point the prophet misrepresents ancient Near Eastern religious beliefs regarding images of the gods. The ancient peoples were not as naive as the prophet suggests. They believed that after an image was consecrated, the spirit of the god represented by the statue inhabited it. The purpose of the image was to help the god and its worshipers to focus their attention on each other. Some statues even had moving parts, allowing priests to give responses to inquiries made by worshipers. The veneration of icons and statues by Christians shows that images of the sacred have power, though people are aware they are human constructions.

The prophet insists that the reality of the Lord is not manifested through a fabricated image but through real people, who are going to make their way from the land of their exile back to their ancestral homeland. Forgiveness of sins and healing of memories equip Judah to be God's witness. Judah serves a God who forgives sins so that it can look to its past without despair and its future with hope. Judah is to regard its past infidelity like the dew that forms in the mornings of the dry season. It dissipates as soon as the sun rises above the horizon. So God's forgiveness makes Judah's sins just as insubstantial. It is not a statue that is the image of the divine but a living people whom God has redeemed. The calling of Judah is to be the living representation of the Lord. Its singing and rejoicing at the prospect of its impending return ought to stimulate nature to join in the praise of God.

The book of Revelation quotes verse 6, putting the words that the prophet attributes to God on the lips of the risen Jesus (Rev 1:8, 17).

44:24–45:13 God's anointed king

Though the prophet has been speaking about the liberation of Jerusalem as a sovereign act of the Lord, he knows that the actual working out of the divine plan will happen through a human instrument. Abraham, Moses,

To the cities of Judah, Be rebuilt!
  I will raise up their ruins.
27I say to the deep, Be dry!
  I will dry up your rivers.
28I say of Cyrus, My shepherd!
  He carries out my every wish,
Saying of Jerusalem, "Let it be
    rebuilt,"
  and of the temple, "Lay its
    foundations."

45 1Thus says the LORD to his
  anointed, Cyrus,
  whose right hand I grasp,
Subduing nations before him,
  stripping kings of their strength,
Opening doors before him,
  leaving the gates unbarred:
2I will go before you
  and level the mountains;
Bronze doors I will shatter,
  iron bars I will snap.
3I will give you treasures of darkness,
  riches hidden away,
That you may know I am the LORD,
  the God of Israel, who calls you
    by name.

4For the sake of Jacob, my servant,
  of Israel my chosen one,
I have called you by name,
  giving you a title, though you
    do not know me.
5I am the LORD, there is no other,
  there is no God besides me.
It is I who arm you, though you do
    not know me,
  6so that all may know, from the
    rising of the sun
  to its setting, that there is none
    besides me.
I am the LORD, there is no other.

7I form the light, and create the
    darkness,
I make weal and create woe;
  I, the LORD, do all these things.
8Let justice descend, you heavens,
    like dew from above,
  like gentle rain let the clouds
    drop it down.
Let the earth open and salvation
    bud forth;
  let righteousness spring up with
    them!
  I, the LORD, have created this.
9Woe to anyone who contends with
    their Maker;
  a potsherd among potsherds of
    the earth!
Shall the clay say to the potter,
  "What are you doing?"
  or, "What you are making has
    no handles"?
10Woe to anyone who asks a father,
  "What are you begetting?"
  or a woman, "What are you
    giving birth to?"
11Thus says the LORD,
  the Holy One of Israel, his
    maker:
Do you question me about my
    children,
  tell me how to treat the work of
    my hands?
12It was I who made the earth
  and created the people upon it;
It was my hands that stretched out
    the heavens;
  I gave the order to all their host.
13It was I who stirred him up for
    justice;
  all his ways I make level.

Joshua, David, and the prophets have all served as the divinely chosen means by which God's will for Israel achieved its ends. Now the prophet is ready to identify the person whom he knows to be the one to effect the

He shall rebuild my city
  and let my exiles go free
Without price or payment,
  says the LORD of hosts.

¹⁴Thus says the LORD:
The earnings of Egypt, the gain of
    Ethiopia,
  and the Sabeans, tall of stature,
Shall come over to you and belong
    to you;
  they shall follow you, coming in
    chains.

Before you they shall bow down,
  saying in prayer:
"With you alone is God; and there
    is none other,
  no other god!
¹⁵Truly with you God is hidden,
  the God of Israel, the savior!
¹⁶They are put to shame and
    disgrace, all of them;
  they go in disgrace who carve
    images.
¹⁷Israel has been saved by the LORD,
  saved forever!

---

newest act of liberation: the redemption of Jerusalem's exiles. The prophet makes a surprising and unexpected identification to say the least.

The prophet begins by repeating the unprecedented nature of what God is about to do. Babylon's diviners did not foresee it. The king's advisors did not even consider the possibility. But it is true that Judah is going to be restored. Its cities—Jerusalem in particular—are going to be rebuilt and repopulated. But who is going to accomplish all this? The surprising answer is Cyrus, the king of Persia. Though the prophet hinted at this earlier (41:2, 25), here he does not use veiled references but makes an explicit identification. In this passage, the prophet mentions Cyrus by name twice (44:28; 45:1) and refers to him with a personal pronoun one more time (45:13).

What is even more surprising, the prophet calls Cyrus the Lord's "messiah" (anointed)—a title that was given to Israel's kings (1 Sam 2:10; 12:3; 2 Sam 23:1; Ps 2:2; 20:7; 132:17). In the book of Isaiah, the term does not have the eschatological connotations that it acquired later. Still, using it to speak of a non-Israelite king is unprecedented. Apparently, the prophet's notion of Jerusalem's liberation did not include the restoration of Judah's native dynasty. God will use Cyrus to free the exiles and enthrone him as king to free the exiles.

Not all the prophet's contemporaries welcomed this message, but he insists that the choice of Cyrus is God's. The only woe oracle that appears in the fourth section of the book (45:8-13) is directed at those who cannot accept the prophet's word about Cyrus. Without the restoration of Judah's native dynasty, there will be no restored Judahite state. By naming Cyrus as God's messiah, the prophet appears to accept a continuing subordinate role for Judah in the political sphere. Though the exiles will be free to return to their land, Judah will remain subject to the Persian king. Apparently,

123

You shall never be put to shame or
    disgrace
  in any future age."

  [18]For thus says the LORD,
The creator of the heavens,
  who is God,
The designer and maker of the
    earth
  who established it,
Not as an empty waste did he
    create it,
  but designing it to be lived in:
I am the LORD, and there is no other.
  [19]I have not spoken in secret
from some place in the land of
    darkness,
I have not said to the descendants
    of Jacob,
  "Look for me in an empty
    waste."

I, the LORD, promise justice,
  I declare what is right.

[20]Come and assemble, gather
    together,
  you fugitives from among the
    nations!
They are without knowledge who
    bear wooden idols
  and pray to gods that cannot
    save.
[21]Come close and declare;
  let them take counsel together:
Who announced this from the
    beginning,
  declared it from of old?
Was it not I, the LORD,
  besides whom there is no other
    God?
  There is no just and saving God
    but me.

---

some of the exiles expected that any restoration of Judah would involve the restoration of the Davidic dynasty and Judahite national state.

Another institution of preexilic Israel that apparently does not have a significant place in the prophet's vision of Jerusalem's restoration is the temple. This is the only time the fourth section of the book of Isaiah mentions the temple (44:28). It follows the description of God's victory over chaotic forces represented by the waters of the seas and rivers (44:27). But victory over chaos and temple building are related activities. A temple makes the heavenly victory manifest to people on earth. Also, temple building was an expression of the king's claims to be divinely chosen. In fact, the decree of Cyrus that allows the exiles to return to Jerusalem states that God chose Cyrus to rebuild the temple of Jerusalem (2 Chr 36:22-23; Ezra 1:2-4).

God's choice of Cyrus as messiah makes it clear that the liberation of Jerusalem does not mean a return to the status quo of Judah's monarchic period. The prophet proclaims that God is about to do something entirely new. The miraculous liberation of Jerusalem will serve to broaden the horizons of Judah's concept of God.

45:14-25 God and the nations

Another important element of the prophet's vision of Jerusalem's future involves the nations. Here too the prophet proclaims something new. The

²²Turn to me and be safe,
all you ends of the earth,
for I am God; there is no other!
²³By myself I swear,
uttering my just decree,
a word that will not return:
To me every knee shall bend;
by me every tongue shall swear,
²⁴Saying, "Only in the LORD
are just deeds and power.
Before him in shame shall come
all who vent their anger against
him.
²⁵In the LORD all the descendants of
Israel
shall have vindication and
glory."

46 **The Gods of Babylon.** ¹Bel bows
down, Nebo stoops,
their idols set upon beasts and
cattle;
They must be borne upon shoulders,
a load for weary animals.
²They stoop and bow down
together;
unable to deliver those who
bear them,
they too go into captivity.

³Hear me, O house of Jacob,
all the remnant of the house of
Israel,
My burden from the womb,
whom I have carried since birth.

previous sections of the book of Isaiah presented the nations as enemies of Judah bent on its destruction. Though they were instruments of divine judgment, the nations often went beyond their mandate and would themselves experience severe judgment for their excesses. Here the prophet has the nations recognize the Lord's role in the fall of Babylon, the rise of Persia, and the liberation of Jerusalem. By defeating Judah, the nations served God's purposes without knowing it, but this new act of God would make it possible for them to recognize Israel's God as the only God.

The nations confess that it is clear that the Lord alone is God and God's intentions for Judah are clear, whereas once they were hidden. God is "hidden" since God has been with Judah in exile, but now that exile is about to end in a glorious and miraculous way. The peoples of exotic lands will leave their countries in order to come to Jerusalem so that they might see the great victory that God has given to Judah, a victory which has meant defeat for those nations that were threats to Judah's existence.

God asserts that God's intentions have always been clear in the creation of the world and through the demand for justice. God's word was not uttered in some secret place but openly. A similar point is made in the book of Acts. During the controversy regarding the obligation of Gentile converts to Christianity to observe the torah, James notes that the Mosaic law had been proclaimed in every city since Moses "has been read in the synagogues every sabbath" (Acts 15:21). Paul too asserts that what the law requires is written on the hearts of the Gentiles (Rom 2:15). Still, the notion that Israel's God is a "hidden God" does help people to recognize the tentativeness of their insights

⁴Even to your old age I am he,
  even when your hair is gray I
    will carry you;
I have done this, and I will lift you
    up,
  I will carry you to safety.

⁵To whom would you liken me as
    an equal,
  compare me, as though we were
    alike?
⁶There are those who pour out gold
    from a purse
  and weigh out silver on the
    scales;
They hire a goldsmith to make it
    into a god
  before which they bow down in
    worship.
⁷They lift it to their shoulders to
    carry;
  when they set it down, it stays,
    and does not move from the
      place.
They cry out to it, but it cannot
    answer;
  it delivers no one from distress.

⁸Remember this and be firm,
  take it to heart, you rebels;
  ⁹remember the former things,
    those long ago:

I am God, there is no other;
  I am God, there is none like me.
¹⁰At the beginning I declare the
    outcome;
  from of old, things not yet done.
I say that my plan shall stand,
  I accomplish my every desire.

¹¹I summon from the east a bird of
    prey,
  from a distant land, one to carry
    out my plan.
Yes, I have spoken, I will
    accomplish it;
  I have planned it, and I will do
    it.
¹²Listen to me, you fainthearted,
  far from the victory of justice:
¹³I am bringing on that victory, it is
    not far off,
  my salvation shall not tarry;
I will put salvation within Zion,
  give to Israel my glory.

47 **The Fall of Babylon.** ¹Come down,
  sit in the dust,
  virgin daughter Babylon;
Sit on the ground, dethroned,
  daughter of the Chaldeans.
No longer shall you be called
  dainty and delicate.
²Take the millstone and grind flour,
  remove your veil;

---

into God's presence and action in the world. While believers look forward to the day of God's final victory over the powers of evil, they recognize that in the meantime it is not always easy to see God's purposes being fulfilled.

The prophet's vision has the nations joining Judah in acknowledging the Lord as the only God. Jerusalem's liberation, when it did come, did not have the effect on the nations that the prophet anticipated. But 45:23b-24a is cited in both Romans 14:11 and Philippians 2:10-11 for Paul believed that the prophet's vision would find its fulfillment in Jesus and the church.

46:1-13 Salvation in Zion

This passage contrasts Babylon and its gods, Bel and Nebo, with Zion and its God. It opens with Bel and Nebo being led away from Babylon in

Strip off your skirt, bare your legs,
  cross through the streams.
³Your nakedness shall be
  uncovered,
and your shame be seen;
I will take vengeance,
  I will yield to no entreaty,
  says ⁴our redeemer,
Whose name is the LORD of hosts,
  the Holy One of Israel.

⁵Go into darkness and sit in silence,
  daughter of the Chaldeans,

No longer shall you be called
  sovereign mistress of kingdoms.
⁶Angry at my people,
  I profaned my heritage
And gave them into your power;
  but you showed them no mercy;
Upon the aged
  you laid a very heavy yoke.
⁷You said, "I shall remain always,
  a sovereign mistress forever!"
You did not take these things to
  heart,
  but disregarded their outcome.

captivity and ends with the affirmation that God "will put salvation within Zion" (46:13).

Bel was a title given to Marduk, Babylon's patron deity. Nebo was the son of Marduk, whose temple was across the Euphrates from Babylon. These gods had to be carried by their worshipers while the Lord "carries" the people of Judah. In drawing this contrast, the prophet expected that the Persians would follow usual practice by carrying off the images of the gods of the conquered cities, but Cyrus had a different policy. He was as tolerant toward the Babylonians and their religion as he was toward the people of Judah. He tried to show himself to the Babylonians as Marduk's chosen instrument to insure the proper service of that god.

The prophet asserts that the Lord's dominion is not like that of the other gods who cannot save because they are manufactured images and nothing more. This passage again ridicules the worship of other gods in order to eliminate rival claimants for Judah's loyalty. The prophet calls skeptics from both Judah and the nations to remember what God has done. Cyrus is the destroyer of Babylon's military power. The destruction of Babylon and the flight of its helpless gods send a clear message to Israel: do not keep yourselves distant from the shrine of the Lord in Zion. The doubters need to be told that the conquest of Babylon by Cyrus, though apparently unrelated to Judah's destiny, was actually an act of God to restore the people of Judah to Jerusalem. The people then are to attend to the fulfillment of prophecy and the exclusive claims of the Lord as manifest through the rise of Cyrus.

47:1-15 Against Babylon

The only way for the liberation of Jerusalem to proceed is for Babylon to fall. The prophet taunts Babylon by asserting that God will strip it of all prerogatives as a royal city. He declares that this pampered daughter of the

[8]Now hear this, voluptuous one,
  enthroned securely,
Saying in your heart,
  "I, and no one else!
I shall never be a widow,
  bereft of my children"—
[9]Both these things shall come to
  you
  suddenly, in a single day:
Complete bereavement and
  widowhood
  shall come upon you
Despite your many sorceries
  and the full power of your spells;
[10]Secure in your wickedness,
  you said, "No one sees me."
Your wisdom and your knowledge
  led you astray,
And you said in your heart,

"I, and no one else!"
[11]But upon you shall come an evil
  you will not be able to charm
  away;
Upon you shall fall a disaster
  you cannot ward off.
Upon you shall suddenly come
  a ruin you cannot imagine.

[12]Keep on with your spells
  and your many sorceries,
  at which you toiled from your
  youth.
Perhaps you can prevail,
  perhaps you can strike terror!
[13]You wore yourself out with so
  many consultations!
Let the astrologers stand forth to
  save you,

Chaldeans, who provided the neo-Babylonian empire with its leadership, will do the work of slaves such as grinding grain into meal. Once an untouchable queen, she will be devastated and subject to sexual harassment like any commoner (compare Hos 2:9-12; Jer 13:20-27). The Lord empowered Babylon to conquer Judah because of the latter's infidelity—not because of Babylon's virtue or because of its military power. Babylon mistook this temporary mission as conferring permanent, privileged status. It thought itself exempt from military defeat and political impotence. It will experience both.

The skills of Babylon's priests and diviners cannot save its empire. Babylon had an international reputation for the skills of its sages and diviners. In the face of the Lord's judgment they are impotent. There are no rituals or charms that can forestall the judgment that awaits Babylon. It is inevitable. Babylon's fall will be quick and spectacular, like fire that consumes dry stubble (47:14). Allies and vassals will leave Babylon to face its fate alone. The book of Revelation imitates the prophet when it taunts Rome, whose fall its author considered inevitable (Rev 17–18). Like Babylon, Rome was the capital of a great empire. Still, both Babylon and Rome were transformed by the power of God. Neither was destroyed, but Babylon became a great center of Jewish learning and Rome became the capital of the Christian world. The visions of both prophets Isaiah and John were fulfilled beyond their expectations.

The stargazers who forecast at each
new moon
what would happen to you.
[14]See, they are like stubble,
fire consumes them;
They cannot deliver themselves
from the spreading flames.
This is no warming ember,
no fire to sit before!
[15]Thus do your wizards serve you
with whom you have toiled
from your youth;
They wander their separate ways,
with none to save you.

48 **Exhortations to the Exiles.** [1]Hear
this, house of Jacob
called by the name Israel,
sprung from the stock of Judah,
You who swear by the name of the
LORD
and invoke the God of Israel

without sincerity, without
justice,
[2]Though you are named after the
holy city
and rely on the God of Israel,
whose name is the LORD of
hosts.
[3]Things of the past I declared long
ago,
they went forth from my mouth,
I announced them;
then suddenly I took action and
they came to be.
[4]Because I know that you are
stubborn
and that your neck is an iron
sinew
and your forehead bronze,
[5]I declared them to you of old;
before they took place I
informed you,

48:1-22 The power of God's word

The prophet's task is to persuade the exiles that his view of Jerusalem's liberation is not just a flight of fancy but the word of God that is going to be fulfilled and soon. What kept people from accepting the prophet's message was their experience—the harsh realities of their lives in exile. To believe that the Lord, the patron deity of a nation and dynasty that no longer existed, was controlling world events strained the people's credulity. Judah was no longer even a minor player on the stage in the ancient Near East. Babylon, whose material culture, military might, and political power far outstripped that of Judah's best days, could not possibly be threatened by any message from the Lord, no matter how convinced the prophet may be.

In this chapter the prophet is venting his frustration at the exiles' unenthusiastic response to his message. He tries to persuade people that the message he is delivering is the word of God, a word that will find fulfillment. There are two parts in this unit: verses 1-11 and verses 12-21. The first embodies a theory of the connection between God's word and God's deeds, and the second applies this theory to the exilic situation and the rise of Cyrus.

The prophet begins by showing that there is a connection between God's word and Israel's experience, as is clear from Israel's past. The prophet also

That you might not say, "My idol
did them,
my statue, my molten image
commanded them."
⁶Now that you have heard, look at
all this;
must you not admit it?
From now on I announce new
things to you,
hidden events you never knew.
⁷Now, not from of old, they are
created,
before today you did not hear of
them,
so that you cannot claim, "I
have known them."
⁸You never heard, you never knew,
they never reached your ears
beforehand.
Yes, I know you are utterly
treacherous,
a rebel you were named from
the womb.
⁹For the sake of my name I restrain
my anger,
for the sake of my renown I hold
it back from you,
lest I destroy you.

¹⁰See, I refined you, but not like
silver;
I tested you in the furnace of
affliction.
¹¹For my sake, for my own sake, I
do this;
why should my name be
profaned?
My glory I will not give to
another.

¹²Listen to me, Jacob,
Israel, whom I called!
I, it is I who am the first,
and am I the last.
¹³Yes, my hand laid the foundations
of the earth;
my right hand spread out the
heavens.
When I summon them,
they stand forth at once.

¹⁴All of you assemble and listen:
Who among you declared these
things?
The one the LORD loves shall do his
will
against Babylon and the
offspring of Chaldea.

---

criticizes a shallow religion that saw Israel's security in its cult and believed that Israel's God had no moral will. He asserts that the word must precede God's actions in Judah's life because of its stubbornness in the past. Judah will know that the Lord is responsible once the word is fulfilled. Unfortunately, the people have shown a tendency to attribute the course of events to some agent other than the Lord. The preexilic prophets contain ample number of threats of judgment on moral grounds, and it was in these that the revealing word of the Lord was contained. The exiles preferred to explain their misfortunes by something other than the moral and religious breakdown of which the prophets spoke.

There is no great act of God without a predictive word to clarify its significance. Judah thinks that it knows who God is and how God acts. It will deny the divine origin of anything that is contrary to its concept of God and the biases connected with it. Of course, this is to be expected since Israel was rebellious from its very beginning. But the Lord is not governed by the

¹⁵I myself have spoken, I have
summoned him,
I have brought him, and his way
succeeds!
¹⁶Come near to me and hear this!
From the beginning I did not
speak in secret;
At the time it happens, I am there:
"Now the Lord GOD has sent
me, and his spirit." *Cyrus*

¹⁷Thus says the LORD, your
redeemer,
the Holy One of Israel:
I am the LORD, your God,
teaching you how to prevail,
leading you on the way you
should go.
¹⁸If only you would attend to my
commandments,
your peace would be like a river,
your vindication like the waves
of the sea,

Prophet's word

¹⁹Your descendants like the sand,
the offspring of your loins like
its grains,
Their name never cut off
or blotted out from my presence.
²⁰Go forth from Babylon, flee from
Chaldea!
With shouts of joy declare this,
announce it;
Make it known to the ends of the
earth,
Say: "The LORD has redeemed
his servant Jacob.
²¹They did not thirst
when he led them through dry
lands;
Water from the rock he set flowing
for them;
he cleft the rock, and waters
welled forth."

²²There is no peace for the wicked,
says the LORD.

---

conduct of Israel. Whether God judges or saves, the motivation is within God's inner being, i.e., God's name. God does not respond to emotional impulse like human beings. The Lord's work will proceed no matter what the popular reaction is.

In the second part of this passage (48:11-22), the prophet applies what he just said about the power of God's word to the situation that Judah faces. The prophet is providing the word and Cyrus is doing the deed. God chose Cyrus to act against Babylon and has guaranteed his success. The fall of Babylon has no significance apart from its manifestation of God's power.

The speaker of verse 16 is Cyrus, who acknowledges that he will conquer Babylon by the power of God's spirit. The messenger formula in the following verse introduces a statement that offers a perspective similar to that undergirding the book of Deuteronomy: if Israel will learn and observe God's teaching, this will guarantee Israel's prosperity, but the "commandments" in verse 18 probably refer to the prophet's words rather than stipulations of the torah. Israel's future is linked to obedience to the authoritative words of the prophet. Using a series of imperatives in verses 20-21, the prophet calls for a new exodus and a new passage through the desert. The prophet summons Israel to action. Verse 22 appears almost verbatim in

B. Expiation of Sin, Spiritual Liberation of Israel

49 **The Servant of the Lord.** [1]Hear me, coastlands,
listen, distant peoples.
Before birth the LORD called me,
from my mother's womb he
gave me my name.
[2]He made my mouth like a
sharp-edged sword,
concealed me, shielded by his
hand.
He made me a sharpened arrow,
in his quiver he hid me.
[3]He said to me, You are my servant,
in you, Israel, I show my glory.

[4]Though I thought I had toiled in
vain,
for nothing and for naught
spent my strength,
Yet my right is with the LORD,
my recompense is with my God.
[5]For now the LORD has spoken
who formed me as his servant
from the womb,
That Jacob may be brought back to
him
and Israel gathered to him;
I am honored in the sight of the
LORD,
and my God is now my
strength!
[6]It is too little, he says, for you to be
my servant,
to raise up the tribes of Jacob,
and restore the survivors of
Israel;

57:21. It is not related to the context here and seems to be a discordant note at the end of a text that shows progressive emotional intensity.

John of Patmos gives advice that is the same as that of the prophet. The book of Revelation calls Christians to "come out" of Rome (Rev 18:4), just as the prophet charges the exiles to leave Babylon (48:20). Believers are called to respond to God's word. They are not to remain passive recipients but active agents of that word. They are to leave behind all that has left them insensitive to the message of God's prophets. John also uses the prophet's epithets "first and last" to speak about Christ (48:12; Rev 1:17; 2:8; see also Isa 44:6).

49:1-6 Israel's mission

The prophet wishes to present his message of Jerusalem's liberation against the widest possible backdrop. It is essential that the exiles do not conceive of their release from captivity as making possible a return to the political, economic, social, and religious conditions of Judah before the fall of Jerusalem. Judah will have a future, but that future consists in bringing the word of God "to the ends of the earth" (49:6). It is for this reason that Israel was chosen as God's people (see Gen 12:3). Jerusalem's restoration will make it possible for the people to present a dramatic and authentic witness of God's power. Luke quotes verse 6 to show that God was controlling the events that led to the decision by Paul and Barnabas to preach to

I will make you a light to the
nations,
that my salvation may reach to
the ends of the earth.
⁷Thus says the LORD,
the redeemer, the Holy One of
Israel,
To the one despised, abhorred by the
nations,
the slave of rulers:
When kings see you, they shall
stand up,
and princes shall bow down
Because of the LORD who is faithful,
the Holy One of Israel who has
chosen you.

**The Liberation and Restoration of
Zion.** ⁸Thus says the LORD:
In a time of favor I answer you,

on the day of salvation I help
you;
I form you and set you
as a covenant for the people,
To restore the land
and allot the devastated
heritages,
⁹To say to the prisoners: Come out!
To those in darkness: Show
yourselves!
Along the roadways they shall find
pasture,
on every barren height shall
their pastures be.
¹⁰They shall not hunger or thirst;
nor shall scorching wind or sun
strike them;
For he who pities them leads them
and guides them beside springs
of water.

---

the Gentiles (Acts 13:47) and he sees the church fulfilling Israel's mission
to proclaim the word of God "to the ends of the earth" (Acts 1:8).

49:7 The reaction of the nations

There will be a dramatic reversal of fortunes following Jerusalem's liberation. The miracle that God will work in and through Judah will be such
that the only possible response will be for kings and princes to acknowledge the sovereignty of Israel's God. While this verse is a testament to the
prophet's faith, it was not fulfilled in the way he expected. The restoration
never achieved the goals that the prophet had for it. This led to further
reflection on and a reinterpretation of the prophet's message. One outcome
of this reinterpretation was the appropriation of the book of Isaiah by the
writers of the New Testament. They believed that the prophet's words finally found their fulfillment in Jesus and the Gospel.

49:8-26 The reaction of the exiles

While the prophet foresees that princes and kings will prostrate themselves before Judah's God when they witness the fulfillment of God's word,
the reaction of God's people to that word is lamentation. The prophet characterizes the days during which he spoke in the name of God as "a time
of favor" (49:8). This was the time that the people of Judah were praying
for. God was answering their prayers and would lead them back to Zion.

¹¹I will turn all my mountains into
    roadway,
    and make my highways level.
¹²See, these shall come from afar:
    some from the north and the
        west,
    others from the land of Syene.

¹³Sing out, heavens, and rejoice,
    earth,
    break forth into song, you
        mountains,
For the LORD comforts his people
    and shows mercy to his
        afflicted.

¹⁴But Zion said, "The LORD has
    forsaken me;
    my Lord has forgotten me."
¹⁵Can a mother forget her infant,
    be without tenderness for the
        child of her womb?
Even should she forget,
    I will never forget you.
¹⁶See, upon the palms of my hands I
    have engraved you;

your walls are ever before me.
¹⁷Your children hasten—
    your levelers, your destroyers
    go forth from you;
¹⁸Look about and see,
    they are all gathering and
        coming to you.
As I live—oracle of the LORD—
    you shall don them as jewels,
    bedeck yourself like a bride.

¹⁹Though you were waste and
    desolate,
    a land of ruins,
Now you shall be too narrow for
    your inhabitants,
    while those who swallowed you
        up will be far away.
²⁰The children of whom you were
    bereft
    shall yet say in your hearing,
"This place is too narrow for me,
    make room for me to live in."
²¹You shall ask yourself:
    "Who has borne me these,
    when I was bereft and barren?

The word that God has for the exiles is "Come out!" (49:9). The return to Jerusalem will be less like a wearisome trek and more like a procession led by God, who will guide the people as a shepherd. Judahite exiles from all over the world, not just Babylon, will stream toward their ancient homeland (49:12: Syene is the modern Aswan in Upper Egypt where there was a Jewish colony).

Inanimate nature recognizes Judah's restoration for what it is: a miraculous demonstration of God's power. It responds with uninhibited joy. The liberation of Jerusalem is no mere political event. The cosmos is caught up in this redemptive act of God that restores the people of Judah not only to their homeland but especially to their unique relationship with God. The people have suffered because of their infidelity, but God's compassion will not allow God's justice to have its full effect on Israel. Judgment was not to be God's last word. The prophet sees the people's redemption on the horizon. Nature too sees this and rejoices.

How do the exiles react to the momentous events in which they are caught up? How do they respond to the prophet's words of hope? Unlike

Exiled and repudiated,
who has reared them?
I was left all alone;
where then do these come from?"
²²Thus says the Lord GOD:
See, I will lift up my hand to the
nations,
and to the peoples raise my
signal;
They shall bring your sons in their
arms,
your daughters shall be carried
on their shoulders.
²³Kings shall be your guardians,
their princesses your
nursemaids;

Face to the ground, they shall bow
down before you
and lick the dust at your feet.
Then you shall know that I am the
LORD,
none who hope in me shall be
ashamed.
²⁴Can plunder be taken from a
warrior,
or captives rescued from a
tyrant?
²⁵Thus says the LORD:
Yes, captives can be taken from a
warrior,
and plunder rescued from a
tyrant;

---

the heavens and the earth, which recognize the significance of God's action, the people of Judah utter words of disbelief. The exiles consider the prophet's message unrealistic—too good to be true. Perhaps they considered them the product of an overwrought religious personality.

To counter the exiles' disbelief, the prophet uses a very poignant metaphor. He asserts that God's love for the people of Judah exceeds that of a nursing mother for her child. While some biblical metaphors can be difficult to understand, the image in verse 15 is impossible to misinterpret. It is difficult to find a more touching image of God's love anywhere else in the Bible. This image underscores the unbreakable bond between God and Israel. While this bond did not exempt Israel from experiencing divine judgment for its infidelity, God's commitment to Israel remains secure. The phrase in verse 16a ("See, upon the palms of my hands I have engraved you . . . ") may refer to tattooing, another image of the permanency of God's commitment to Israel. The prophet promises that Jerusalem will be rebuilt and repopulated. He then returns to a familiar motif: the reversal of the fortunes of Judah and Babylon leading all peoples to recognize that the Lord's power saved Judah.

Paul cited 49:8 to urge the people of Corinth to respond to God's grace at work in them (see 2 Cor 6:2). Like the prophet, Paul believed that apart from the believers' response the transforming power of God's word would not have concrete effect.

50:1-3 The purpose of the exiles

To counter the exiles' lack of hope regarding their future, the prophet assures them that the purpose of the exile was not to end Jerusalem's

Those who oppose you I will
oppose,
and your sons I will save.
²⁶I will make your oppressors eat
their own flesh,
and they shall be drunk with
their own blood
as though with new wine.
All flesh shall know
that I, the LORD, am your savior,
your redeemer, the Mighty One
of Jacob.

50 **Salvation Through the Lord's Servant.** ¹Thus says the LORD:
Where is the bill of divorce
with which I dismissed your
mother?
Or to which of my creditors
have I sold you?
It was for your sins you were sold,
for your rebellions your mother
was dismissed.

²Why was no one there when I
came?
Why did no one answer when I
called?
Is my hand too short to ransom?
Have I not the strength to
deliver?
See, with my rebuke I dry up the sea,
I turn rivers into wilderness;
Their fish rot for lack of water,
and die of thirst.
³I clothe the heavens in black,
and make sackcloth their
covering.

⁴The Lord GOD has given me
a well-trained tongue,
That I might know how to answer
the weary
a word that will waken them.
Morning after morning
he wakens my ear to hear as
disciples do;

---

relationship with God but to discipline its people. Both Hosea and Jeremiah use the metaphor of divorce (Hos 2:4; Jer 3:1, 8) to speak about the consequences that Israel will have to pay for its infidelity, but the prophet rejects this comparison. He maintains that there was no divorce between Jerusalem ("your mother") and God since no bill of divorce was given (see Deut 24:1-4). He also asserts that, despite appearances, the people were not sold into slavery, since that would imply that God needed to sell Israel to settle debts. God has no creditors. What happened to the people of Judah happened because they did not recognize the power of their God, who alone overcame the mighty waters to bring order out of chaos. God's power will now liberate Jerusalem from its exile.

50:4-11 Light and darkness

The prophet identifies himself with all those whom God sent to bring light to those who preferred to live in darkness. This passage is reminiscent of a thanksgiving psalm (e.g., Ps 34) with its description of distress and the affirmation that God saved the prophet. In the midst of humiliating treatment, the prophet asserts that God was with him, so that in the end he will be vindicated. The prophet then turns to his audience and tells them that they may enjoy the same divine protection. The prophet agrees that he

⁵The Lord God opened my ear;
    I did not refuse,
    did not turn away.
⁶I gave my back to those who beat
        me,
    my cheeks to those who tore out
        my beard;
My face I did not hide
    from insults and spitting.

⁷The Lord God is my help,
    therefore I am not disgraced;
Therefore I have set my face like
        flint,
    knowing that I shall not be put
        to shame.
⁸He who declares my innocence is
        near.
    Who will oppose me?
    Let us appear together.
Who will dispute my right?
    Let them confront me.
⁹See, the Lord God is my help;
    who will declare me guilty?
See, they will all wear out like a
        garment,
    consumed by moths.
¹⁰Who among you fears the Lord,
    heeds his servant's voice?
Whoever walk in darkness,
    without any light,
Yet trust in the name of the Lord
    and rely upon their God!
¹¹All you who kindle flames
    and set flares alight,
Walk by the light of your own fire

and by the flares you have
        burnt!
This is your fate from my hand:
    you shall lie down in a place of
        torment.

51 **Exhortation to Trust in the Lord.**
    ¹Listen to me, you who pursue
justice,
    who seek the Lord;
Look to the rock from which you
        were hewn,
    to the quarry from which you
        were taken;
²Look to Abraham, your father,
    and to Sarah, who gave you
        birth;
Though he was but one when I
        called him,
    I blessed him and made him
        many.
³Yes, the Lord shall comfort Zion,
    shall comfort all her ruins;
Her wilderness he shall make like
        Eden,
    her wasteland like the garden of
        the Lord;
Joy and gladness shall be found in
        her,
    thanksgiving and the sound of
        song.

⁴Be attentive to me, my people;
    my nation, give ear to me.
For teaching shall go forth from me,
    and my judgment, as light to the
        peoples.

---

walks in the darkness of the exile, but he urges his audience to trust in God so that they might join him in the light. This passage has been listed among the "Servant Songs," though the word "servant" does not appear here.

51:1-8 Salvation is coming

Here the prophet takes a more positive tack as he exhorts his fellow exiles to believe in the future of Jerusalem. He addresses his audience as "you who pursue justice," i.e., those actively committed to the establishment

137

⁵I will make my victory come
   swiftly;
 my salvation shall go forth
   and my arm shall judge the
      nations;
In me the coastlands shall hope,
   and my arm they shall await.

⁶Raise your eyes to the heavens,
   look at the earth below;
Though the heavens vanish like
      smoke,
   the earth wear out like a
      garment
   and its inhabitants die like flies,
My salvation shall remain forever
   and my victory shall always be
      firm.
⁷Hear me, you who know justice,

you people who have my
   teaching at heart:
Do not fear the reproach of others;
   remain firm at their revilings.
⁸They shall be like a garment eaten
      by moths,
   like wool consumed by grubs;
But my victory shall remain forever,
   my salvation, for all generations.

⁹Awake, awake, put on strength,
   arm of the LORD!
Awake as in the days of old,
   in ages long ago!
Was it not you who crushed Rahab,
   you who pierced the dragon?
¹⁰Was it not you who dried up the
      sea,
   the waters of the great deep,

of a just society. He goes on to show that their dreams are realistic despite what appear to be great obstacles to their fulfillment.

Those who believe only a miracle could restore Judah ought to remember the story of Abraham and Sarah, their ancestors. God's promises to them were fulfilled although it appeared impossible for them ever to have children. God will effect another miracle to save the people of Jerusalem in exile. God will transform the city and its people in a way that is similar to the transformation of the desert into a beautiful garden.

Though the prophet uses the mythical image of Eden as a metaphor for the liberated Jerusalem, it is clear that he expects the transformation to take place through justice and the torah. Again recalling the words of 2:2-4, the prophet assures the exiles that all nations will recognize this triumph of justice. Though the heavens suggest permanency, they will be swept away before God's salvation and deliverance for Zion will fail. The people need to live by the torah and be unafraid of those who do not. The latter will be gone soon, but God's deliverance will be lasting. God's victory over the powers of chaos is another reason for the people's confidence. What God did once God can do again.

51:9–52:12 Awake!

The prophet's language is becoming more intense as he urges his fellow exiles to action. Three times in this passage he tells them to awake (51:9, 17; 52:1). The prophet again reminds the exiles of the power of God

You who made the depths of the
sea into a way
for the redeemed to pass
through?
[11]Those whom the LORD has
ransomed will return
and enter Zion singing,
crowned with everlasting joy;
They will meet with joy and
gladness,
sorrow and mourning will flee.

[12]I, it is I who comfort you.
Can you then fear mortals who
die,
human beings who are just grass,
[13]And forget the LORD, your maker,
who stretched out the heavens
and laid the foundations of
earth?
All the day you are in constant dread
of the fury of the oppressor
When he prepares himself to
destroy;
but where is the oppressor's
fury?

[14]The captives shall soon be
released;
they shall not die and go down
into the pit,
nor shall they want for bread.
[15]For I am the LORD, your God,
who stirs up the sea so that its
waves roar;
the LORD of hosts by name.

[16]I have put my words into your
mouth,
I covered you, shielded by my
hand,
Stretching out the heavens,
laying the foundations of the
earth,
saying to Zion: You are my
people.

The Cup of the Lord. [17]Wake up, wake
up!
Arise, Jerusalem,
You who drank at the LORD's hand
the cup of his wrath;
Who drained to the dregs
the bowl of staggering!
[18]She has no one to guide her
of all the children she bore;
She has no one to take her by the
hand,
of all the children she reared!—
[19]Your misfortunes are double;
who is there to grieve with you?
Desolation and destruction, famine
and sword!
Who is there to comfort you?
[20]Your children lie helpless
at every street corner
like antelopes in a net.
They are filled with the wrath of
the LORD,
the rebuke of your God.

[21]But now, hear this, afflicted one,
drunk, but not with wine,

---

in creation. First, by using mythological imagery similar to that in 27:1, the prophet wants the exiles to see God as victorious in a primeval combat with the chaos monster Rahab (51:9-16). Confidence in God's power to liberate Jerusalem then is well founded. The exiles will return to Jerusalem. They should not fear what human beings can do to them because of what God promised to do for them. Their oppressors' power will end, and they will be released from captivity very soon. Using the same imagery as in 40:8, the prophet declares that God has assured Zion of its deliverance and the word of the Creator can be depended on.

²²Thus says the LORD, your Master,
  your God, who defends his
      people:
See, I am taking from your hand
  the cup of staggering;
The bowl of my wrath
  you shall no longer drink.
²³I will put it into the hands of your
    tormentors,
  those who said to you,
  "Bow down, that we may walk
      over you."
So you offered your back like the
    ground,
  like the street for them to walk
      on.

52 Let Zion Rejoice. ¹Awake, awake!
Put on your strength, Zion;
Put on your glorious garments,
  Jerusalem, holy city.
Never again shall the uncircumcised
  or the unclean enter you.
²Arise, shake off the dust,
  sit enthroned, Jerusalem;
Loose the bonds from your neck,
  captive daughter Zion!

³For thus says the LORD:
For nothing you were sold,
  without money you shall be
      redeemed.

⁴For thus says the Lord GOD:
To Egypt long ago my people went
    down,
  to sojourn there;
  Assyria, too, oppressed them for
      nought.
⁵But now, what am I to do here?
  —oracle of the LORD.
My people have been taken away
    for nothing;
  their rulers mock, oracle of the
      LORD;
  constantly, every day, my name
      is reviled.
⁶Therefore my people shall know
    my name
  on that day, that it is I who
      speaks: Here I am!
⁷How beautiful upon the
    mountains
  are the feet of the one bringing
      good news,

Second, Jerusalem, which has experienced divine judgment, should realize that judgment was not God's last word to it (51:17-23). Though Jerusalem experienced the loss of its children and military and natural disasters, there is a new day that is about to dawn. Zion will no longer have to drink the cup of judgment. That cup will pass to those nations that have been Zion's tormentors.

Finally, Zion has to rouse itself after the stupor caused by having to drink the cup of judgment (52:1-12). As it rises from the humiliation of captivity, the city will no longer be vulnerable to attack from outsiders. It will no longer be occupied by aliens nor tainted by the ritually impure. The bonds that have kept Zion captive are now falling away. The people whom God abandoned to slavery and captivity will experience the power of God's presence. The deliverance that Zion will experience will testify to the power and presence of God. Those returning from exile will bring good news to Jerusalem. From a distance, those who protect the city from surprise attack will see the procession of Jerusalem's exiles. They will be the

Announcing peace, bearing good
news,
announcing salvation, saying to
Zion,
"Your God is King!"

[8]Listen! Your sentinels raise a cry,
together they shout for joy,
For they see directly, before their
eyes,
the LORD's return to Zion.
[9]Break out together in song,
O ruins of Jerusalem!
For the LORD has comforted his
people,
has redeemed Jerusalem.
[10]The LORD has bared his holy arm
in the sight of all the nations;
All the ends of the earth can see
the salvation of our God.

[11]Depart, depart, go out from there,
touch nothing unclean!
Out from there! Purify yourselves,
you who carry the vessels of the
LORD.
[12]But not in hurried flight will you
go out,
nor leave in headlong haste,
For the LORD goes before you,
and your rear guard is the God
of Israel.

**Suffering and Triumph of the Servant
of the Lord.** [13]See, my servant shall
prosper,
he shall be raised high and
greatly exalted.
[14]Even as many were amazed at
him—
so marred were his features,
beyond that of mortals
his appearance, beyond that of
human beings—
[15]So shall he startle many nations,
kings shall stand speechless;
For those who have not been told
shall see,
those who have not heard shall
ponder it.

53 [1]Who would believe what we
have heard?
To whom has the arm of the
LORD been revealed?
[2]He grew up like a sapling before
him,
like a shoot from the parched
earth;
He had no majestic bearing to catch
our eye,
no beauty to draw us to him.
[3]He was spurned and avoided by
men,
a man of suffering, knowing
pain,

---

first to hear the good news of the city's deliverance, so they will announce
that deliverance by singing of God's great victory over the powers that kept
Zion in subjection. The people who return must make themselves ritually
clean, because they will be entering the city made holy by God's presence.

The book of Revelation assumes that the prophet's vision of a new Jerusalem will be fulfilled only at the end of this age with the descent of the
heavenly Jerusalem to earth (52:7; Rev 21:27). In Romans 10:15 Paul applies
52:7 to Christian preachers who bring the good news of Jesus to the Jews.

52:13–53:12 The Suffering Servant

After using feminine metaphors to describe the plight of Zion in some
detail in chapters 51 and 52, the prophet returns to the masculine image of

Like one from whom you turn your
face,
spurned, and we held him in no
esteem.

⁴Yet it was our pain that he bore,
our sufferings he endured.
We thought of him as stricken,
struck down by God and
afflicted,
⁵But he was pierced for our sins,
crushed for our iniquity.
He bore the punishment that makes
us whole,
by his wounds we were healed.
⁶We had all gone astray like sheep,
all following our own way;
But the LORD laid upon him
the guilt of us all.

⁷Though harshly treated, he
submitted
and did not open his mouth;
Like a lamb led to slaughter
or a sheep silent before shearers,
he did not open his mouth.
⁸Seized and condemned, he was
taken away.
Who would have thought any
more of his destiny?
For he was cut off from the land of
the living,
struck for the sins of his people.
⁹He was given a grave among the
wicked,
a burial place with evildoers,
Though he had done no wrong,
nor was deceit found in his
mouth.

---

the Servant. Taking on the persona of God, the prophet proclaims the exaltation of the servant after his total humiliation. This will happen before the eyes of the kings responsible for the servant's suffering. Again the prophet announces the end of Judah's degradation.

In 53:1, the prophet speaks in the person of the kings who are witnessing the servant's exaltation. They cannot believe what they are seeing since they considered the servant of no account, someone who could be looked upon only with contempt. The kings then make an astonishing statement in verses 4-5. These verses appear to speak of vicarious atonement, i.e., that one person can bear the sin of another so as to remove the guilt of the second person. Such an idea is found nowhere else in the Old Testament. While this does not eliminate the possibility that the prophet was speaking about vicarious suffering, it should lead one to consider other possibilities. Perhaps what the prophet's rhetoric is expressing is an idea similar to that in Lamentations 5:7, i.e., that the preexilic generation actually committed the sin, but the exiles are the ones who have to bear the consequences.

Another way to understand 53:4-5 is to see these verses as the prophet's attempt to broaden his contemporaries' understanding of their suffering beyond punishment for sin. While the prophet did affirm more than once that Jerusalem's suffering was God's judgment on its infidelity (42:18-22, 24-25; 43:24; 47:6), he also maintained that the city's punishment was out of proportion to its guilt (40:2). What then was the point of the exile?

◄ ¹⁰But it was the LORD's will to crush
    him with pain.
By making his life as a reparation
    offering,
    he shall see his offspring, shall
      lengthen his days,
and the LORD's will shall be
    accomplished through
    him.
◄ ¹¹Because of his anguish he shall see
    the light;
    because of his knowledge he
      shall be content;

My servant, the just one, shall
    justify the many,
    their iniquity he shall bear.
¹²Therefore I will give him his   ▶
    portion among the many,
and he shall divide the spoils
    with the mighty,
Because he surrendered himself to
    death,
was counted among the
    transgressors,
Bore the sins of many,
    and interceded for the
      transgressors.

Jerusalem's suffering was part of God's work in the world. The nations will see what God has done and will do for Zion and be led to join Judah in the worship of its God. The people's suffering and exaltation then enable them to be God's witnesses (43:9-10) as they fulfill their mission to be "a light to the nations" (42:6; 49:6).

The poem concludes with God speaking in the first person just as the poem began (52:13-14; 53:11-13). God describes the vindication of the servant. In fact, the poem as a whole is a dramatization of the servant's final triumph. This is reminiscent of a thanksgiving psalm, but with certain modifications. In thanksgiving psalms, the person who has been rescued speaks. Here the servant is silent. God describes the servant's vindication. Second, people listen to the testimony of the one rescued in a thanksgiving psalm, but here the people themselves testify to the marvels that they have witnessed.

Of all Isaianic texts, this one has resonated most with the Christian belief in Jesus and in the significance of his suffering and death. There are about forty citations or allusions to this text in the New Testament. This testifies to the power of the prophetic word. Matthew also cites this text in commenting on Jesus' healing of Peter's mother-in-law (Matt 8:17).

The problem of suffering is one of those issues that confronts believers in every religious tradition. It was a special problem for the first Christians, who had to make sense of the tragic death of Jesus. They found this passage especially meaningful. The prophet was able to help the exiles see that their suffering was more than a judgment upon the sins of their elders. It was the means by which Judah could fulfill its mission as a light to the nations. The prophet has articulated one of the great paradoxes of the biblical tradition: victory comes through defeat, exaltation through humiliation, life from death. This is how the first Christians came to understand the cross.

143

54 **The New Zion.** ¹Raise a glad cry,
you barren one who never bore a
child,
> break forth in jubilant song, you
> who have never been in
> labor,
For more numerous are the
> children of the deserted wife
> than the children of her who has
> a husband,
> says the LORD.
²Enlarge the space for your tent,
> spread out your tent cloths
> unsparingly;
> lengthen your ropes and make
> firm your pegs.
³For you shall spread abroad to the
> right and left;
> your descendants shall
> dispossess the nations
> and shall people the deserted
> cities.

⁴Do not fear, you shall not be put to
> shame;

do not be discouraged, you shall
> not be disgraced.
For the shame of your youth you
> shall forget,
> the reproach of your
> widowhood no longer
> remember.
⁵For your husband is your Maker;
> the LORD of hosts is his name,
Your redeemer, the Holy One of
> Israel,
> called God of all the earth.

⁶The LORD calls you back,
> like a wife forsaken and grieved
> in spirit,
A wife married in youth and then
> cast off,
> says your God.
⁷For a brief moment I abandoned
> you,
> but with great tenderness I will
> take you back.
⁸In an outburst of wrath, for a
> moment

54:1-17 Zion is reconciled with God

The focus of this passage is on reconciliation and its effects. A husband promises never again to lose his temper, never again to walk out on his wife, never again to leave her childless and humiliated. Though the cause of the rift was partly the woman's fault, the husband takes primary responsibility for the tragedy and swears that he will never again be angry with her. The reconciliation makes possible "enduring love" and a "covenant of peace" that is more lasting than the hills (54:8, 10). The woman is physically weaker and is socially and economically dependent on her husband. He has the power to punish, humiliate, and abuse her; he also has the power to make her happy and to give her dignity and freedom. He has to convince her that he really loves her and that she can trust him. The image of God painted by the prophet here is that of a husband who gives in to a temporary fit of anger but whose love of his wife is forever. Of course, Zion represents the exiles as verse 17 makes clear. Also, the verb in verse 7, translated as "I will take you back," is a technical term for the ingathering of the exiles and points to a collective interpretation of the woman.

The prophet articulates one of the great paradoxes of the biblical tradition: victory comes through defeat, life from death. This is how the first Christians came to understand the Cross. (See Isaiah 53:4:ff.)

I hid my face from you;
But with enduring love I take pity
on you,
   says the Lord, your redeemer.

9This is for me like the days of
Noah:
As I swore then that the waters of
Noah
   should never again flood the
earth,
So I have sworn now not to be
angry with you,
   or to rebuke you.
10Though the mountains fall away
and the hills be shaken,
My love shall never fall away from
you
   nor my covenant of peace be
shaken,
   says the Lord, who has mercy
on you.

11O afflicted one, storm-battered
and unconsoled,
I lay your pavements in
carnelians,
   your foundations in sapphires;
12I will make your battlements of
rubies,
   your gates of jewels,
   and all your walls of precious
stones.
13All your children shall be taught
by the Lord;
   great shall be the peace of your
children.
14In justice shall you be established,

far from oppression, you shall
not fear,
from destruction, it cannot come
near.
15If there be an attack, it is not my
doing;
   whoever attacks shall fall before
you.

16See, I have created the smith
   who blows on the burning coals
   and forges weapons as his work;
It is I also who have created
   the destroyer to work havoc.
17Every weapon fashioned against
you shall fail;
   every tongue that brings you to
trial
   you shall prove false.

This is the lot of the servants of the
Lord,
   their vindication from me—
   oracle of the Lord.

55 **An Invitation to Grace.** 1All you
who are thirsty,
   come to the water!
You who have no money,
   come, buy grain and eat;
Come, buy grain without money,
   wine and milk without cost!
2Why spend your money for what
is not bread;
   your wages for what does not
satisfy?
Only listen to me, and you shall eat
well,
   you shall delight in rich fare.

Following the lead of the Septuagint, Paul applies verse 1 to Sarah (see Gen 15), who becomes the mother of Isaac and ultimately to all the children of the promise as he applies this text to the church, the new Jerusalem (Gal 4:27-28).

55:1-13 The return to Zion

The prophet urges the exiles to return to Jerusalem. His appeal begins with an offer of food and drink to the hungry and thirsty. This food and

³Pay attention and come to me;
  listen, that you may have life.
I will make with you an everlasting
    covenant,
  the steadfast loyalty promised
      to David.
⁴As I made him a witness to peoples,
  a leader and commander of
      peoples,
⁵So shall you summon a nation you
    knew not,
  and a nation that knew you not
      shall run to you,
Because of the LORD, your God,
  the Holy One of Israel, who has
      glorified you.

⁶Seek the LORD while he may be
    found,
  call upon him while he is near.
⁷Let the wicked forsake their way,

and sinners their thoughts;
Let them turn to the LORD to find
    mercy;
  to our God, who is generous in
      forgiving.
⁸For my thoughts are not your
    thoughts,
  nor are your ways my ways—
      oracle of the LORD.
⁹For as the heavens are higher than
    the earth,
  so are my ways higher than
      your ways,
  my thoughts higher than your
      thoughts.

¹⁰Yet just as from the heavens
  the rain and snow come down
And do not return there
  till they have watered the earth,
  making it fertile and fruitful,

---

drink bring life, the source of which is the covenant made between God and those invited to the feast. While the prophet speaks of the "everlasting covenant" made with David, he does not envision the restoration of the Davidic dynasty. He transforms the Davidic covenant by asserting that the role once played by Judah's kings in the past will be fulfilled by a much wider circle in the future. The second person plural "you" in verse 3 makes it clear that the exiles, who are returning to Jerusalem, will be the witnesses to God's power. Those who accept God's invitation to the banquet (the experience of God's presence in Jerusalem) have life through the covenant, which makes God's glory shine through them.

Through the prophet, God summons the exiles to God's sanctuary in Jerusalem. But to enter the sanctuary is to enter into God's presence. Those who come into God's presence must reject patterns of inappropriate behavior (see Pss 15; 25; Isa 33:14-16). While Jerusalem is not mentioned specifically, the clear implication of this text is that an authentic encounter with God can take place only in Zion (see Jer 29:10-14). The time of exile was a special circumstance, but once Babylon has fallen, Jerusalem can be restored to its unique status in Israel. Just as all physical life on earth is dependent upon the moisture that comes from the sky, so Jerusalem's restoration is dependent upon God. But God has spoken. Zion's future is assured.

Giving seed to the one who sows
and bread to the one who eats,
[11]So shall my word be
that goes forth from my mouth;
It shall not return to me empty,
but shall do what pleases me,
achieving the end for which I
sent it.

[12]Yes, in joy you shall go forth,
in peace you shall be brought
home;
Mountains and hills shall break out
in song before you,
all trees of the field shall clap
their hands.
[13]In place of the thornbush, the
cypress shall grow,
instead of nettles, the myrtle.

This shall be to the LORD's renown,
as an everlasting sign that shall
not fail.

III. Isaiah 56–66

56 **Salvation for the Just.** [1]Thus says
the LORD:
Observe what is right, do what is
just,
for my salvation is about to
come,
my justice, about to be revealed.
[2]Happy is the one who does this,
whoever holds fast to it:
Keeping the sabbath without
profaning it,
keeping one's hand from doing
any evil.

The prophet calls the exiles to take the first steps back to Jerusalem where the Lord can be found. The desert that stands between Babylon and Judah has been stripped of its power to interfere with the glorious procession that will bring the exiles back to Zion. This is a reprise of the opening vision of the prophecy (40:3-5). The image that the prophet is creating is one which sees God at the head of a great throng of Israelites who are making their way back to their homeland after years of exile. Nature is transformed miraculously to ease their journey. They are returning to Zion where they can seek and find God (see Isa 33:20-22).

Paul quotes verse 10 as he tries to motivate the Corinthians to contribute to the collection that he is making for the poor of Jerusalem (2 Cor 9:10-11).

THE NEW JERUSALEM

Isaiah 56:1–66:24

The image of the Creator who subdued the powers of chaos, leading the exiles back to Jerusalem and initiating a glorious restoration that will amaze the nations, gives way to a more realistic picture in the final section of the book of Isaiah. Some exiles have returned to Jerusalem, but the restoration is sputtering. The prophet observes that the old social trappings are reemerging, that the people are not committed to their identity as Jews, and that their religious observance is inauthentic because it is not founded on a commitment to justice. Despite this, the prophet is still able to speak

Obligations and Promises to Share in the Covenant. ³The foreigner joined to the LORD should not say,
"The LORD will surely exclude me from his people";
Nor should the eunuch say,
"See, I am a dry tree."
⁴For thus says the LORD:
To the eunuchs who keep my sabbaths,
who choose what pleases me,
and who hold fast to my covenant,
⁵I will give them, in my house and within my walls, a monument and a name
Better than sons and daughters;
an eternal name, which shall not be cut off, will I give them.

⁶And foreigners who join themselves to the LORD,
to minister to him,
To love the name of the LORD,
to become his servants—
All who keep the sabbath without profaning it
and hold fast to my covenant,
⁷Them I will bring to my holy mountain
and make them joyful in my house of prayer;
Their burnt offerings and their sacrifices
will be acceptable on my altar,
For my house shall be called
a house of prayer for all peoples.
⁸Oracle of the Lord GOD,
who gathers the dispersed of Israel—

about the future of Jerusalem in a lyrical and expansive mode. He envisions a new Jerusalem repopulated with those who pursue righteousness and joined in the worship of Yahweh by all nations.

56:1-8 The sabbath

The prophet uses a strategy that presents sabbath observance as an element of Jewish identity and then goes on to expand the parameters of that identity. The observance of the sabbath came to have great significance in the Jewish community as an identity-marker. The preexilic markers of Judahite identity such as the national state and native dynasty were gone. Traditional practices such as sabbath observance, circumcision, and the dietary laws began to take on new significance. This passage mentions the need to keep the sabbath three times (56:2, 4, 6). It also broadens the scope of the people of God. The community, of course, includes the descendants of Abraham (see 48:1; 51:2; 63:16), but also those people who can claim no such descent but who, nonetheless, observe the sabbath and keep the covenant. God will bring these people to Jerusalem and to the temple, which is here called a "house of prayer for all peoples" (56:7; see 1 Kgs 8:41-43). God will not only bring the exiles back to Jerusalem but will call the nations to become part of God's people. What is important for inclusion among this people, then, is not physical descent from a common ancestor but careful observance of God's will.

Others will I gather to them
    besides those already gathered.

Unworthy Shepherds. ⁹All you beasts
of the field,
    come to devour,
    all you beasts in the forest!
¹⁰All the sentinels of Israel are blind,
    they are without knowledge;
They are all mute dogs,
    unable to bark;
Dreaming, reclining,
    loving their sleep.

¹¹Yes, the dogs have a ravenous
    appetite;
    they never know satiety,
Shepherds who have no
    understanding;
    all have turned their own way,
    each one covetous for gain:
¹²"Come, let me bring wine;
    let us fill ourselves with strong
      drink,
And tomorrow will be like today,
    or even greater."

Verses 3b-5 mention eunuchs, i.e., castrated males. In the monarchic period, eunuchs were members of the royal court (see 1 Sam 8:15; 1 Kgs 22:9; 2 Kgs 8:6). This passage focuses not on their social position but on their physical condition. Deuteronomic law excluded eunuchs from Judah's religious assemblies (Deut 23:1). The prophet did not. Also, eunuchs, who were afraid that they would be forgotten without descendants to remember them, are promised "a monument and a name" in the new Jerusalem. The Hebrew phrase *yad vashem* ("a monument and a name") is the title given to Jerusalem's memorial to the Holocaust. The title is inspired by verse 5 and the memorial is so named because entire families were exterminated in the Holocaust, leaving no one to remember them.

In the story of Jesus' cleansing of the temple, the Synoptic Gospels have Jesus cite verse 7 as a justification for his action, though only Mark cites that part of the prophet's words which call the temple a place of prayer "for all peoples" (Matt 21:13; Mark 11:17; Luke 19:46). But the allusion to the Isaianic text sees the universalism of the messianic age fulfilled through the proclamation of the gospel.

56:9-12 Corrupt leaders

The restored Jerusalem community was not blessed with good leadership. Too often its "watchmen" used their position to enrich themselves at the expense of those over whom they were to watch. What was worse was that their appetite had no limits. The prophet refers to them as "dogs" (56:11). This was a particularly insulting affront. Dogs were not kept as pets but were scavengers living on the outskirts of cities and towns, living off refuse and carrion. The prophet also accuses the community's leaders for toasting to their good fortune and their plans for more profits at the expense of the poor.

57 ¹The just have perished,
but no one takes it to heart;
The steadfast are swept away,
while no one understands.
Yet the just are taken away from the
presence of evil,
²and enter into peace;
They rest upon their couches,
the sincere, who walk in integrity.

An Idolatrous People. ³But you,
draw near,
you children of a sorceress,
offspring of an adulterer and a
prostitute!
⁴Against whom do you make sport,
against whom do you open
wide your mouth,
and stick out your tongue?
Are you not rebellious children,
deceitful offspring—
⁵You who burn with lust among the
oaks,
under every green tree;
You who immolate children in the
wadies,
among the clefts of the rocks?

⁶Among the smooth stones of the
wadi is your portion,
they, they are your allotment;
Indeed, you poured out a drink offering to them,
and brought up grain offerings.
With these things, should I be
appeased?
⁷Upon a towering and lofty
mountain
you set up your bed,
and there you went up to offer
sacrifice.
⁸Behind the door and the doorpost
you set up your symbol.
Yes, deserting me, you carried up
your bedding;
and spread it wide.
You entered an agreement with
them,
you loved their couch, you
gazed upon nakedness.
⁹You approached the king with oil,
and multiplied your perfumes;
You sent your ambassadors far
away,
down even to deepest Sheol.

57:1-13 Against idolatry

The prophet associates an unjust social system with the worship of other gods. He continues his criticism of a corrupt leadership class by noting that these leaders do not pay any attention to the death of just people. Their passing goes unnoticed by those whose attention is centered on their own aggrandizement. The prophet has no use for Jerusalem's religious leadership and accuses them of idolatry and associated practices including child sacrifice. The intensity of the language here makes it clear that there was a serious division in the Jewish community. Clearly the prophet aligns himself not with the leaders but with those who are oppressed by an incompetent and unjust upper class. The prophet concludes his diatribe by ridiculing idolatry. He claims that gods other than the Lord are powerless to help their worshipers. Only those who remain faithful to Israel's ancestral deity will be secure. Serving other gods is a prelude to destruction.

The prophet's words likely reflect a genuine social and religious conflict between those elements of early Jewish society who wished to remain true

¹⁰Though worn out with the length
    of your journey,
        you never said, "It is hopeless";
You found your strength revived,
    and so you did not weaken.
¹¹Whom did you dread and fear,
    that you told lies,
And me you did not remember
    nor take to heart?
Am I to keep silent and conceal,
    while you show no fear of me?
¹²I will proclaim your justice
    and your works;
        but they shall not help you.
¹³When you cry out,
    let your collection of idols save
        you.
All these the wind shall carry off,
    a mere breath shall bear them
        away;
But whoever takes refuge in me
    shall inherit the land,
        and possess my holy mountain.

The Way to Peace for God's People.
¹⁴And I say:
Build up, build up, prepare the way,
    remove every obstacle from my
        people's way.
¹⁵For thus says the high and lofty
        One,
    the One who dwells forever,
        whose name is holy:

I dwell in a high and holy place,
    but also with the contrite and
        lowly of spirit,
To revive the spirit of the lowly,
    to revive the heart of the crushed.
¹⁶For I will not accuse forever,
    nor always be angry;
For without me their spirit fails,
    the life breath that I have given.
¹⁷Because of their wicked avarice I
        grew angry;
    I struck them, hiding myself
        from them in wrath.
But they turned back, following the
        way
    of their own heart.
¹⁸I saw their ways,
    but I will heal them.
I will lead them and restore full
        comfort to them
    and to those who mourn for
        them,
¹⁹creating words of comfort.
Peace! Peace to those who are far
        and near,
    says the LORD; and I will heal
        them.
²⁰But the wicked are like the tossing
        sea
    which cannot be still,
Its waters cast up mire and mud.
²¹There is no peace for the
        wicked! says my God.

to their ancestral religious traditions and those who were ready to accommodate themselves to the political, social, and economic realities of the day. Their accommodation expresses itself in their willingness to abandon their own religious traditions in favor of those of their occupiers.

57:14-21 The two ways

Although the corrupt leadership of Judah had control of the religious symbols of Judaism (e.g., the temple of Jerusalem), the prophet assures people that God dwells with the humble and contrite. The prophet, speaking in the name of God, asserts that the road of repentance is always open to those who have abandoned their religious traditions. Still, the wicked

58 **Reasons for Judgment.** [1]Cry out
full-throated and unsparingly,
lift up your voice like a trumpet
blast;
Proclaim to my people their
transgression,
to the house of Jacob their sins.
[2]They seek me day after day,
and desire to know my ways,
Like a nation that has done what is
just
and not abandoned the
judgment of their God;
They ask of me just judgments,
they desire to draw near to God.
[3]"Why do we fast, but you do not
see it?
afflict ourselves, but you take no
note?"
See, on your fast day you carry out
your own pursuits,
and drive all your laborers.
[4]See, you fast only to quarrel and
fight
and to strike with a wicked fist!
Do not fast as you do today
to make your voice heard on
high!

[5]Is this the manner of fasting I
would choose,
a day to afflict oneself?
To bow one's head like a reed,
and lie upon sackcloth and ashes?
Is this what you call a fast,
a day acceptable to the LORD?

**Authentic Fasting That Leads to
Blessing.** [6]Is this not, rather, the fast
that I choose:
releasing those bound unjustly,
untying the thongs of the yoke;
Setting free the oppressed,
breaking off every yoke?
[7]Is it not sharing your bread with
the hungry,
bringing the afflicted and the
homeless into your
house;
Clothing the naked when you see
them,
and not turning your back on
your own flesh?
[8]Then your light shall break forth
like the dawn,
and your wound shall quickly
be healed;

---

who refuse to repent cannot expect peace from God. The contrast between the "dejected" and the wicked is reminiscent of other descriptions of the "two ways," such as Psalm 1 and Jeremiah 17:5-8. The community in Jerusalem was experiencing a recurrence of the divisions that the prophet believes led to the fall of the city and the end of its political and religious institutions. He reaffirms his belief that God is with the poor and will judge their oppressors.

58:1-12 Fasting

Jerusalem's restoration was not proceeding according to expectations. The people had been fasting to elicit God's mercy, but to no avail. In early Judaism, fasting was not an ascetical practice. It was associated with mourning. The purpose of the fasts that came into vogue during the restoration (see Zech 8:18) was to move God to pity Jerusalem and hasten the day of its complete renewal. What the prophet decries here is not the practice of

Your vindication shall go before
you,
and the glory of the LORD shall
be your rear guard.
⁹Then you shall call, and the LORD
will answer,
you shall cry for help, and he
will say: "Here I am!"
If you remove the yoke from
among you,
the accusing finger, and
malicious speech;
¹⁰If you lavish your food on the
hungry
and satisfy the afflicted;
Then your light shall rise in the
darkness,
and your gloom shall become
like midday;
¹¹Then the LORD will guide you
always
and satisfy your thirst in
parched places,
will give strength to your bones
And you shall be like a watered
garden,

like a flowing spring whose
waters never fail.
¹²Your people shall rebuild the
ancient ruins;
the foundations from ages past
you shall raise up;
"Repairer of the breach," they shall
call you,
"Restorer of ruined dwellings."

Authentic Sabbath Observance That Leads to Blessing. ¹³If you refrain from
trampling the sabbath,
from following your own
pursuits on my holy day;
If you call the sabbath a delight,
the LORD's holy day glorious;
If you glorify it by not following
your ways,
seeking your own interests, or
pursuing your own
affairs—
¹⁴Then you shall delight in the
LORD,
and I will make you ride upon
the heights of the earth;

---

fasting but the ignorance of those who engaged in this practice. After all that the people of Judah have been through, they still have not learned that God expects them to create and maintain a society of justice and equity for all. The performance of ritual actions, no matter how well intentioned, is not a substitute for such a society. As long as injustice, oppression, and internal conflicts plague Judah, the restoration will be stalled. God wants Judah to "fast" from injustice. God wants the people of means to share their food, clothing, and shelter with their brothers and sisters who lack them. When Judah becomes a society based on compassion rather than oppression, justice rather than injustice, the restoration will go forward. Until then, Judah can expect nothing but divine judgment on an unjust and uncaring society. God will honor a just society with the divine presence.

58:13-14 The sabbath

The observance of the sabbath became a significant form of Jewish self-identity following the return from Babylon. The national state and dynasty were not going to be restored. Despite encouragement and support from

I will nourish you with the heritage
of Jacob, your father,
for the mouth of the LORD has
spoken.

59 **Salvation Delayed.** ¹No, the hand of
the LORD is not too short to save,
nor his ear too dull to hear.
²Rather, it is your crimes
that separate you from your
God,
It is your sins that make him hide
his face
so that he does not hear you.
³For your hands are defiled with
blood,
and your fingers with crime;
Your lips speak falsehood,
and your tongue utters deceit.
⁴No one brings suit justly,
no one pleads truthfully;
They trust an empty plea and tell
lies;
they conceive mischief and
bring forth malice.

⁵They hatch adders' eggs,
and weave spiders' webs:
Whoever eats the eggs will die,
if one of them is crushed, it will
hatch a viper;
⁶Their webs cannot serve as clothing,
nor can they cover themselves
with their works.
Their works are evil works,
and deeds of violence are in
their hands.
⁷Their feet run to evil,
and they hasten to shed
innocent blood;
Their thoughts are thoughts of
wickedness,
violence and destruction are on
their highways.
⁸The way of peace they know not,
and there is no justice on their
paths;
Their roads they have made crooked,
no one who walks in them
knows peace.

Rom 3,15-17

---

the Persians, more than twenty years elapsed before the temple was rebuilt. The sabbath then came to have new meaning. It was not simply a day of rest; it became a symbol of commitment to Judah's ancestral religion. The prophet suggests that if the people of Judah neglect the sabbath, they are rejecting their identity as the people of God. Observance of the sabbath, then, is an essential component of Jerusalem's restoration.

59:1-21 God will establish justice

Though God has ended the power of Judah's enemies and brought back its people from exile, the restoration was a profound disappointment. What was disappointing was not the lack of God's action but the people's response to it. Instead of creating a new society, the people were at war with each other. The old social and economic divisions that tore apart Israelite society in the monarchic period were beginning to reassert themselves. This social conflict had the power to destroy Judah again as it had before.

The first step in reversing this process is the community's confession of sin. People have to take responsibility for creating a society that is self-destructive. The sad state of Judahite society is testimony to the failure of its people to incarnate the prophet's vision, a vision of a society of justice

Acknowledgment of Transgressions.

⁹That is why judgment is far from
us
and justice does not reach us.
We look for light, but there is
darkness;
for brightness, and we walk in
gloom!
¹⁰Like those who are blind we grope
along the wall,
like people without eyes we feel
our way.
We stumble at midday as if at
twilight,
among the vigorous, we are like
the dead.
¹¹Like bears we all growl,
like doves we moan without
ceasing.
We cry out for justice, but it is not
there;
for salvation, but it is far from
us.
¹²For our transgressions before you
are many,
our sins bear witness against us.
Our transgressions are present to
us,
and our crimes we acknowledge:
¹³Transgressing, and denying the
LORD,
turning back from following our
God,
Planning fraud and treachery,

uttering lying words conceived
in the heart.
¹⁴Judgment is turned away,
and justice stands far off;
For truth stumbles in the public
square,
and uprightness cannot enter.
¹⁵Fidelity is lacking,
and whoever turns from evil is
despoiled.

Divine Intervention.

The LORD saw
this, and was aggrieved
that there was no justice.
¹⁶He saw that there was no one,
was appalled that there was
none to intervene;
Then his own arm brought about
the victory,
and his justice sustained him.
¹⁷He put on justice as his breastplate,
victory as a helmet on his head;
He clothed himself with garments
of vengeance,
wrapped himself in a mantle of
zeal.
¹⁸According to their deeds he
repays his enemies
and requites his foes with wrath;
to the coastlands he renders
recompense.
¹⁹Those in the west shall fear the
name of the LORD,
and those in the east, his glory,

---

and truth. The people's failures cause God to act since God cannot ignore what the people are doing to themselves. God's judgment will come again on Jerusalem since God always acts for the sake of the oppressed. The prophet affirms that God's intention to restore Judah will not be frustrated by the people's actions. Since God has chosen Zion, God will restore Zion in spite of the failures of some of the people.

In speaking about the universal dominion of sin, Paul strings together several citations from the Old Testament, among them are verses 7-8 (Rom 3:15-17). He also uses the images of "righteousness as a breastplate" and "the helmet of salvation" (59:17) in Ephesians 6:14-17 and 1 Thessalonians 5:8.

Coming like a pent-up stream
   driven on by the breath of the
     Lord.
²⁰Then for Zion shall come a
   redeemer,
     to those in Jacob who turn from
       transgression—oracle of
       the Lord.
²¹This is my covenant with them,
   which I myself have made, says
     the Lord:
My spirit which is upon you
   and my words that I have put in
     your mouth
Shall not depart from your mouth,
   nor from the mouths of your
     children
Nor the mouths of your children's
   children
     from this time forth and forever,
     says the Lord.

60 **The Dawning of Divine Glory for Zion.** ¹Arise! Shine, for your light
has come,
   the glory of the Lord has
     dawned upon you.
²Though darkness covers the earth,
   and thick clouds, the peoples,
Upon you the Lord will dawn,
   and over you his glory will be
     seen.
³Nations shall walk by your light,
   kings by the radiance of your
     dawning.

The Nations Come to Zion. ⁴Raise
your eyes and look about;
   they all gather and come to
     you—
Your sons from afar,
   your daughters in the arms of
     their nurses.
⁵Then you shall see and be radiant,
   your heart shall throb and
     overflow.
For the riches of the sea shall be
   poured out before you,
   the wealth of nations shall come
     to you.
⁶Caravans of camels shall cover you,
   dromedaries of Midian and
     Ephah;
All from Sheba shall come
   bearing gold and frankincense,
   and heralding the praises of the
     Lord.
⁷All the flocks of Kedar shall be
   gathered for you,
   the rams of Nebaioth shall serve
     your needs;
They will be acceptable offerings on
   my altar,
   and I will glorify my glorious
     house.
⁸Who are these that fly along like a
   cloud,
   like doves to their cotes?
⁹The vessels of the coastlands are
   gathering,
   with the ships of Tarshish in the
     lead,
To bring your children from afar,
   their silver and gold with
     them—

60:1-22 The glory of the new Jerusalem

The prophet shifts abruptly from a description of Jerusalem's halting restoration to a utopian picture of the new Jerusalem. Zion here is personified as a woman basking in the glow of God's light. The city, which has been a vassal of more powerful states for more than three hundred years, will be the place from which Yahweh rules the world. In fact, the rulers of those states that held Jerusalem in subjection will serve as workmen in

For the name of the LORD, your God,
for the Holy One of Israel who has glorified you.

Honor and Service for Zion.

[10]Foreigners shall rebuild your walls,
their kings shall minister to you;
Though in my wrath I struck you,
yet in my good will I have shown you mercy.
[11]Your gates shall stand open constantly;
day and night they shall not be closed
So that they may bring you the wealth of nations,
with their kings in the vanguard.
[12]For the nation or kingdom that will not serve you shall perish;
such nations shall be utterly destroyed!
[13]The glory of Lebanon shall come to you—
the juniper, the fir, and the cypress all together—

To bring beauty to my sanctuary,
and glory to the place where I stand.
[14]The children of your oppressors shall come,
bowing before you;
All those who despised you,
shall bow low at your feet.
They shall call you "City of the LORD,"
"Zion of the Holy One of Israel."
[15]No longer forsaken and hated,
with no one passing through,
Now I will make you the pride of the ages,
a joy from generation to generation.
[16]You shall suck the milk of nations,
and be nursed at royal breasts;
And you shall know that I, the LORD, am your savior,
your redeemer, the Mighty One of Jacob.
[17]Instead of bronze I will bring gold,
instead of iron I will bring silver;
Instead of wood, bronze;
instead of stones, iron.

---

rebuilding the city's walls. The nations will contribute to the outfitting of the new temple. Prosperity and security will be the marks of "the city of Yahweh" and "Zion of the Holy One of Israel." As is clear from chapters 58–59, the prophet's vision has yet to be transformed into reality. Still, he is certain that God will bring all this about "swiftly" (60:22).

Two aspects of the prophet's vision call for comment. First is what has been described as "universalism." The nations are welcomed in Jerusalem. In fact, those nations that do not see the hand of the Lord in Zion's restoration will be no more. The surviving nations, however, are clearly subordinate to Judah. They bring their wealth to Jerusalem and serve its people. What this text reflects is not universalism but religious nationalism.

Second, a critical element in the prophet's vision is his expectation that the people of Jerusalem will be just. This is the foundation of the new Jerusalem. Gone will be the social distinctions of the past, the economic op-

I will appoint peace your governor,
and justice your ruler.
¹⁸No longer shall violence be heard
of in your land,
or plunder and ruin within your
borders.
You shall call your walls "Salvation"
and your gates "Praise."

Eternal Light for Zion. ¹⁹No longer
shall the sun
be your light by day,
Nor shall the brightness of the
moon
give you light by night;
Rather, the LORD will be your light
forever,
your God will be your glory.
²⁰No longer will your sun set,
or your moon wane;
For the LORD will be your light
forever,
and the days of your grieving
will be over.
²¹Your people will all be just;
for all time they will possess the
land;

They are the shoot that I planted,
the work of my hands, that I
might be glorified.
²²The least one shall become a clan,
the smallest, a mighty nation;
I, the LORD, will swiftly accomplish
these things when the time
comes.

61 The Anointed Bearer of Glad Tidings.
¹The spirit of the Lord GOD is upon ▶
me,
because the LORD has anointed
me;
He has sent me to bring good news
to the afflicted,
to bind up the brokenhearted,
To proclaim liberty to the captives,
release to the prisoners,
²To announce a year of favor from
the LORD
and a day of vindication by our
God;
To comfort all who mourn;
³to place on those who mourn in
Zion
a diadem instead of ashes,

---

pression, and the political domination of the poor by the people of means. This new society will be God's doing. Of course, the prophet recognizes that this new society is a long way from being realized. It is not surprising that the book of Revelation uses this text to speak about the heavenly Jerusalem (60:3, 11, 19; Rev 21:23, 25-26).

61:1-3 The prophet's mission

Isaiah describes his mission in terms of justice for the oppressed in language similar to 42:1-4, 49:1-6, and 50:4-11. While the "captives" are the people of Judah still in exile in Babylon, the prophet certainly sees his mission in broader terms. The "afflicted" and the "brokenhearted" in verse 1 are the victims of the corrupt and incompetent leadership that the prophet condemned in 56:9-12 and 58:1-9. Here he comes back to a significant Isaianic motif: justice for the poor. Judah is condemned to exile because of the injustice of its economic and social system. God will recreate Judahite society according to justice, and the prophet has a central role in the working out of God's plan.

To give them oil of gladness instead
of mourning,
a glorious mantle instead of a
faint spirit.

Restoration and Blessing. They will
be called oaks of justice,
the planting of the LORD to
show his glory.
⁴They shall rebuild the ancient ruins,
the former wastes they shall
raise up
And restore the desolate cities,
devastations of generation upon
generation.

⁵Strangers shall stand ready to
pasture your flocks,
foreigners shall be your farmers
and vinedressers.
⁶You yourselves shall be called
"Priests of the LORD,"
"Ministers of our God" you
shall be called.
You shall eat the wealth of the
nations
and in their riches you will
boast.
⁷Because their shame was twofold
and disgrace was proclaimed
their portion,

"The Spirit of the LORD" is a characteristic Isaianic expression used to describe the presence and power of God in the world. The prophet uses this phrase to underscore his belief that Jerusalem's liberation and restoration are the work of God, not a human achievement. Jerusalem's future will not be determined by any king, Judahite or Persian. It will be the result of miraculous transformation of society. Though the prophet has a role in that transformation, he exercises that role only because of the anointing of God's Spirit on his life.

Luke has Jesus read this text during synagogue worship and then assert that it had been fulfilled in him (Luke 4:17-19). The evangelist reflects the early Christian belief that God's Spirit has been poured out upon Jesus in a unique way to accomplish the divine plan that will effect the salvation of Israel and the nations. Luke believes that the prophet's vision was fulfilled in Jesus—but fulfilled in a way that far exceeded the prophet's profoundest hopes and wildest expectations.

61:4-11 The priesthood of the poor

The prophet does not describe the political and religious institutions of the new Jerusalem in any detail as Ezekiel does. He prefers language that is more evocative than descriptive. For example, the prophet implies that in the new Jerusalem the role of the king will be taken by the people as a whole (55:3-5). Did this mean that the prophet did not envision the restoration of Judah's native dynasty? Here the prophet speaks to the people of the new Jerusalem and asserts that they "shall be named priests of the Lord" (61:6). Does this mean that he did not envision the restoration of the Zadokite priesthood, the descendants of Aaron and keepers of the temple,

They will possess twofold in their own land;
everlasting joy shall be theirs.

God's Word of Promise. [8]For I, the LORD, love justice,
I hate robbery and wrongdoing;
I will faithfully give them their recompense,
an everlasting covenant I will make with them.
[9]Their offspring shall be renowned among the nations,
and their descendants in the midst of the peoples;
All who see them shall acknowledge them:
"They are offspring the LORD has blessed."

Thanksgiving for God's Deliverance.
[10]I will rejoice heartily in the LORD,
my being exults in my God;
For he has clothed me with garments of salvation,
and wrapped me in a robe of justice,
Like a bridegroom adorned with a diadem,
as a bride adorns herself with her jewels.
[11]As the earth brings forth its shoots,
and a garden makes its seeds spring up,
So will the Lord GOD make justice spring up,
and praise before all the nations.

---

to its unique position in the new Jerusalem? What the prophet describes is the priestly role that the people of the new Jerusalem will play in regard to the nations. These "priests" will lead the nations to serve Judah's God. The rebuilding of the temple and the renewal of priestly service do not appear to be priorities for the prophet. What is more significant for him is the renewal of Judahite society on the basis of justice. A just society brings with it God's blessing and is the embodiment of the covenant between God and Jerusalem.

The prophet understands his mission to Israel to be the creation of a just society, one that will be the envy of the whole world. God has anointed him, i.e., designated him solemnly to overcome the social problems that are keeping Judah from becoming the type of community that can enjoy all God's benefits. Once that new society is created, the people can proceed with the restoration of their villages and cities that were devastated by Judah's political, military, and economic collapse.

Judah can free itself from foreign domination by creating a new society without religious hierarchy and social status. All the people will be priests and all the people will have access to the wealth with which God has blessed Judah. This new society will turn Judah's oppressors into its servants. This new society will bring wealth to its entire people. This new society is precisely what God wants Judah to establish. God will make an everlasting covenant with that new, just community, not with people who are devouring themselves through internal societal conflicts.

161

62 A New Name for Zion.

¹For Zion's sake I will not be silent,
for Jerusalem's sake I will not keep still,
Until her vindication shines forth like the dawn
and her salvation like a burning torch.
²Nations shall behold your vindication,
and all kings your glory;
You shall be called by a new name bestowed by the mouth of the LORD.
³You shall be a glorious crown in the hand of the LORD,
a royal diadem in the hand of your God.
⁴No more shall you be called "Forsaken,"
nor your land called "Desolate,"
But you shall be called "My Delight is in her,"
and your land "Espoused."
For the LORD delights in you,
and your land shall be espoused.
⁵For as a young man marries a virgin,
your Builder shall marry you;
And as a bridegroom rejoices in his bride
so shall your God rejoice in you.
⁶Upon your walls, Jerusalem,
I have stationed sentinels;
By day and by night,
they shall never be silent.
You who are to remind the LORD, take no rest,
⁷And give him no rest,
until he re-establishes Jerusalem
And makes it the praise of the earth.

The book of Revelation asserts that the members of the Christian community are priests serving their God, thus fulfilling the prophet's vision (61:6; Rev 1:6; 5:10). The Magnificat, Mary's song in Luke, is a collage of Old Testament text that begins with a paraphrase of verse 10 (Luke 1:46).

62:1-5 The new Jerusalem: The Lord's Bride

The prophet recognizes that his vision of a new Jerusalem has not been realized. Instead of retracting or modifying his argument, he restates his points in a more forceful fashion. There will be a new Jerusalem for all peoples to see. Then using feminine grammatical forms for Jerusalem, the prophet addresses the city and asserts that it will be Yahweh's queen. The city's reversal of fortunes will be marked by its new names: "My Delight" and "Espoused" (62:4). The prophet exploits the image of Jerusalem as a woman to speak about the city's coming restoration and glorification. God is being reconciled with Jerusalem as a husband is reconciled with his estranged wife. This union will bring fertility to the land and the rebuilding of the city.

62:6-12 Daughter Zion

The prophet calls upon the people of Jerusalem to remind the Lord of the promises made to Jerusalem. They are to be so intemperate in their pleading that God will have no rest from their petitions. He concludes this

The Blessings of Salvation for God's People. ⁸The Lord has sworn by his
right hand
and by his mighty arm:
No more will I give your grain
as food to your enemies;
Nor shall foreigners drink the wine,
for which you toiled.
⁹But those who harvest shall eat,
and praise the Lord;
Those who gather shall drink
in my holy courts.
¹⁰Pass through, pass through the
gates,
prepare a way for the people;
Build up, build up the highway,
clear it of stones,
raise up a standard over the
nations.
¹¹The Lord has proclaimed
to the ends of the earth:
Say to daughter Zion,
"See, your savior comes!
See, his reward is with him,
his recompense before him."
¹²They shall be called "The Holy
People,"
"The Redeemed of the Lord."
And you shall be called "Cared For,"
"A City Not Forsaken."

63 **The Divine Warrior.** ¹Who is this
that comes from Edom,
in crimsoned garments, from
Bozrah?
Who is this, glorious in his apparel,
striding in the greatness of his
strength?
"It is I, I who announce vindication,
mighty to save."
²Why is your apparel red,
and your garments like one who
treads the wine press?
³"The wine press I have trodden
alone,
and from the peoples no one
was with me.
I trod them in my anger,
and trampled them down in my
wrath;
Their blood spurted on my
garments,
all my apparel I stained.
⁴For a day of vindication was in my
heart,
my year for redeeming had
come.
⁵I looked about, but there was no
one to help,
I was appalled that there was no
one to lend support;

---

chapter by assuring "daughter Zion" that her salvation is coming. The
prophet addressed these words to people who considered themselves heirs
to the promises made about the restoration of Judah, the liberation of Jerusalem, and the reversal of the fortunes of the poor. Though the prophet's
visions have not come to fulfillment, he refuses to abandon them. While
Jerusalem and Judah were economically depressed and politically impotent, the prophet speaks of the city's splendor. While that splendor is yet
to be revealed, it is coming. The prophet can see God coming; he can see
the new Jerusalem.

63:1-6 The Lord, the warrior

It is hard to imagine a more stunning shift in mood than the one that
occurs here. The prophet leaves behind the poignant image of a husband
reconciling with his wife. In this passage, God is a warrior returning from

163

So my own arm brought me victory
and my own wrath lent me
support.
⁶I trampled down the peoples in
my anger,
I made them drunk in my
wrath,
and I poured out their blood
upon the ground."

Prayer for the Return of God's Favor.
⁷The loving deeds of the LORD I will
recall,
the glorious acts of the LORD,
Because of all the LORD has done
for us,
the immense goodness to the
house of Israel,
Which he has granted according to
his mercy
and his many loving deeds.
⁸He said: "They are indeed my
people,
children who are not disloyal."
So he became their savior
⁹in their every affliction.
It was not an envoy or a messenger,
but his presence that saved
them.
Because of his love and pity
the LORD redeemed them,
Lifting them up and carrying them

all the days of old.
¹⁰But they rebelled
and grieved his holy spirit;
So he turned to become their enemy,
and warred against them.

¹¹Then they remembered the days of old,
of Moses, his servant:

Where is the one who brought up
out of the sea
the shepherd of his flock?
Where is the one who placed in
their midst
his holy spirit,
¹²Who guided Moses by the hand,
with his glorious arm?
Where is the one who divided the
waters before them—
winning for himself an
everlasting renown—
¹³Who guided them through the
depths,
like horses in open country?
¹⁴As cattle going down into the
valley,
they did not stumble.
The spirit of the LORD guided
them.
Thus you led your people,
to make for yourself a glorious
name.

---

the battlefield with his clothes soaked with the blood of the enemy. Edom and its capital Bozrah symbolize the forces pressuring Judah and preventing the restoration from proceeding as the prophet envisioned it. But God is determined to restore Judah so that a new, just society can emerge there. God will not allow any interference. Any nation that stands in the way of Judah's restoration will be subject to God's judgment and swept aside. God will accomplish this without the help of anyone—least of all Judah itself which has yet to create the kind of society that God is making possible.

In speaking of the final battle with the powers of evil, the book of Revelation describes the coat of the rider on the white horse as "dipped in blood," implying that the prophet's words will find their fulfillment at the end of this age (63:1; Rev 19:13).

¹⁵Look down from heaven and
regard us
from your holy and glorious
palace!
Where is your zealous care and
your might,
your surge of pity?
Your mercy hold not back!
¹⁶For you are our father.
Were Abraham not to know us,
nor Israel to acknowledge us,
You, LORD, are our father,
our redeemer you are named
from of old.
¹⁷Why do you make us wander,
LORD, from your ways,
and harden our hearts so that
we do not fear you?
Return for the sake of your
servants,
the tribes of your heritage.
¹⁸Why have the wicked invaded
your holy place,
why have our enemies trampled
your sanctuary?
¹⁹Too long have we been like those
you do not rule,
on whom your name is not
invoked.
Oh, that you would rend the
heavens and come down,
with the mountains quaking
before you,

64 ¹As when brushwood is set
ablaze,
or fire makes the water boil!
Then your name would be made
known to your enemies

and the nations would tremble
before you,
²While you worked awesome deeds
we could not hope for,
³such as had not been heard of
from of old.
No ear has ever heard, no eye ever
seen,
any God but you
working such deeds for those
who wait for him.
⁴Would that you might meet us
doing right,
that we might be mindful of you
in our ways!
Indeed, you are angry; we have
sinned,
we have acted wickedly.
⁵We have all become like something
unclean,
all our just deeds are like
polluted rags;
We have all withered like leaves,
and our crimes carry us away
like the wind.
⁶There are none who call upon your
name,
none who rouse themselves to
take hold of you;
For you have hidden your face
from us
and have delivered us up to our
crimes.

A Final Plea. ⁷Yet, LORD, you are our
father;
we are the clay and you our
potter:
we are all the work of your hand.

63:7–64:11 A lament

The prophet shifts moods again as he prays for the restoration of Jerusalem. The prophet adopts the lament form which tries to move God to act by reminding God of acts on Israel's behalf in the past and then by describing the difficulties experienced by Zion.

⁸Do not be so very angry, Lord,
    do not remember our crimes
      forever;
    look upon us, who are all your
      people!
⁹Your holy cities have become a
    wilderness;
    Zion has become wilderness,
      Jerusalem desolation!

¹⁰Our holy and glorious house
    in which our ancestors praised
      you
Has been burned with fire;
    all that was dear to us is laid
      waste.
¹¹Can you hold back, Lord, after all
    this?
    Can you remain silent, and
      afflict us so severely?

The prophet begins by singing of God's actions for Judah. God has been faithful, loving, and good to Israel. The people of Israel are God's people, so God suffered when they suffered and God saved them when they were about to be extinguished. Despite this, Judah has still continued its path of self-destruction. God did not abandon Judah to its fate but acted toward it as God did toward the exodus generation. That generation too failed to respond faithfully toward the marvelous deeds that God worked for them in freeing them from slavery in Egypt. They murmured in the wilderness. Still, God saved them through Moses. God saved them from themselves.

Just as Moses interceded for the freed but rebellious Hebrew slaves, so the prophet intercedes for the freed but rebellious exiles and their descendants. The prophet calls God the "Father" of the Judahites because their ancient ancestors Abraham and Jacob will not acknowledge them. The prophet is mystified by his people's pattern of rebellion and asks God to be Judah's king by rebuilding the temple so that Judah can once again call on God's name in God's sanctuary. The prophet's cry that God "rend the heavens and come down" (63:19) asks God to take immediate and decisive action to establish the new Jerusalem.

In chapter 64, the prophet continues his prayer on Judah's behalf, pleading that the people experience God's presence and power as their ancestors did long before. The prophet is confident because God saves those who are righteous. Still, the prophet's overwhelming fear is that Israel's infidelity and sin have the power to keep God from restoring Judah. Zion now experiences God's absence because of its infidelity.

The prophet uses all his skill to move God to compassion and forgiveness. The people are God's creation. Can God continue to ignore the fate of the chosen people? Jerusalem and its temple have been devastated. Can God continue to allow these to remain in ruins? God should not allow this terrible situation to continue. Forgiveness and restoration are what the prophet asks of God. In assessing the reasons for the failure of the restora-

"Lord, you are our father; we are the clay and you our potter: we are all the work of your hand." (See Isaiah 64:7.)

65 ¹I was ready to respond to those
who did not ask,
    to be found by those who did
      not seek me.
I said: Here I am! Here I am!
    To a nation that did not invoke
      my name.
²I have stretched out my hands all
    day
    to a rebellious people,
Who walk in a way that is not
    good,
    following their own designs;
³A people who provoke me
    continually to my face,
Offering sacrifices in gardens
    and burning incense on bricks,
⁴Sitting in tombs
    and spending the night in caves,
Eating the flesh of pigs,
    with broth of unclean meat in
      their dishes;
⁵Crying out, "Hold back,
    do not come near me, lest I
      render you holy!"
These things are smoke in my
    nostrils,
    a fire that burns all the day.
⁶See, it stands written before me;

I will not remain quiet until I
    have repaid in full
⁷Your crimes and the crimes of your
    ancestors as well,
    says the LORD.
Since they burned incense on the
    mountains,
    and insulted me on the hills,
I will at once pour out in full
    measure
    their recompense into their laps.

Fate of the Just and Unjust in Israel.
    ⁸Thus says the LORD:
As when the juice is pressed from a
    cluster,
    and someone says, "Do not
      destroy it,
    for there is still good in it,"
So will I do for the sake of my
    servants:
    I will not destroy them all.
⁹From Jacob I will bring forth
    offspring,
    from Judah, those who are to
      possess my mountains;
My chosen ones shall possess the
    land,
    my servants shall dwell there.

---

tion, the prophet does not find fault with God but with Judah (64:5), and so has the people confess their sins. Similar confessions became common in early Jewish prayer (e.g., Neh 9:1-37). Also, the prophet does not approach God as a righteous judge who must deal with Judah's sins, but as a father whose love for his erring children remains constant (63:16).

Jesus used this image of God frequently and the prayer that he taught his disciples addresses God as "our father" just as Isaiah's prayer does (see Matt 5:9). In speaking about the spiritual wisdom of the believer, Paul imitates the language of 64:3 (see 1 Cor 2:9).

65:1-16 God's response

The preceding prayer tried to move God to action, but, speaking in the name of God, the prophet affirms that God has always been ready to act. The Judahites themselves ignored their God. But they have done more

¹⁰Sharon shall become a pasture for
    the flocks,
    the Valley of Achor a resting
        place for the cattle,
    for my people who have sought
      me.
¹¹But you who forsake the LORD,
    who forget my holy mountain,
Who spread a table for Fortune
    and fill cups of mixed wine for
      Destiny,
¹²You I will destine for the sword;
    you shall all bow down for
      slaughter;
Because I called and you did not
      answer,
    I spoke and you did not listen,
But did what is evil in my sight
    and things I do not delight in,
      you chose,
¹³therefore thus says the Lord
    GOD:
My servants shall eat,

but you shall go hungry;
My servants shall drink,
    but you shall be thirsty;
My servants shall rejoice,
    but you shall be put to shame;
¹⁴My servants shall shout
    for joy of heart,
But you shall cry out for grief of
    heart,
    and howl for anguish of spirit.
¹⁵You will leave your name for a
    curse to my chosen ones
    when the Lord GOD slays you,
    and calls his servants by another
      name.
¹⁶Whoever invokes a blessing in the
    land
    shall bless by the God of truth;
Whoever takes an oath in the land
    shall swear by the God of truth;
For the hardships of the past shall
    be forgotten
    and hidden from my eyes.

---

than this. They have provoked God through aberrant religious practices including the violation of dietary laws that, along with sabbath observance and circumcision, became the marks of Jewish self-identity. By ignoring the dietary laws, some Judahites effectively placed themselves outside the Jewish community. There is only one possible response: divine judgment. Judah experienced it in the past; it will experience it anew. But there are those in the community whom the prophet calls God's "servants." These will not experience judgment but the blessings of the land that will provide what is necessary for their survival, food, and drink.

The Judahites then will not have a single destiny. There are those who "walk in evil paths," and there are God's "servants." Each group will have its own destiny in accordance with its response to the God who freed the exiles of Zion. There are two ways: one leads to life and the other to death. The prophet reminds the wicked what they have to look forward to.

In verses 1-2, the prophet is speaking about God's intention to seek out those Jews who have given up their ancestral religion; Paul applies these verses to the Gentiles whom God has "sought out" through Paul's mission (Rom 10:20).

A World Renewed. ¹⁷See, I am creating
new heavens
and a new earth;
The former things shall not be
remembered
nor come to mind.
¹⁸Instead, shout for joy and be glad
forever
in what I am creating.
Indeed, I am creating Jerusalem to
be a joy
and its people to be a delight;
¹⁹I will rejoice in Jerusalem
and exult in my people.
No longer shall the sound of
weeping be heard there,
or the sound of crying;
²⁰No longer shall there be in it
an infant who lives but a few
days,
nor anyone who does not live a
full lifetime;
One who dies at a hundred years
shall be considered a youth,
and one who falls short of a
hundred shall be thought
accursed.
²¹They shall build houses and live
in them,

they shall plant vineyards and
eat their fruit;
²²They shall not build and others
live there;
they shall not plant and others
eat.
As the years of a tree, so the years
of my people;
and my chosen ones shall long
enjoy
the work of their hands.
²³They shall not toil in vain,
nor beget children for sudden
destruction;
For they shall be a people blessed
by the LORD
and their descendants with them.
²⁴Before they call, I will answer;
while they are yet speaking, I
will hear.
²⁵The wolf and the lamb shall
pasture together,
and the lion shall eat hay like
the ox—
but the serpent's food shall be
dust.
None shall harm or destroy
on all my holy mountain, says
the LORD.

65:17-25 The new world

The Jerusalem that the prophet envisions is clearly not the city he lives in. It will be part of the new world that God is about to bring into existence. The prophet concluded that this world would not be the place of the ultimate triumph of God's justice. God will create a new world and, of course, a new Jerusalem. This is the first step in the direction of Revelation's "new Jerusalem, coming down out of heaven" (Rev 21:1-3). The new Jerusalem that the prophet expects will be a joy and a delight, not the feeble and forlorn city of this world.

For the prophet, Jerusalem has become a symbol of the new world that God will bring into existence. It is a world in which there will be no infant mortality. People will live into old age. They will enjoy their homes and vineyards and their children will grow into honorable adulthood. God

66 True and False Worship.

¹Thus says the LORD:

The heavens are my throne,
the earth, my footstool.
What house can you build for me?
Where is the place of my rest?
²My hand made all these things
when all of them came to be—
oracle of the LORD.
This is the one whom I approve:
the afflicted one, crushed in
spirit,
who trembles at my word.
³The one slaughtering an ox,
striking a man,
sacrificing a lamb, breaking a
dog's neck,
Making an offering of pig's blood,
burning incense, honoring an
idol—
These have chosen their own ways,
and taken pleasure in their own
abominations.
⁴I in turn will choose affliction for
them
and bring upon them what they
fear.
Because when I called, no one
answered,
when I spoke, no one listened.
Because they did what was evil in
my sight,
and things I do not delight in
they chose,
⁵Hear the word of the LORD,
you who tremble at his word!
Your kin who hate you
and cast you out because of my
name say,
"May the LORD show his glory,
that we may see your joy";
but they shall be put to shame.

will answer their prayers before they finish making them. In short, this passage describes a perfect world where "the wolf and the lamb pasture together"(65:25), the kind of world the lyrical text of Isaiah 11:6-9 imagines. The utopian visions of chapters 11 and 65 were born of the disappointments experienced by the people of Jerusalem at very difficult periods of their lives. The disappointment of the Jerusalem community made it possible for texts such as 2 Peter 3:13 to reinterpret the prophet's vision of the "new heavens and a new earth" (65:17, see also Isa 66:22) as coming when Jesus returns.

66:1-6 Worship and justice

This text severs the fate of Jerusalem from that of the temple. Verses 1-6 are as negative a statement on temple worship as is found in the Bible. Together with 1:10-20 they frame the book of Isaiah and suggest that one goal of the final form of the book as a whole reflected a conflict within the early Jewish community. On one side were the priests who believed that the rituals of the temple were the guarantees of Israel's future. On the other side were those who believed that a just social and moral order was more significant than any ritual. Verse 5 is a clear reference to that conflict, and the following verse asserts that those for whom the temple is so important will hear the voice of the Lord who comes to redress the injustices done to the poor.

⁶A voice roaring from the city,
a voice from the temple;
The voice of the LORD
rendering recompense to his
enemies!

**Blessings of Prosperity and
Consolation.** ⁷Before she is in labor,
she gives birth;
Before her pangs come upon her,
she delivers a male child.
⁸Who ever heard of such a thing,
or who ever saw the like?
Can a land be brought forth in one
day,
or a nation be born in a single
moment?
Yet Zion was scarcely in labor
when she bore her children.
⁹Shall I bring a mother to the point
of birth,
and yet not let her child be
born? says the LORD.
Or shall I who bring to birth
yet close her womb? says your
God.
¹⁰Rejoice with Jerusalem and be
glad because of her,
all you who love her;
Rejoice with her in her joy,
all you who mourn over her—
¹¹So that you may nurse and be
satisfied
from her consoling breast;

That you may drink with delight
at her abundant breasts!
¹²For thus says the LORD:
I will spread prosperity over her
like a river,
like an overflowing torrent,
the wealth of nations.
You shall nurse, carried in her
arms,
cradled upon her knees;
¹³As a mother comforts her child,
so I will comfort you;
in Jerusalem you shall find your
comfort.
¹⁴You will see and your heart shall
exult,
and your bodies shall flourish
like the grass;
The LORD's power shall be revealed
to his servants,
but to his enemies, his wrath.
¹⁵For see, the LORD will come in fire,
his chariots like the stormwind;
To wreak his anger in burning rage
and his rebuke in fiery flames.
¹⁶For with fire the LORD shall enter
into judgment,
and, with his sword, against all
flesh;
Those slain by the LORD shall be
many.

¹⁷Those who sanctify and purify themselves to go into the gardens, following

---

The imagery of verse 1 must have passed into Jewish religious speech since Jesus calls heaven God's "throne" and the earth God's "footstool" (Matt 5:35; 23:22). Stephen cites verses 1-2 to argue that the building of the temple by Solomon was a mistake (Acts 7:49-50).

66:7-17 Jerusalem, our mother

Once Jerusalem is free from those who look to ritual as support for their injustice, Jerusalem will be able to fulfill its destiny as a mother to all believers. After God's judgment has purged the guilty, Jerusalem will give birth miraculously to many children "in a single moment" (66:8).

one who stands within, eating pig's flesh, abominable things, and mice, shall all together come to an end, with their deeds and purposes—oracle of the LORD.

God Gathers the Nations. [18]I am coming to gather all nations and tongues; they shall come and see my glory. [19]I will place a sign among them; from them I will send survivors to the nations: to Tarshish, Put and Lud, Mosoch, Tubal and Javan, to the distant coastlands which have never heard of my fame, or seen my glory; and they shall proclaim my glory among the nations. [20]They shall bring all your kin from all the nations as an offering to the LORD, on horses and in chariots, in carts, upon mules and dromedaries, to Jerusalem, my holy mountain, says the LORD, just as the Israelites bring their grain offering in a clean vessel to the house of the LORD. [21]Some of these I will take as priests and Levites, says the LORD.

[22]Just as the new heavens and the
new earth
which I am making
Shall endure before me—oracle of
the LORD—
so shall your descendants and
your name endure.
[23]From new moon to new moon,
and from sabbath to sabbath,
All flesh shall come to worship
before me, says the LORD.
[24]They shall go out and see the
corpses
of the people who rebelled
against me;
For their worm shall not die,
their fire shall not be
extinguished;
and they shall be an abhorrence
to all flesh.

The picture of "mother Zion" surrounded by her children is followed by another announcement of judgment on those who have perverted temple worship. Here the prophet concludes the transformation of Jerusalem from the woman who "was dismissed" (50:1) by her husband to the woman reunited with him and becoming a mother to his children.

66:18-24 The pilgrimage of the nations

The book of Isaiah ends with a familiar Isaianic theme: the pilgrimage of the nations to Jerusalem. They will join Israel in worship at "Yahweh's house," where new priests and Levites will replace those who have been purged because of their venality. This is a part of the new world that God is creating to effect the restoration of Israel—a restoration that will include all humanity except those who have rebelled. Jesus uses the imagery of verse 24 to speak about the punishment of those who lead others into sin (Mark 9:48).

The book ends on a negative note as it speaks about the fate of those who rebel against God. In rabbinic tradition, the public reading of the book of Isaiah concludes with the repetition of verse 23 to leave the hearers on a note of promise, not judgment.

173

REVIEW AIDS AND DISCUSSION TOPICS

Introduction *(pages 5–9)*

1. What is the significance of the book of Isaiah in Judaism?

2. How have Christians tied the book of Isaiah to the life, death, and resurrection of Jesus? As you read the book of Isaiah, keep a list of the passages that you have heard used as predictions of the arrival of Jesus as the very presence of God come to save Israel.

3. What theme in Isaiah contributed to doctrine issued by the Second Vatican Council?

4. What three periods of Israel's history are covered by the book of Isaiah?

5. How is the message from Isaiah regarding the Babylonian exile and return to Jerusalem different from other prophets and the books of the Deuteronomic History?

6. How is the book of Isaiah related to the books of Daniel and Revelation?

Jerusalem's future: Isaiah 1:1–12:6 *(pages 11–43)*

1. Chapter 1: What is the meaning of the name "Isaiah" and how might it relate to his message?

2. We are told that 1:9 introduces an important theme in the book: "the remnant," a group saved or spared judgment to carry on as the chosen people. What are your associations with this term? What might be dangerous about it? Why might it be used in this book?

3. Make a list of Israel's wrongdoings. On what basis will God judge Israel and punish the people with exile?

4. Chapter 2: What is the ultimate future God has planned for Jerusalem and Judah?

5. Chapter 6: What verse becomes an important text recited by the people during Mass? Isaiah is quoted in the New Testament more than any other book but Psalms. It is also the source for Handel's *Messiah*, which is heard often at Christmas. Be aware of other passages that are familiar and think about how they work in their original and new contexts.

6. Chapter 6: Make a list of the elements of Isaiah's "call." What does this passage tell you about Isaiah? What does it tell you about the God who called him?

7. Verse 6:10: The idea of open or closed eyes and ears recurs often in the New Testament. Why might the prophecy of Isaiah be hard for the people of Judah and Israel to hear and understand?

8. Chapter 7: Who is Immanuel? What is suggested by the use of this passage in Matthew 1:22-23?

9. Chapter 10: What is God's attitude toward power in the case of the people of Israel and the nation of Assyria?

10. Chapter 12: Why do you think this part ends with a hymn of praise and thanksgiving?

Jerusalem and the nations: Isaiah 13:1–27:13 *(pages 44–72)*

1. What is the importance of Babylon to the history of Israel?

2. Compare the oracle against Babylon in chapters 13:1–14:22 and chapter 21 with Revelation 18. What are their similarities? What are the differences?

3. Why do you think Isaiah spent so much time outlining the judgment against the nations?

4. Chapter 14 tells of the fall of a tyrant. In literature this tyrant has become "Lucifer," the devil, a fallen angel. What do you think of this interpretation?

5. Chapters 24–27: These chapters are often called the "Isaiah Apocalypse." For the people of the Babylonian exile, it must certainly have felt like the end of the world was near. What elements of the poetry here appeal to you? Where is the vision of hope in all this destruction? Why might this text appeal to oppressed people today?

Jerusalem's judgment and salvation: Isaiah 28:1–39:8 *(pages 73–103)*

1. Identify the message of social justice in these chapters. What kind of kingdom will God destroy and what kind of kingdom will be raised in its place?

2. What is the effect of reading these alternating accounts of judgment and salvation?

3. Chapter 35:1-10: Verses in this passage are found in at least six places in the New Testament, including Matthew, Mark, and Luke's Gospels, Acts, Hebrews, and Revelation. Can you identify why these verses are associated with Jesus?

4. Read 2 Kings 18:13–20:19 and compare it to Isaiah 36:1–37:9a. How do you account for the differences?

5. What is the primary message from Isaiah about the exile in Babylon?

Jerusalem's liberation: Isaiah 40:1–55:13 *(pages 103–148)*

1. Trace the two metaphors through these chapters: the servant and the woman Zion. How is the prophet using them? Why do you think the servant metaphor is associated with Jesus in the New Testament?

2. What images and names of God do these chapters contribute? Which ones have the most meaning for you? How can they be used in contemplation and prayer?

3. Chapters 41–42: What is the mission of the servant?

4. How are we to understand the military imagery in chapter 42? How does it work with or against the image of God as a woman in labor in the same chapter?

5. Chapters 43–44 and 48: Why does Isaiah use the exodus story in his account of the judgment and salvation of Israel?

6. Chapters 40:12-31 and 42:6-22: In these two places, Isaiah criticizes the nations for worshiping idols made of wood and iron. How do we understand the place of images and statues in Christian worship? What is the prophet's message about the difference between the nations' gods and the God of Israel?

7. Who is Cyrus? What role does he play in God's plan of salvation?

8. What does the term "messiah" mean? Can there be more than one?

9. Chapter 48: How does the prophet see his own role?

10. Chapter 49: What are the family metaphors in this chapter (mother, father, child, bride, etc.)? How are they being used?

11. What are the feminine metaphors in chapters 51–52? How do they expand our concept of who God is and how God acts?

12. How are the domestic images of these chapters resolved in chapter 54?

13. What action does the prophet want the exiles to take? How might this apply to oppressed people of other times and places?

The new Jerusalem: Isaiah 56:1–66:24 *(pages 148–173)*

1. How does the postexilic community in Jerusalem match up to the prophet's predictions of a new Jerusalem?

2. What role do sabbath observance, circumcision, and dietary restrictions play in the new community?

3. Chapter 58: What might it mean to "fast from injustice"? How might we enact such a fast today?

4. How does the prophet describe sin in chapter 59?

5. How does our current community of faith and secular community reflect the vision of Isaiah? What are we called to do to make the new Jerusalem a reality?

6. What do these chapters suggest is the role of the people and what is the role of God in bringing about a just society and a new world?

INDEX OF CITATIONS FROM THE
CATECHISM OF THE CATHOLIC CHURCH

The arabic number(s) following the citation refer(s) to the paragraph number(s)
in the *Catechism of the Catholic Church.*

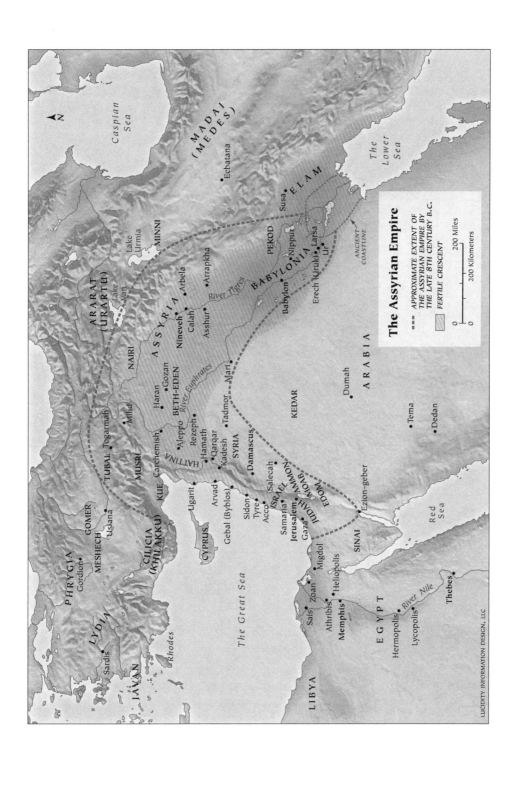

The Assyrian Empire

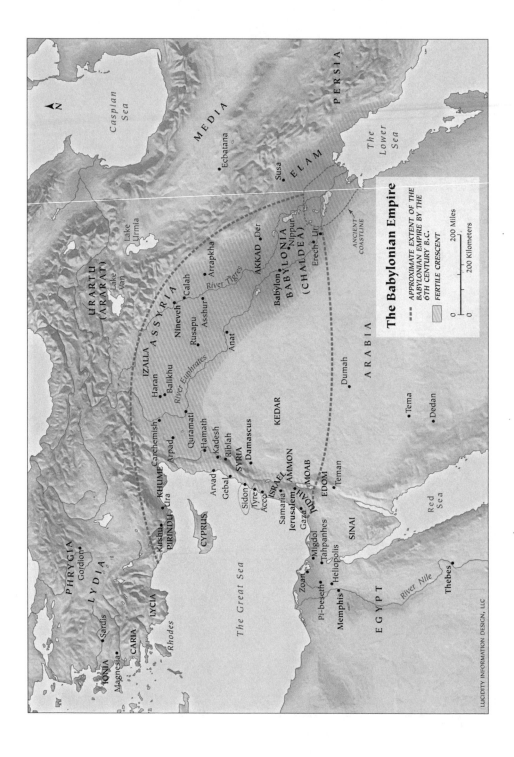

The Babylonian Empire

- - - APPROXIMATE EXTENT OF THE
BABYLONIAN EMPIRE BY THE
6TH CENTURY B.C.
▨ FERTILE CRESCENT

0   200 Miles
0   200 Kilometers

ANCIENT
COASTLINE

PERSIA

MEDIA

Caspian Sea

Ecbatana

The Lower Sea

ELAM

Susa

Lake Urmia

Lake Van

URARTU (ARARAT)

IZALLA

ASSYRIA

River Tigres

Arrapkha

Calah

Nineveh

Rusapu

Asshur

Anat

Der

AKKAD

Babylon

BABYLONIA (CHALDEA)

Nippur

Erech

Ur

Haran

Balikhu

River Euphrates

Carchemish

Quramati

Hamath

Kadesh

Riblah

Arpad

SYRIA

Damascus

KEDAR

Dumah

ARABIA

Tema

Dedan

KHUME

Ura

Arvad

Gebal

Sidon

Tyre

Acco

Samaria

ISRAEL

Jerusalem

JUDAH

Gaza

AMMON

MOAB

EDOM

Teman

Kirshu

PIRINDU

CYPRUS

PHRYGIA

Gordion

LYDIA

Sardis

LYCIA

Rhodes

CARIA

Magnesia

IONIA

The Great Sea

SINAI

Red Sea

Migdol

Tahpanhes

Zoan

Pi-beseth

Heliopolis

Memphis

EGYPT

River Nile

Thebes

LUCIDITY INFORMATION DESIGN, LLC

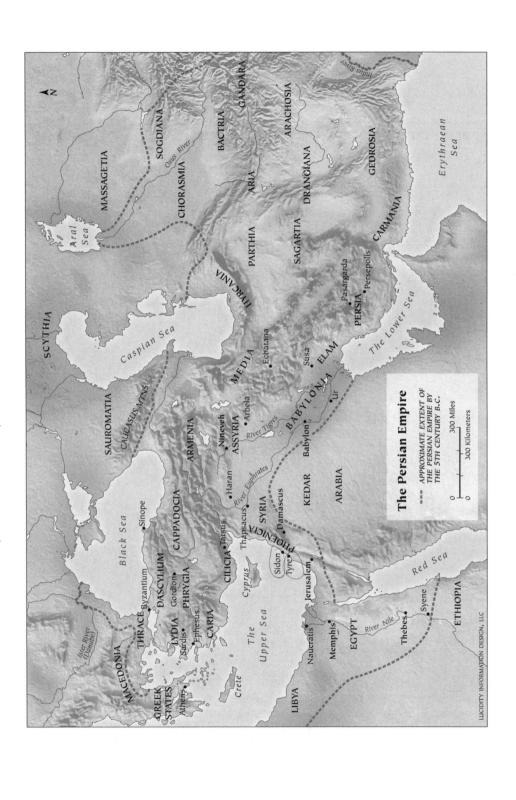

The Persian Empire

APPROXIMATE EXTENT OF
THE PERSIAN EMPIRE BY
THE 5TH CENTURY B.C.

300 Miles

300 Kilometers

0

0

LUCIDITY INFORMATION DESIGN, LLC

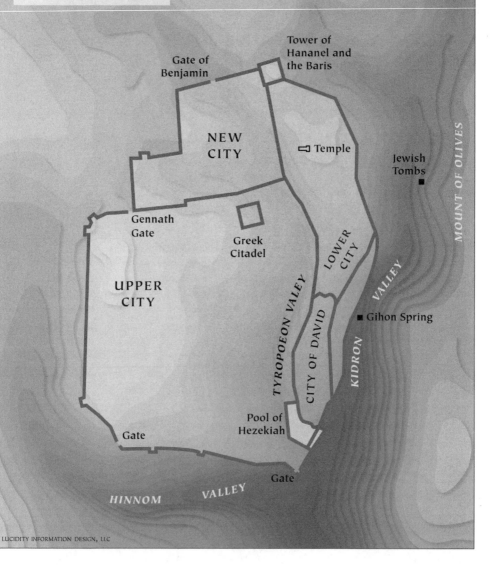

Jerusalem in the Time of the Old Testament

PROBABLE ALIGNMENT OF ANCIENT WALL

| 0 | | | 1000 Feet |
| 0 | | | 300 Meters |

N

Gate of Benjamin

Tower of Hananel and the Baris

NEW CITY

Temple

Jewish Tombs

MOUNT OF OLIVES

Gennath Gate

Greek Citadel

LOWER CITY

UPPER CITY

TYROPOEON VALLEY

CITY OF DAVID

KIDRON

VALLEY

Gihon Spring

Pool of Hezekiah

Gate

Gate

HINNOM VALLEY

LUCIDITY INFORMATION DESIGN, LLC